iOS Development with Xamarin Cookbook

Over 100 exciting recipes to help you develop iOS applications with Xamarin

Dimitris Tavlikos

PUBLISHING

BIRMINGHAM - MUMBAI

iOS Development with Xamarin Cookbook

First published: December 2011

Second edition: May 2014

Production reference: 1160514

Published by Packt Publishing Ltd.
Livery Place
35 Livery Street
Birmingham B3 2PB, UK.

ISBN 978-1-84969-892-4

www.packtpub.com

Cover image by Kelly Gibson (gibsonkelly36@yahoo.com)

Credits

Author

Dimitris Tavlikos

Reviewers

Ryan Alford

Yaroslav Bigus

William Smith

Acquisition Editors

Joanne Fitzpatrick

Usha Iyer

Content Development Editor

Amit Ghodake

Technical Editors

Neha Mankare

Humera Shaikh

Faisal Siddiqui

Copy Editors

Dipti Kapadia

Sayanee Mukherjee

Deepa Nambiar

Karuna Narayanan

Stuti Srivastava

Laxmi Subramanian

Project Coordinator

Amey Sawant

Proofreaders

Simran Bhogal

Bridget Braund

Lauren Harkins

Indexer

Mariammal Chettiyar

Production Coordinators

Aparna Bhagat

Arvindkumar Gupta

Saiprasad Kadam

Nilesh R. Mohite

Aditi Gajjar Patel

Cover Work

Nilesh R. Mohite

About the Author

Dimitris Tavlikos is a freelance software developer living in Greece. With over 10 years of professional experience as a programmer, he specializes in mobile development with clients all over the world. Dimitris has a passion for programming, and has recently been awarded the Xamarin MVP designation for his work. He has written a book on iOS development and various articles on his blog.

About the Reviewers

Ryan Alford is a .NET software engineer who works from home. Ryan has been a .NET developer for over 7 years, with the majority of his focus being on C#. In his early years, he worked almost exclusively on WinForms and Windows Mobile. He then started working with ASP.Net, AJAX, and Silverlight. In the past few years, as mobile development really started to take off, he took an interest in Xamarin and MonoTouch.

Ryan was able to help convince the management at his employer to use Xamarin for their upcoming enterprise application on iOS, as the company was using .Net and C# in other projects. It was at this point that Ryan was added to the three-person development team to write the new iOS enterprise application.

Ryan has written and released two Android applications: MotoTorch LED and Phase 10 Score Center. MotoTorch LED has more than 500,000 downloads and was one of the first applications on Android that used the camera LEDs as a flashlight.

Today, Ryan is currently rewriting Phase 10 Score Center in Xamarin.Android to ease the development of new features. He is still on his iOS team and continues to add new features to his company's enterprise application.

Yaroslav Bigus is an expert in building cross-platform web and mobile applications. He has over 4 years experience in development and has worked for companies in Leeds and New York. He has been using the .NET Framework stack for developing backend systems, JavaScript for the frontend side, and Xamarin for mobile devices.

He is now working for an Israeli startup called yRuler. Previously, Yaroslav reviewed *Xamarin Mobile Application Development for iOS, Paul F. Johnson, Packt Publishing*.

I am thankful to my family and friends.

William Smith has been developing with Xamarin Studio for over 3 years and has been developing software since 2001. He currently works as a Geospatial Developer at Geographic Information Services, Inc., specializing in mobile-platform development. He is also the founder of Websmiths, LLC (`www.websmithsllc.com`), a consulting firm that offers services in cross-platform mobile application development and web development. William holds two BSc degrees in Computer Science and Business Administration from the University of Maryland.

www.PacktPub.com

Support files, eBooks, discount offers, and more

You might want to visit www.PacktPub.com for support files and downloads related to your book.

Did you know that Packt offers eBook versions of every book published, with PDF and ePub files available? You can upgrade to the eBook version at www.PacktPub.com and as a print book customer, you are entitled to a discount on the eBook copy. Get in touch with us at service@packtpub.com for more details.

At www.PacktPub.com, you can also read a collection of free technical articles, sign up for a range of free newsletters, and receive exclusive discounts and offers on Packt books and eBooks.

http://PacktLib.PacktPub.com

Do you need instant solutions to your IT questions? PacktLib is Packt's online digital book library. Here, you can access, read, and search across Packt's entire library of books.

Why subscribe?

- Fully searchable across every book published by Packt
- Copy and paste, print and bookmark content
- On demand and accessible via web browser

Free access for Packt account holders

If you have an account with Packt at www.PacktPub.com, you can use this to access PacktLib today and view nine entirely free books. Simply use your login credentials for immediate access.

Table of Contents

Preface

This book will provide you with all the necessary skills to develop and deploy rich and powerful applications for the iPhone and iPad, with the C# programming language. Xamarin.iOS, formerly known as MonoTouch, is already established as a powerful software development kit that brings iOS development to .NET programmers. Packed with easy-to-understand and detailed examples, this book will be your best companion in your iOS development journey.

What this book covers

Chapter 1, Development Tools, teaches you how to install and use the development tools necessary to create your first iOS app. From there, you will create and debug your first Xamarin.iOS project.

Chapter 2, User Interface – Views, discusses the essential User Interface components of the iOS SDK. Covering the most commonly used views and controls and many more in detail, we will get familiar with the platform through a number of example projects. We will also discuss the similarities and differences with standard .NET components.

Chapter 3, User Interface – View Controllers, introduces you to the view controllers, the objects that are responsible for providing the interaction mechanism between your app and the user. Explained with simple step-by-step processes, you will start creating complete apps that can run on both the iPhone and iPad devices.

Chapter 4, Data Management, covers data management practices available on the iOS platform and how to use them efficiently with the convenience of C#. You will learn to manage locale SQLite database files, but also work on using iCloud to store data across different devices.

Chapter 5, Displaying Data, focuses on another important part of data management. Through a series of simple and complete projects, you will learn about the available components to display data on the screen of the iPhone, which are smaller than computer screens. Displaying various types of data in a user-friendly manner is essential for mobile devices, and by the time you finish reading this chapter, you will certainly be more skillful in this area.

Chapter 6, Web Services, guides you through .NET SOAP, WCF, and REST services for creating apps that connect the user to the world. These powerful .NET features would not have been part of iOS development without Xamarin.iOS.

Chapter 7, Multimedia Resources, will teach you to create applications that capture, reproduce, and manage multimedia content through the device's hardware. You will not only learn to use the camera to capture images and video, but also learn how to play back and record audio.

Chapter 8, Integrating iOS Features, will walk you through the ways to incorporate the platform's native applications and components. You will learn how to provide e-mail, text messaging, and address book features in your application and how to use the native calendar to create events.

Chapter 9, Interacting with Device Hardware, discusses creating applications that are fully aware of their surrounding environment through the device's sensors. You will learn to adjust the User Interface according to device orientations and respond to accelerometer and gyroscope events.

Chapter 10, Location Services and Maps, is a detailed guide for using the built-in location services to create applications that provide location information to the user. You will not only learn to use the GPS hardware, but also how to display and layout information on maps.

Chapter 11, Graphics and Animation, introduces 2D graphics and animation. You will learn to animate components and draw simple graphics on the screen. By the end of this chapter, you will create a small finger-drawing application.

Chapter 12, Multitasking, will walk you through the details of implementing multitasking in iOS applications. This dramatically enhances the user experience by executing code behind the scenes.

Chapter 13, Localization, discusses how to provide localized content in applications. You will learn how to prepare your application to target users worldwide.

Chapter 14, Deploying, will not only walk you through the required steps to deploy your finished application to devices, but also to prepare and distribute it to the App Store.

Chapter 15, Advanced Features, introduces some of the key features introduced in newer iOS versions, such as implementing physics to User Interface components through the power of iOS 7's UIKit Dynamics, customizing animated transitions between view controllers, and more!

What you need for this book

The minimum requirement for this book is a Mac computer running at least Mac OS X Lion (10.7.*). Almost all projects you will create with the help of this book work on iOS Simulator. However, some projects will require a device to work properly. You will find all the appropriate details in *Chapter 1, Development Tools*.

Who this book is for

This book is essential for C# and .NET developers with no previous experience in iOS development, but it is also for Objective-C developers who want to make a transition to the benefits of Xamarin.iOS and C# language to create complete, compelling iPhone, iPod, and iPad applications and deploy them to the App Store.

Conventions

In this book, you will find a number of styles of text that distinguish between different kinds of information. Here are some examples of these styles, and an explanation of their meaning.

Code words in text, cookbook names, recipe names, scripts, database table names, folder names, filenames, file extensions, and pathnames are shown as follows: "The `Register` attribute is used to expose classes to the underlying Objective-C runtime."

A block of code is set as follows:

```
using System;
using System.Collections.Generic;
using System.Linq;
using MonoTouch.Foundation;
using MonoTouch.UIKit;
```

When we wish to draw your attention to a particular part of a code block, the relevant lines or items are set in bold:

```
EKEvent newEvent = EKEvent.FromStore(evStore);
newEvent.StartDate = DateTime.Now.AddDays(1);
newEvent.EndDate = DateTime.Now.AddDays(1.1);
newEvent.Title = "Xamarin event!";
```

Any command-line input or output is written as follows:

```
cd <code_directory>/CH06_code/WcfService/WcfService
./start_wcfservice.sh
```

New terms and **important words** are shown in bold. Words you see on the screen, in menus or dialog boxes, for example, appear in the text like this: "Go to the **Library** pane and select **Objects** from the drop-down list."

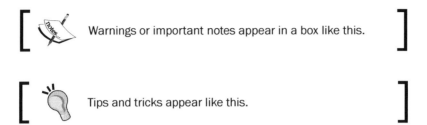

Warnings or important notes appear in a box like this.

Tips and tricks appear like this.

Reader feedback

Feedback from our readers is always welcome. Let us know what you think about this book—what you liked or may have disliked. Reader feedback is important for us to develop titles that you really get the most out of.

To send us general feedback, simply send an e-mail to feedback@packtpub.com, and mention the book title via the subject of your message.

If there is a topic that you have expertise in and you are interested in either writing or contributing to a book, see our author guide on www.packtpub.com/authors.

Customer support

Now that you are the proud owner of a Packt book, we have a number of things to help you to get the most from your purchase.

Downloading the example code

You can download the example code files for all Packt books you have purchased from your account at http://www.packtpub.com. If you purchased this book elsewhere, you can visit http://www.packtpub.com/support and register to have the files e-mailed directly to you.

Errata

Although we have taken every care to ensure the accuracy of our content, mistakes do happen. If you find a mistake in one of our books—maybe a mistake in the text or the code—we would be grateful if you would report this to us. By doing so, you can save other readers from frustration and help us improve subsequent versions of this book. If you find any errata, please report them by visiting `http://www.packtpub.com/submit-errata`, selecting your book, clicking on the **errata submission form** link, and entering the details of your errata. Once your errata are verified, your submission will be accepted and the errata will be uploaded on our website, or added to any list of existing errata, under the Errata section of that title. Any existing errata can be viewed by selecting your title from `http://www.packtpub.com/support`.

Piracy

Piracy of copyrighted material on the Internet is an ongoing problem across all media. At Packt, we take the protection of our copyright and licenses very seriously. If you come across any illegal copies of our works, in any form, on the Internet, please provide us with the location address or website name immediately so we can pursue a remedy.

Please contact us at `copyright@packtpub.com` with a link to the suspected pirated material.

We appreciate your help in protecting our authors, and our ability to bring you valuable content.

Questions

You can contact us at `questions@packtpub.com` if you are having a problem with any aspect of the book, and we will do our best to address it.

1

Development Tools

In this chapter, we will cover:

- ▶ Installing prerequisites
- ▶ Creating an iOS project with Xamarin Studio
- ▶ Interface Builder
- ▶ Creating the UI
- ▶ Accessing the UI with Outlets
- ▶ Adding Actions to controls
- ▶ Compiling an iOS project
- ▶ Debugging our application

Introduction

One of the most important things professionals care about is the tools that are required to complete their work with. Just like carpenters need a chisel to scrape wood, or photographers need a camera to capture light, we developers need certain tools which we cannot work without.

In this chapter, we will provide information on what **IDEs** (**Integrated Development Environments**) and **SDKs** (**Software Development Kits**) are needed to develop applications for iOS, Apple's operating system, for the company's mobile devices. We will describe what the role of every tool in the development cycle is, and go through the features that are essential to develop our first application.

The following are the tools needed to develop applications with Xamarin.iOS:

- ▶ **An Apple Mac computer running at least the Lion (10.7.*) operating system**: The essential programs we need cannot be installed on other computer platforms.

Xamarin also offers Visual Studio development integration for their products. A Mac computer is still required for compiling, testing, debugging, and distributing the application. More information can be found on Xamarin's website at `http://docs.xamarin.com/guides/ios/getting_started/introduction_to_xamarin_ios_for_visual_studio/`.

▸ **Latest iOS SDK**: To be able to download iOS SDK, a developer must be registered as an Apple developer. iOS SDK, among other things, includes two essential components:

    ❑ **Xcode**: This is Apple's IDE for developing native applications for iOS and Mac with the *Objective-C* programming language.

    ❑ **iOS Simulator**: This is an essential program to debug iOS apps on the computer, without the need of a device. Note that there are many iOS features that do not work on the simulator. Hence, a device is needed if an app uses these features.

Both the registration and SDK download are free of charge from Apple's developer portal (`http://developer.apple.com`). If we want to run and debug our apps on the device or distribute them on the App Store, we need to enroll to iOS Developer Program, which requires a subscription fee.

▸ **Xamarin Installer**: Xamarin offers all their necessary tools in one installation bundle. This bundle includes the Xamarin.iOS SDK and Xamarin Studio, the IDE for developing iOS applications with C#. A free registration is required for downloading the Xamarin Installer, and it can be found by clicking on the link `http://xamarin.com/download`.

This chapter will also describe how to create our first iPhone project with Xamarin Studio, construct its UI with Xcode, and access the app's user interface from within our code, with the concepts of **Outlets** and **Actions**.

Last, but not least, we will learn how to compile our app, the available compilation options we have, and how to debug on the simulator.

Installing prerequisites

This section gives you information on how to download and install the necessary tools to develop with Xamarin.iOS.

Getting ready

We need to download all the necessary components on our computer. The first thing to do is register as an Apple developer on `http://developer.apple.com`. The registration is free and easy, and it provides access to all the necessary development resources. After the registration is confirmed through e-mail, we can login and download the iOS SDK from the address `https://developer.apple.com/devcenter/ios/index.action#downloads`. At the time of writing, Xcode's latest version is 5.0.1 and iOS SDK's latest version is 7.0.3.

How to do it...

To prepare our computer for iOS development, we need to download and install the necessary components in the following order:

- ▶ **Xcode and iOS SDK**: A login to the Mac App Store is required. You can either search for Xcode in the App Store or click on the **Download Xcode** button in the iOS developer portal's download section. After the download is complete, follow the onscreen instructions to install Xcode. The following screenshot shows Xcode in the Mac App Store:

▶ **Xamarin Starter Edition**: Download and run the Xamarin Starter Edition from Xamarin's website `http://xamarin.com/download`. Follow the onscreen instructions to install Xamarin Studio and Xamarin.iOS.

The Xamarin Starter Edition is free, but there are some restrictions, such as a limit on the maximum app bundle size and no Visual Studio support. It does support, however, deploying to a device and to the App Store. At the time of writing, all recipes shown in this book are fully supported by the Starter Edition, except for the *Using WCF services* recipe in *Chapter 6, Web Services*. A Business or Enterprise Edition is needed for WCF support.

How it works...

Now that we have everything ready, let's see what each component is needed for.

Xcode

Xcode is Apple's IDE for developing applications for both iOS and Mac platforms. It is targeted on the Objective-C programming language, which is the main language to program in with the iOS SDK. Since Xamarin.iOS is an SDK for the C# language, one might ask what we would need it for. Apart from providing various tools for debugging iOS apps, Xcode provides us with the **Organizer** window. Shown in the following screenshot, we can use it to view a device's console logs, install and manage the necessary provisioning profiles, and even view the device's crash logs. To open the **Organizer** window, navigate to **Window | Organizer** on the menu bar, or press *Cmd + Shift + 2* on the keyboard.

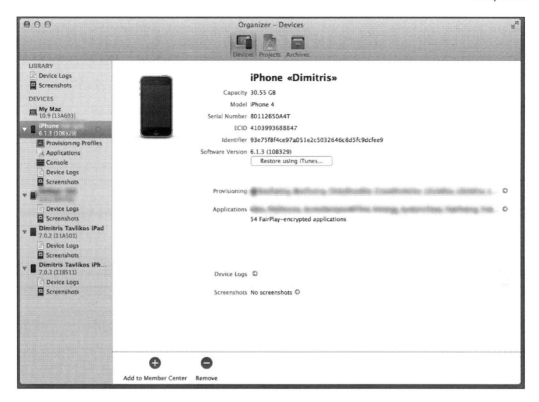

Interface Builder

The second component is Interface Builder. This is the user interface designer, which was formerly a standalone application. Starting with Xcode 4.0, it is integrated into the IDE. Interface Builder provides all the necessary functionality to construct an application user interface. It is also quite different from what .NET developers are accustomed to.

iOS Simulator

The third component is iOS Simulator. It is exactly what its name suggests: a device simulator that we can use to run our apps on, without the need for an actual device. The most important thing about iOS Simulator is that it has the option of simulating older iOS versions (if they are installed on the computer), both iPhone and iPad interfaces and device orientations. However, the simulator lacks some device features that are dependent on hardware such as the compass or accelerometer. Applications using these features must be tested and debugged on an actual device.

Xamarin.iOS is the SDK that allows .NET developers to develop apps for iOS, using the C# programming language. All APIs available to Objective-C developers are also available to C# developers through Xamarin.iOS. It is not a standalone framework with its own APIs for, say, user interfaces. A Xamarin.iOS programmer can use the same UI elements as an Objective-C programmer, along with the added benefits of C# such as generics, LINQ, and asynchronous programming with async/await.

There's more...

Applications developed with Xamarin.iOS have the same chances of making it to the App Store as all other applications developed with the native Objective-C programming language. This means that if an app does not conform to Apple's strict policy about app acceptance, it will fail, whether is written in Objective-C or C#. The Xamarin.iOS team has done a great job in creating an SDK that leaves the developer to worry only about the design and best practice of the code, and nothing else.

Useful links

The following are useful links that you can go through:

- **Apple iOS developer portal**: `http://developer.apple.com/devcenter/ios/index.action`
- **Xamarin.iOS**: `http://xamarin.com/ios`
- **Xamarin installation guide for Mac**: `http://docs.xamarin.com/guides/ios/getting_started/installation/mac/`
- **Information about Apple developer tools**: `http://developer.apple.com/technologies/tools/xcode.html`

Updates

Xamarin Studio has a feature for checking available updates. Whenever a program starts, it checks for updates of Xamarin.iOS. It can be turned off, but this is not suggested since it helps with staying up to date with the latest versions. It can be found under **Xamarin Studio | Check for Updates**.

See also

- The *Compiling an iOS project* and *Debugging our application* recipes
- The *Preparing our app for the App Store* recipe in *Chapter 14, Deploying*

Creating an iOS project with Xamarin Studio

In this recipe, we will discuss how to create our first iOS project with Xamarin Studio.

Getting ready...

Now that we have all the prerequisites installed, we will discuss how to create our first iOS project with Xamarin Studio.

Start Xamarin Studio. It can be found in the `Applications` folder. Xamarin Studio's default project location is `/Users/{yourusername}/Projects`. If it does not exist on the hard disk, it will be created when we create out first project. If you want to change the folder, go to **Xamarin Studio | Preferences** from the menu bar. Select **Load/Save** in the pane on the left, enter the preferred location for the projects in the **Default Solution location** field, and click on **OK**.

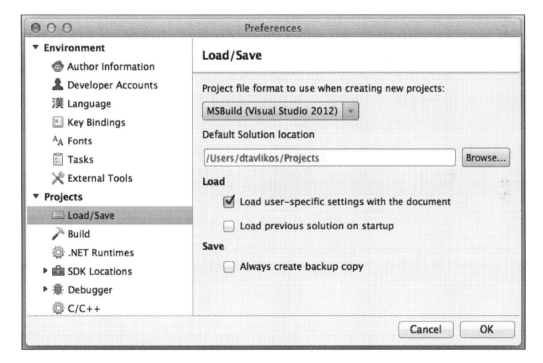

How to do it...

The first thing that is loaded when starting Xamarin Studio is its start page. Perform the following steps to create an iOS project with Xamarin Studio:

1. Navigate to **File | New | Solution...** from the menu bar. A window that provides us with the available project options will appear.

2. In the pane on the left of this window, go to **C#** | **iOS** | **iPhone**. The iPhone project templates will be presented on the middle pane.

3. Select **Single View Application**.

4. Finally, enter `MyFirstiOSProject` for **Solution name** and click on **OK**. The following screenshot displays the **New Solution** window:

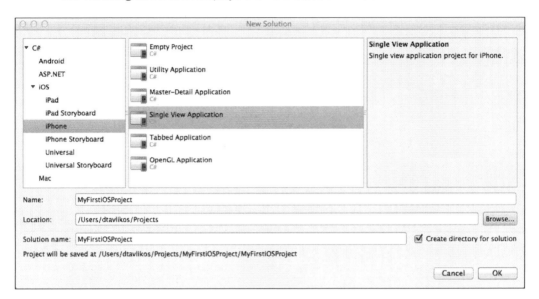

That was it. You just created your first iPhone project. You can build and run it; iOS Simulator will start, with a blank light-gray screen nevertheless.

 The project templates may be different from the ones shown in the preceding screenshot.

How it works...

Let's see what goes on behind the scenes.

When Xamarin Studio creates a new iOS project, it creates a series of files. The solution files can be viewed in the **Solution** pad on the left side of Xamarin Studio window. If the **Solution** pad is not visible, it can be activated by checking on **View** | **Pads** | **Solution** from the menu bar.

The files shown in the following screenshot are the essential files that form an iPhone project:

MyFirstiOSProjectViewController.xib

`MyFirstiOSProjectViewController.xib` is the file that contains the view of the application. XIB files are basically XML files with a specific structure that Xcode can read. The files contain information about the user interface, such as the type of controls it contains, their properties, and Outlets.

 If `MyFirstiPhoneProjectViewController.xib`, or any other file with the .xib suffix, is double-clicked, Xamarin Studio automatically opens the file in Xcode's Interface Builder.

When we create a new interface with Interface Builder and save it, it is saved in the XIB format.

MyFirstiOSProjectViewController.cs

`MyFirstiOSProjectViewController.cs` is the file that implements the view's functionality. These are the contents of the file when it is created:

```
using System;
using System.Drawing;
using MonoTouch.Foundation;
using MonoTouch.UIKit;

namespace MyFirstiOSProject
{
    public class MyFirstiOSProjectViewController :
        UIViewController
    {
```

```
public MyFirstiOSProjectViewController () :
    base ("MyFirstiOSProjectViewController", null)
{
}

public override void DidReceiveMemoryWarning ()
{
    // Releases the view if it doesn't have a superview.
    base.DidReceiveMemoryWarning ();

    // Release any cached data, images, etc that aren't in
    use.
}

public override void ViewDidLoad ()
{
    base.ViewDidLoad ();

    // Perform any additional setup after loading
    the view, typically from a nib.
}
}
}
```

Xamarin.iOS was formerly known as MonoTouch. For proper code compatibility, the namespaces have not been renamed.

The code in this file contains the class which corresponds to the view that will be loaded, along with some default method that overrides. These methods are the ones that we will use more frequently when we create view controllers. A brief description of each method is listed as follows:

- **ViewDidLoad**: This method is called when the view of the controller is loaded. This is the method we use to initialize any additional component.

- **DidReceiveMemoryWarning**: This method is called when the app receives a memory warning. This method is responsible for releasing resources that are not needed at the time.

MyFirstiOSProjectViewController.designer.cs

MyFirstiOSProjectViewController.designer.cs is the file that holds our main window's class information in C# code. Xamarin Studio creates one .designer.cs file for every XIB that is added in a project. The file is autogenerated every time we save a change in our XIB through Interface Builder. This is taken care of by Xamarin Studio so that the changes we make in our interface are reflected right away in our code. We must not make changes to this file directly, since when the corresponding XIB is saved with Interface Builder, they will be lost. Also, if nothing is saved through Interface Builder and if changes are made to it manually, it will most likely result in a compilation error.

These are the contents of the file when a new project is created:

```
//
// This file has been generated automatically by MonoDevelop to
  store outlets and
// actions made in the Xcode designer. If it is removed, they will
  be lost.
// Manual changes to this file may not be handled correctly.
//
using MonoTouch.Foundation;

namespace MyFirstiOSProject
{
    [Register ("MyFirstiOSProjectViewController")]
    partial class MyFirstiOSProjectViewController
    {
        void ReleaseDesignerOutlets ()
        {
        }
    }
}
```

This file contains the other partial declaration of our MyFirstiOSProjectViewController class. It is decorated with the Register attribute.

The Register attribute is used to expose classes to the underlying Objective-C runtime. The string parameter declares by what name our class will be exposed to the runtime. It can be whatever name we want it to be, but it is a good practice to always set it to our C# class' name. The attribute is used heavily in the internals of Xamarin.iOS, since it is what binds all the native NSObject classes with their C# counterparts.

> NSObject is a root class or base class. It is the equivalent of System.Object in the .NET world. The only difference between the two is that all .NET objects inherit from System.Object, but most, not all, Objective-C objects inherit from NSObject in Objective-C. The C# counterparts of all native objects that inherit from NSObject also inherit from its Xamarin.iOS NSObject counterpart.

AppDelegate.cs

The AppDelegate.cs file contains the AppDelegate class. The contents of the file are listed below:

```
using System;
using System.Collections.Generic;
using System.Linq;
using MonoTouch.Foundation;
using MonoTouch.UIKit;

namespace MyFirstiOSProject
{
    // The UIApplicationDelegate for the application. This class
    is responsible for launching the
    // User Interface of the application, as well as listening
    (and optionally responding) to
    // application events from iOS.
    [Register ("AppDelegate")]
    public partial class AppDelegate : UIApplicationDelegate
    {
        // class-level declarations
        UIWindow window;
        MyFirstiOSProjectViewController viewController;
        //
        // This method is invoked when the application has loaded
        and is ready to run. In this
        // method you should instantiate the window, load the UI
        into it and then make the window
        // visible.
        //
        // You have 17 seconds to return from this method,
        or iOS will terminate your application.
```

```
        //
        public override bool FinishedLaunching (UIApplication app,
            NSDictionary options)
        {
            window = new UIWindow (UIScreen.MainScreen.Bounds);

            viewController =
                new MyFirstiOSProjectViewController ();
            window.RootViewController = viewController;
            window.MakeKeyAndVisible ();

            return true;
        }
    }
}
```

The first part is familiar to .NET developers and consists of the appropriate using directives that import the required namespaces to use. Consider the following code:

```
using System;
using System.Collections.Generic;
using System.Linq;
using MonoTouch.Foundation;
using MonoTouch.UIKit;
```

The first three using directives allow us to use the specific and familiar namespaces from the .NET world with Xamarin.iOS.

> System, System.Collections.Generic, System.Linq: Although the functionality that the three namespaces provide is almost identical to their well-known .NET counterparts, they are included in assemblies specifically created for use with Xamarin. iOS and shipped with it, of course. An assembly compiled with .NET cannot be directly used in a Xamarin.iOS project.

The MonoTouch.Foundation namespace is a wrapper around the native Objective-C Foundation Framework, which contains classes that provide basic functionality. These objects' names share the same NS prefix that is found in the native Foundation Framework. Some examples are NSObject, NSString, NSValue, and so on. Apart from the NS-prefixed objects, the MonoTouch.Foundation namespace contains all of the attributes that are used for binding to native objects, such as the Outlet and Register attributes we saw earlier. The MonoTouch.UIKit namespace is a wrapper around the native Objective-C UIKit Framework. As its name suggests, the namespace contains classes, delegates, and events that provide us with interface functionality. Almost all the objects' names share the same UI prefix. It should be clear at this point that these two namespaces are essential for all Xamarin. iOS apps, and their objects will be used quite frequently.

The class inherits from the `UIApplicationDelegate` class, qualifying it as our app's delegate object.

 The concept of a delegate object in the Objective-C world is somewhat different from `delegate` in C#. It will be explained in detail in *Chapter 2, User Interface – Views*.

The `AppDelegate` class contains two fields and one method:

```
UIWindow window;
MyFirstiOSProjectViewController viewController;
//..
public override bool FinishedLaunching (UIApplication app,
    NSDictionary options) {
```

The `UIWindow` object defines the main window of our application, while the `MyFirstiOSProjectViewController` object is the variable that will hold the app's view controller.

 An iOS app typically has only one window of type `UIWindow`. `UIWindow` is the first control that is displayed when an app starts, and every subsequent view is hierarchically added below it.

The `FinishedLaunching` method, as its name suggests, is called when the app has completed its initialization process. This is the method where we must present the user interface to the user. The implementation of this method must be lightweight; if it does not return in time from the moment it is called, iOS will terminate the app. This provides faster user interface loading time to the user by preventing developers from performing complex and long-running tasks upon initialization, such as connecting to a web service to receive data. The `app` parameter is the application's `UIApplication` object, which is also accessible through the `static` property `UIApplication.SharedApplication`. The `options` parameter may or may not contain information about the way the app was launched. We do not need it for now.

The default implementation of the `FinishedLaunching` method for this type of project is as follows:

▶ The `UIWindow` object is initialized with the size of the screen as follows:

```
window = new UIWindow (UIScreen.MainScreen.Bounds);
```

▶ The view controller is initialized and set as the window's root view controller as follows:

```
viewController = new MyFirstiPhoneProjectViewController();
window.RootViewController = viewController;
window.MakeKeyAndVisible ();
return true;
```

The window is displayed on the screen with the `window.MakeKeyAndVisible()` call and the method returns. This method must be called inside the `FinishedLaunching` method, otherwise the app's user interface will not be presented as it should be to the user. Last but not least, the `return true` line returns the method by marking its execution completion.

Main.cs

Inside the `Main.cs` file is where the runtime life cycle of the program starts as shown in the following code:

```
namespace MyFirstiOSProject
{
    public class Application
    {
        // This is the main entry point of the application.
        static void Main (string[] args)
        {
            // if you want to use a different Application
                Delegate class from "AppDelegate"
            // you can specify it here.
            UIApplication.Main (args, null, "AppDelegate");
        }
    }
}
```

It is much like the following call in a .NET System.Windows.Forms application:

```
Application.Run(new Form1());
```

The `UIApplication.Main` method starts the message loop or run loop that is responsible for dispatching notifications to the app through the `AppDelegate` class with event handlers that we can override. Event handlers such as `FinishedLaunching`, `ReceiveMemoryWarning`, or `DidEnterBackground` are only some of these notifications. Apart from the notification dispatching mechanism, the `UIApplication` object holds a list of all `UIWindow` objects that exist, typically one. An iOS app must have one `UIApplication` object, or a class that inherits from it, and this object must have a corresponding `UIApplicationDelegate` object. This is the `AppDelegate` class implementation we saw earlier.

Info.plist

The `Info.plist` file is basically the app's settings file. It has a simple structure of properties with values that define various settings for an iOS app, such as the orientations it supports, its icons, supported iOS versions, what devices it can be installed on, and so on. If we double-click on this file in Xamarin Studio, it will open in the embedded editor specifically designed for this file. Our file in a new project looks like the following screenshot:

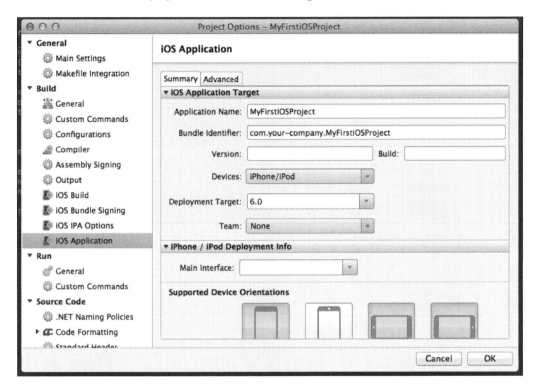

We can also access `Info.plist` through the project's options window under **iOS Application**.

There's more...

Xamarin Studio provides many different project templates for developing iOS apps. Here is a list that describes what each project template is for:

- ▶ **Empty project**: This is an empty project without any views.
- ▶ **Utility application**: This is a special type of iOS app that provides one screen for functionality and, in many cases, another one for configuration.
- ▶ **Master-detail application**: This type of project creates a template that supports navigating through multiple screens. It contains two view controllers.
- ▶ **Single view application**: This template type is the one we used in this recipe.

- **Tabbed application**: This is a template that adds a tab bar controller, which manages two view controllers in a tab-like interface.

- **OpenGL application**: This is a template for creating OpenGL-powered applications or games.

These templates are available for the iPhone, iPad, and Universal (both iPhone and iPad) projects. They are also available in Interface Builder's storyboarding app design.

 Unless stated, all project templates referring to the iPhone are suitable for the iPod Touch as well.

List of Xamarin.iOS assemblies

Xamarin.iOS-supported assemblies can be found at `http://ios.xamarin.com/Documentation/Assemblies`.

See also

- The *Creating the UI* and *Accessing the UI with Outlets* recipes

- The *Adding and customizing views* recipe in *Chapter 2, User Interface – Views*

Interface Builder

In this recipe, we will take a look at Xcode's Interface Builder. Since we cannot use Xcode to write our code, Xamarin Studio provides a transparent way of communicating with Xcode when it comes to user interface files.

How to do it...

Let's take a look at Interface Builder by performing the following steps:

1. If you have installed the iOS SDK, then you already have Xcode with Interface Builder installed on your computer. Go to Xamarin Studio and open the project `MyFirstiOSProject` we created earlier.

2. In the **Solution** pad on the left, double-click on **MyFirstiOSProjectViewController.xib**. Xamarin Studio starts Xcode with the file loaded in Interface Builder.

3. On the top of the Xcode window in the right side of the toolbar, select the appropriate editor and viewing options, as shown in the following screenshot:

4. The following screenshot demonstrates what Interface Builder looks like with an XIB file open:

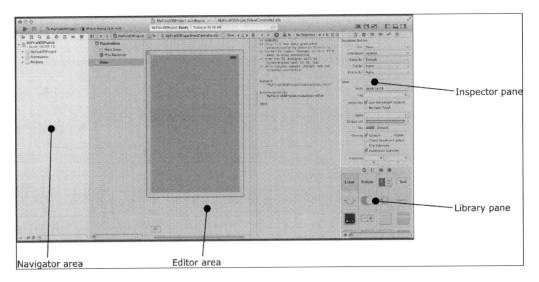

Now that we have loaded Interface Builder with the view controller of our app, let's familiarize ourselves with it.

The user interface designer is directly connected to an Xcode project. When we add an object, Xcode automatically generates code to reflect the change we made. Xamarin Studio takes care of this for us, so that when we double-click on an XIB file, it automatically creates a temporary Xcode project. This allows us to make the changes we want in the user interface. Therefore, we have nothing more to do than just design the user interface for our app.

Interface Builder is divided into three areas. A brief description of each area is given as follows:

- ▶ **Navigator area**: In this area, we can see the files included in the Xcode project.
- ▶ **Editor area**: This area is where we design the user interface. The editor area is divided into two sections. The one on the left is the designer, and the one on the right is the assistant editor. Inside the assistant editor, we see the underlying Objective-C source code file that corresponds to the selected item in the designer. Although we do not need to edit the Objective-C source, we will need the assistant editor later.
- ▶ **Utility area**: This area contains the inspector and library panes. The inspector pane is where we configure each object, and the library pane is where we find the objects.

There's more...

We saw what an XIB file looks like in Interface Builder, but there is more as far as these files are concerned. We mentioned earlier that XIB files are XML files with appropriate information readable by Interface Builder. The thing is that when a compilation is done in a project, the compiler compiles the XIB file converting it to its binary equivalent, the NIB file. Both XIB and NIB files contain the same information. The only difference between them is that XIB files are in a human-readable form while the NIB files are not. For example, when we compile the project we created, the `MyFirstiOSProjectViewController.xib` file will become `MyFirstiOSProjectViewController.nib` in the output folder. Apart from the binary conversion, the compiler also performs a compression on NIB files. So, NIB files will be significantly smaller in size than XIB files.

That's not all about XIB files. The way a developer manages the XIB files in a project is very important in an app's performance and stability. It is better to have many small-sized XIB files, instead of one or two large ones. This is because of the way iOS manages its memory. This can be accomplished by dividing the user interface into many XIB files. It may seem a bit difficult, but as we'll see later in this book, it is actually very easy.

When an app starts, iOS loads the NIB files as a whole in memory, and all the objects in it are instantiated. So, it is a waste of memory to keep objects in NIB files that are not always going to be used. Also, remember that you are developing for a mobile device whose available resources are not a match against that of desktop computers, no matter what its capabilities are.

As of iOS 5, Apple introduced storyboarding, which simplifies user interface design.

More information

You may have noticed that in the **Attributes** tab of the **Inspector** pane, there is a section called **Simulated Metrics**. Options under this section help us see directly what our interface looks like in the designer area with the device's status bar, a toolbar, or a navigation bar. Although these options are saved in the XIB files, they have nothing to do with the actual app at runtime. For example, if we set the **Status Bar** option to **None**, it does not mean that our app will start without a status bar.

 Status Bar is the bar that is shown on the top portion of the device's screen, which displays certain information to the user, such as the current time, battery status, and carrier name on the iPhone.

See also

> ▶ The *Creating the UI, Accessing the UI with Outlets*, and *Adding Actions to controls* recipes

> ▶ The *Adding and customizing views* recipe in *Chapter 2, User Interface – Views*

> ▶ The *Loading a view with a view controller* recipe in *Chapter 3, User Interface – View Controllers*

Creating the UI

In this recipe, we will learn how to add and manage controls in the user interface.

Getting ready

Let's add a few controls in an interface. Start by creating a new iPhone single view application project in Xamarin Studio. Name the project `ButtonInput`. When it opens, double-click on **ButtonInputViewController.xib** in the **Solution** pad to open it with Interface Builder.

How to do it...

Now that we have a new project, and Interface Builder has opened the `ButtonInputViewController.xib` file, we'll add some controls to it.

Adding a label

Perform the following steps:

1. Go to the **Library** pane and select **Objects** from the drop-down list, if it is not already selected.

2. Select the **Label** object. Drag-and-drop **Label** onto the gray space of the view in the designer, somewhere in the top half.

3. Select and resize the **Label** object from both the left and right sides so that it snaps to the dashed line that will show up when you reach close to the edges of the view.

4. Again, with the **Label** object selected, go to the **Inspector** pane, select the **Attributes** tab, and in the **Layout** section, click on the middle alignment button.

Congratulations, you have just added **Label** in your app's main view!

Adding a button

We will perform similar steps to add a button in our interface, using the following steps:

1. Again, in the **Library** pane, in the **Objects** section, select the **Button** object. It is next to the **Label** object. Drag-and-drop it onto the bottom half of the view. Align its center with the center of **Label** we added earlier.

2. A dashed line will show up, and the **Button** object will snap to it when the centers of the two controls are almost aligned.

3. Resize the **Button** object to the same width as that of **Label**. Since **Label** has a transparent background, and you cannot see how wide it is exactly, you will know when the **Button** object is of the same width when three dashed lines show up while you are resizing it.

4. Now, let's add some text to **Button**. Select it and go to **Inspector** pane.

5. In the **Attributes** tab of the **Title** field, enter `Tap here please!`.

6. After adding the button, save the document by navigating to **File | Save** in the menu bar. The main view should now look like the following screenshot:

How it works...

As you can see, although some concepts of Interface Builder seem difficult, it is quite easy to use. It also provides a lot of feedback. When we drag objects, guidelines that basically act as snap points for positioning the control properly, appear. Also, when we resize a control, we see its dimensions next to it.

You can also resize and position the controls by modifying the values in the **Size** tab of the **Inspector** pane. Another useful feature in the **Size** tab is **Autosizing**. **Autosizing** provides layout options for the controls, and it can be very useful when we want our app to support different device orientations. You can select a control you want, and then click on the lines that are outside or inside of the square on the left in the **Autosizing** section. The image next to it animates to give you an impression of how the control will behave when the layout changes.

There's more...

Now, let's try running the app on iOS Simulator. Back in Xamarin Studio, select the project configuration **Debug** if it is not already selected. Depending on the version of iOS SDK you have installed, the following screenshot shows the available options of debugging targets:

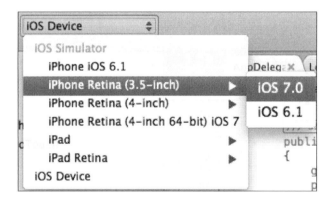

Select your preferred target and click on the **Run** button. When the compilation finishes, iOS Simulator will automatically start and run the app we just created. You can even tap on **Button** by clicking on it with the mouse, and see it responding. Of course, our app does not have any other functionality right now.

Setting titles on Buttons

Setting the title of a Button or Label can be done by simply double-clicking on it and typing the preferable title. Do it, and watch how Interface Builder behaves to show you what action is to be performed.

See also

▶ The *Compiling an iOS project* and *Debugging our application* recipes

▶ The *Receiving user input with buttons* recipe in *Chapter 2, User Interface – Views*

Accessing the UI with Outlets

In this recipe, we will discuss the concept of Outlets and their usage with Xamarin.iOS.

Getting ready

In the previous recipe, we learned how to add controls to form a basic interface for our app. In this recipe, we will discuss how to access and use these controls in our code. Launch Xamarin Studio and open the project `ButtonInput` we created earlier. Open the project's `ButtonInputViewController.xib` in Interface Builder by double-clicking on it in the **Solution** pad.

How to do it...

Perform the following steps to access the UI with Outlets:

1. In the assistant editor, select the `ButtonInputViewController.h` file, press the *Ctrl* key, and drag it from **Label** to the Objective-C source file, as displayed in the following screenshot:

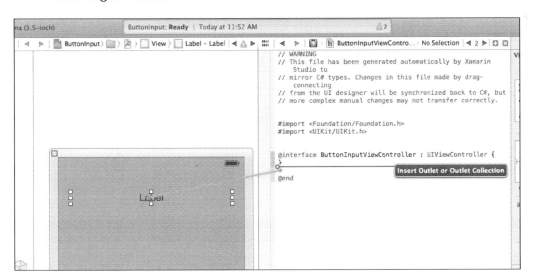

2. When you release the cursor, a context window will appear similar to the one in the following screenshot:

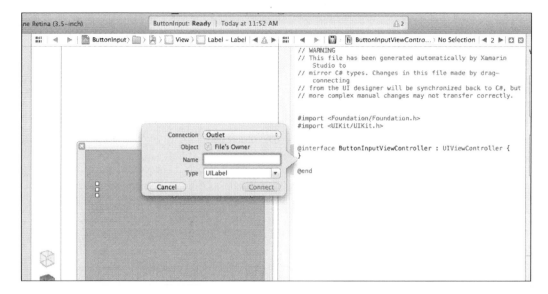

3. In the **Name** field of the context window, enter `labelStatus` and click on **Connect**.

4. Do the same for **Button**, and name it `buttonTap`. Save the Interface Builder document by navigating to **File | Save** in the menu bar or by pressing *Cmd + S* on the keyboard.

5. Back in Xamarin Studio, enter the following code in the `ViewDidLoad` method of the `ButtonInputViewController` class:

```
// Create and hook a handler to our button's
  TouchUpInside event
// through its outlet
this.buttonTap.TouchUpInside += delegate(object sender,
  EventArgs e) {
  this.labelStatus.Text = "Button tapped!";
};
```

This code snippet adds a handler to the button's `TouchUpInside` event. This event is similar to the `Clicked` event of a `Button` control in `System.Windows.Forms`. It also displays the usage of an anonymous method, which just shows how Xamarin.iOS provides C# features to .NET developers.

That was it! Our app is now ready with functional controls. Compile and run it on the simulator. See the label changing its text when you tap on the button.

How it works...

The Outlet mechanism is basically a way of connecting Interface Builder objects with the code. It is necessary since it is the only way we can access user interface objects that we create with Interface Builder. This is how Interface Builder works, and it is not just a Xamarin.iOS workaround. An Outlet of an object provides a variable of this object so that we will be able to use it in a project. Xamarin.iOS makes a developer's life much easier because when we create Outlets in Interface Builder and connect them, Xamarin Studio works in the background by autogenerating code regarding these Outlets. This is what the `ButtonInputViewController.designer.cs` file has added to provide us access to the controls we created:

```
[Outlet]
MonoTouch.UIKit.UILabel labelStatus { get; set; }

[Outlet]
MonoTouch.UIKit.UIButton buttonTap { get; set; }
```

These are the properties which provide us access to the controls. They are decorated with the `Outlet` attribute. You can see that the names of the properties are exactly the same names we entered for our Outlets. This is very important since we only have to provide names once for the Outlets, and we do not have to worry about repeating the same naming conventions in different parts of our code. Also, notice that the types of variables of the controls are exactly the same as the types of controls we dragged-and-dropped in our user interface. This information is stored in the XIB file, and Xamarin Studio reads this information accordingly.

There's more...

To remove Outlets, you first have to disconnect them. For example, to remove the `buttonTap` Outlet, press *Ctrl* and click on the button. In the panel that will appear, click on the **x** button next to the Outlet, as shown in the following screenshot. This will disconnect the Outlet.

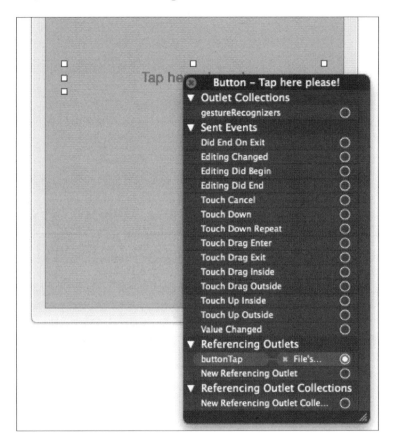

After this, delete the following code from the Objective-C source file:

```
@property (retain, nonatomic) IBOutlet UIButton *buttonTap;
```

When you save the document, the Outlet will be removed from the Xamarin Studio project.

Adding Outlets through code

Another way of adding Outlets is to create a property in your C# class and decorate it with the `Outlet` attribute:

```
[Outlet]
UIButton ButtonTap { get;    set; }
```

When you open the XIB file in Interface Builder, the Outlet will be added to the user interface. However, you would still have to connect it to the corresponding control. The easiest way to do this is to press *Ctrl*, click on the control the Outlet corresponds to, and click-and-drag from **New Referencing Outlet** to the **File's Owner** object on the left of the designer area, as shown in the following screenshot:

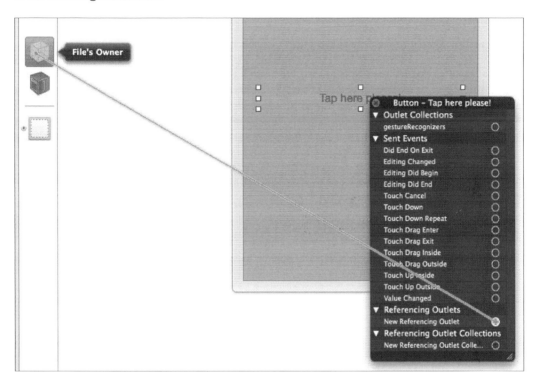

When you release the cursor, select the **ButtonTap** Outlet from the small context menu that will appear.

 Note that it is Xamarin Studio that monitors for changes made in Interface Builder, and not the other way around. When making changes in the Xamarin project, make sure to always open the XIB file from Xamarin Studio.

See also

▶ The *Interface Builder*, *Creating the UI*, and *Adding Actions to controls* recipes

▶ The *Adding and customizing views* recipe in *Chapter 2, User Interface – Views*

Adding Actions to controls

In this recipe, we discuss the concept of Actions and their usage with Xamarin.iOS.

Getting ready

In this recipe, we will discuss how to use Actions with the controls of the user interface.

1. Create a new iPhone single view application project in Xamarin Studio and name it `ButtonInputAction`.

2. Open `ButtonInputActionViewController.xib` in Interface Builder, and add the same controls, Outlets, and connections as the ones from the project `ButtonInput` from the previous recipe. Do not add any code in the project for now.

How to do it...

Adding Actions to interface objects is similar to adding Outlets, as follows:

1. In Interface Builder, press *Ctrl* and drag from the button to the source code file.

2. In the context window that will be shown, change the **Connection** field from **Outlet** to **Action**.

3. Enter `OnButtonTap` in the **Name** field, and select **Touch Up Inside** in the **Event** field, if it is not already selected.

4. Click on the **Connect** button and save the document.

5. In the `ButtonInputActionViewController` class, add the following method:

```
partial void OnButtonTap(NSObject sender)
{

    this.labelStatus.Text = "Button tapped!";

}
```

The app is ready! Compile and run it in the simulator. Tap on the button and see the text in the label change, just like in the previous app we created.

How it works...

Actions in Objective-C are the equivalent of control events in C#. They are responsible for delivering notification signals of various objects. In this example, instead of hooking up a handler on the `TouchUpInside` event of the button, we have added an action for it. As you may already have noticed, the method we added to act as a handler for the action was declared as `partial`; this is because Xamarin Studio already declared a partial method declaration for us. This is the code that was produced when we saved the document in Interface Builder:

```
[Action ("OnButtonTap:")]
partial void OnButtonTap (MonoTouch.Foundation.NSObject sender);
```

The partial declaration of the method is marked with the `Action` attribute. This is another attribute from the `MonoTouch.Foundation` namespace that allows us to expose methods as Objective-C Actions. You see that the string parameter passed in the attribute is exactly the same as the action name we entered in Interface Builder, with only an appended colon (:) to it.

 Colons in Objective-C indicate the presence of parameters. For example, `doSomething` is different from `doSomething;`. The difference is that the first does not accept any parameters, and the second accepts one parameter.

The colon at the end of the action name indicates that there is one parameter, in this case, the parameter `MonoTouch.Foundation.NSObject` sender. This is what our app looks like when we have tapped on the button in the simulator:

There's more...

The example in the preceding section was created just to show how to implement actions in Xamarin.iOS projects. Replacing an event with an action is basically at the discretion of the developer.

See also

▶ The *Interface Builder, Creating the UI*, and *Accessing the UI with Outlets* recipes

Compiling an iOS project

In this recipe, we will discuss how to compile a project with Xamarin.iOS.

Getting ready

Xamarin Studio provides many different options for compiling. In this recipe, we will discuss these options. We will be working with the project `ButtonInput` we created earlier in this chapter.

How to do it...

Perform the following steps to compile an iOS project with Xamarin.iOS:

1. With the project loaded in Xamarin Studio, go to **Project | ButtonInput Options**.
2. In the window that appears, select **iOS Build** from the **Build** section on the left pad. Select **Debug** as project configuration and **iPhoneSimulator** as a platform.
3. In the **Linker behavior** field, select **Link all assemblies** from the combo box.
4. In the **SDK version** field, select **Default** if it is not already selected.
5. Now go to **iOS Application** on the left pad.

6. In the **Summary** tab, enter `Button Input` in the **Application Name** field and `1.0` in the **Version** field. Select version **6.0** in the **Deployment Target** combo box. The **iOS Application** options window is shown in the following screenshot:

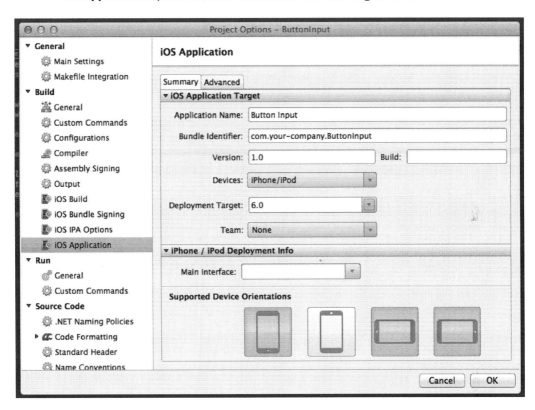

7. Click on the **OK** button and compile the project by navigating to **Build | Build All** in the menu bar.

How it works...

We have set up some options for our project. Let's see what these options provide for compilation customization:

iOS build options

The first option we set up relates to the **linker**. The linker is a tool that was developed by the Xamarin.iOS team and is provided in the SDK. Every time a Xamarin.iOS project is compiled, the compiler does not only compile the project, it also needs all the assemblies of the Xamarin.iOS Framework so that the final app will be able to run on the device (or the simulator). This actually means that every app comes with its own compiled version of the Xamarin.iOS Framework. The final application bundle is quite large in size. This is where the linker comes in. What it does is strips down the assemblies of all the unused code so that the compiler will only compile what is needed and used by the app. This results in much smaller app bundles, a precious asset when it comes to mobile apps. The following are the linker options:

> ▶ **Don't Link**: Use this option when debugging on the simulator. The linker is turned off and all the assemblies are compiled as they are. It provides faster compilation time.

> ▶ **Link SDK assemblies only**: The linker only strips down the Xamarin.iOS Framework assemblies. The project assemblies remain intact. It effectively reduces the final size of the app.

> ▶ **Link all assemblies**: The linker is activated on all assemblies. This reduces the size a bit more. Care needs to be taken when using this option if reflection or serialization is used in the code. Types and methods that are used through reflection in the code are transparent to the linker. If a situation like this exists in the code, decorate these types or methods with the `Preserve` attribute. This attribute basically informs the linker to be left out of the stripping-down process.

In the **SDK version** field, we set the iOS SDK version that will be used to compile the app. Setting it to **Default** automatically selects the highest SDK version installed on the system.

> When compiling for the simulator, turning the linker on is not suggested. This is because the compiler is not compiling the Xamarin.iOS assemblies in the iPhoneSimulator platform, hence, they are being used directly. Turning the linker on only causes compilation to take more time to complete. It has no effect in reducing the final app bundle size.

iOS application options

In the **iOS Application** window of the **Build** section in the project options, we set up three options:

> ▶ The first option is **Application Name**. This is the name of the application bundle that will be displayed on the simulator, the device, and on the App Store. As we can see here, we can normally add spaces to the name.

> ▶ The second option, **Version**, defines the version of the app. It is what will be displayed as the app's version when it is finally distributed through the App Store.

> ▶ The third option, **Deployment Target**, is the minimum iOS version the app can be installed on.

There's more...

There are two more option windows. These are **iOS Bundle Signing** and **iOS IPA Options**. They will be discussed thoroughly in the recipes in *Chapter 14, Deploying*.

See also

> ▸ The *Preparing our app for the App Store* recipe in *Chapter 14, Deploying*

Debugging our application

This recipe provides information on debugging a Xamarin.iOS app on the simulator.

Getting ready

Xamarin.iOS, in combination with Xamarin Studio, provides a debugger for debugging apps either on the simulator or on the device. In this recipe, we'll see how to use the debugger for debugging Xamarin.iOS apps. Open Xamarin Studio and load the `ButtonInput` project. Make sure to set the project configuration to **Debug | iPhone**.

How to do it...

Perform the following steps to debug your application:

1. Xamarin Studio supports breakpoints. To activate a breakpoint on a line, click on the space on the left of the line number to set it. Set a breakpoint on the following line in the `ButtonInputViewController.cs` file:

   ```
   this.labelStatus.Text = "Button tapped!";
   ```

   The following screenshot shows what a breakpoint in Xamarin Studio looks like:

   ```
   23   public override void ViewDidLoad ()
   24   {
   25       base.ViewDidLoad ();
   26
   27       // Create and hook a handler to our button's TouchUpInside event
   28       // through its outlet
   29       this.buttonTap.TouchUpInside += delegate(object sender, EventArgs e) {
   30           this.labelStatus.Text = "Button tapped!";
   31       };
   32
   33   }
   ```

2. Compile and debug the project by clicking on the **Run** button or by navigating to **Run | Start Debugging** on the menu bar. Xamarin Studio's status will display the message **Waiting for debugger to connect...**.

3. When the simulator is opened and the app is loaded, watch the information that is provided in the **Application Output** pad.

4. Tap on the app button. Execution will pause and Xamarin Studio will highlight the breakpoint in yellow. Move the mouse over the `labelStatus` variable in the breakpoint line. A window will be displayed with all the evaluated variable's members, as shown in the following screenshot:

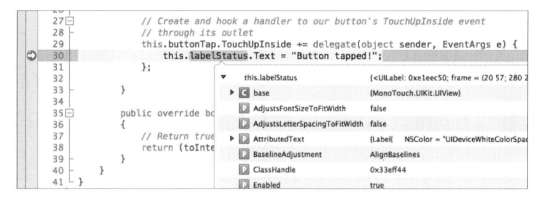

5. To stop debugging, click on the **Stop** button in the toolbar.

How it works...

The debugger that is used is called **soft debugger**. It is called so because it depends on both the runtime and Xamarin Studio, combined to provide one unified debugging platform. When the debugging process starts, Xamarin Studio begins listening for debugging information from the app. The same applies for debugging on both the simulator and the device. When the app executes, it starts sending information back to Xamarin Studio. It then displays that information in the **Application Output** pad, which is automatically activated. A typical application output when debugging is the information on the assemblies that are loaded, the threads that begin execution, and the breakpoints, if any, that are available.

There's more...

The `Console.WriteLine()` method can also be used for debugging purposes. The debugger takes care of this and redirects the output of the method to Xamarin Studio's **Application Output** pad.

App performance when debugging

When compiling for debugging purposes, the compiler produces larger and slower code. This is because it generates extra code that is needed to provide the appropriate debugging information. That's why, when debugging an app, the execution of the app is much slower than on simple running situations. Before producing a release copy of the app, remember to compile it with the **Release | iPhone** project configuration to avoid slow runtime execution.

Breakpoints in FinishedLaunching

One more reason for not to have complicated code in the `FinishedLaunching` method is that, in most cases, you will not be able to debug it. If you set a breakpoint in `FinishedLaunching`, app execution will pause, but iOS will terminate the app when the time limit is reached.

See also

▶ The *Creating profiles* recipe in *Chapter 14, Deploying*

2
User Interface – Views

In this chapter, we will cover the following topics:

- ► Adding and customizing views
- ► Receiving user input with buttons
- ► Displaying images
- ► Displaying and editing text
- ► Using the keyboard
- ► Displaying progress
- ► Displaying content larger than the screen
- ► Navigating through the content divided into pages
- ► Displaying alerts
- ► Creating a custom view
- ► Styling views

Introduction

An application's **User Interface** (**UI**) is essential for providing the user with an easy way of communicating with a device, be it a computer, a mobile phone, or a tablet. On a mobile device, the user interface is not only essential but the only way to interact with the user. Developers have to cope with various limitations and restrictions when developing applications for mobile devices. The processing power of mobile devices does not match that of desktop CPUs, and the screens are smaller, making the process of choosing what sort of information will be displayed each time somewhat more difficult.

In this chapter, we will discuss the key components of an iOS application's UI. We will see how to use and customize these components to create rich application user interfaces and discuss the similarities and differences they have with their desktop equivalents. The following is a list of these components:

- ▸ **UIView**: This is a customizable container that is the base object of most iOS user interface controls

- ▸ **UIButton**: This is the equivalent of a Button in the .NET world

- ▸ **UILabel**: This is the equivalent of a Label in the .NET world

- ▸ **UIImageView**: This is a view that allows us to display and create basic animations with images

- ▸ **UITextView**: This is a view that allows us to display editable text

- ▸ **UITextField**: This is similar to .NET's TextBox control

- ▸ **UIProgressView**: This displays the known length progress

- ▸ **UIScrollView**: This provides the ability to display scrollable content

- ▸ **UIPageControl**: This provides navigation functionality to the content that is divided into different pages or screens

- ▸ **UIAlertView**: This is the default iOS control for displaying a message box to the user

We will also talk about how to programmatically create instances of these components and how to style and use them efficiently.

Adding and customizing views

In this recipe, we will discuss how to add and customize UIView with Xcode's Interface Builder.

Getting ready

Adding views with Interface Builder is a simple task. Let's start by creating a new iPhone Single View Application project in Xamarin Studio. Name the project FirstViewApp and open the FirstViewAppViewController.xib file with Interface Builder.

How to do it...

Perform the following steps:

1. To add a view to the project, drag-and-drop a UIView object from the **Library** pad onto the main view. Make sure that it fits the entire window area. To make UIView accessible, create an outlet for it and name it subView.

The concept of outlets and how to use them is discussed in detail in *Chapter 1, Development Tools*.

2. Select the view that we have just added and go to the **Inspector** pad. Select the **Attributes** tab, and select **Dark Gray Color** in the **Background** drop-down list. Now, select the **Size** tab and reduce the view's height by 60 points. Save the document.

3. Compile and run the app on the simulator. The result should look like the one shown in the following screenshot:

The dark gray portion of the simulator's screen is the view that we have just added.

How it works...

We have successfully created an app that contains one view. Of course, this app does not provide any functionality. It is only meant to show how to add a view and display it.

Views are the essential components of an iOS app interface. Every visual user interface object inherits from the UIView class. The concept is somewhat different from a form in .NET. A view manages content drawing, accepts other views as subviews, provides autosizing features, can accept touch events for itself and its subviews, and many of its properties can even be animated. Even UIWindow inherits from UIView. It is this class or its inheritors that iOS developers will use most frequently.

When a view that is added with Interface Builder is first instantiated at runtime, it sets its `Frame` property with values that are set through the **Inspector** pad's **Size** tab. The `Frame` property is of the `RectangleF` type, and it defines the location of the view in its superview's coordinate system (in our case, the main window) and its size in points.

> In Objective-C, the `frame` property of UIView is of the `CGRect` type. This type has not been bound in Xamarin.iOS, and the more familiar `System.Drawing.RectangleF` was used instead.
>
> A superview is a view's parent view, while subviews are its child views. Views that have the same superview are described as siblings.

The default coordinate system in iOS originates from the top-left corner and extends towards the bottom and the right. The coordinate origin is always the same and cannot be changed programmatically.

The coordinate system of iOS is displayed in the following diagram:

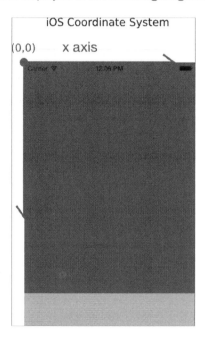

When the `Frame` property is set, it adjusts the `Bounds` property. The `Bounds` property defines the location of the view in its own coordinate system and its size in points. It is also of the `RectangleF` type. The default location for the `Bounds` property is (0,0), and its size is always the same as the view's `Frame` value. Both these properties' sizes are connected to each other, so when you change the size of `Frame`, the size of `Bounds` changes accordingly and vice versa. You can change the `Bounds` property to display different parts of the view.

A view's frame can exceed the screen in both location and position. That is, a view's frame with values *(x = -50, y = -50, width = 1500, height = 1500)* is perfectly acceptable, although it will not be completely visible on the screen of an iPhone.

There's more...

Another thing to note is that the `UIView` class inherits from the `UIResponder` class. The `UIResponder` class is responsible for responding to and handling events. When a view is added to a superview, it becomes part of its responder chain. The `UIView` class exposes the properties and methods of `UIResponder`, and the ones we are interested in describing for now are the following two:

- **IsFirstResponder property**: This returns a Boolean value indicating whether the view is the first responder. Basically, it indicates if the view has focus.

- **ResignFirstResponder():** This causes the view to lose focus.

Adding views programmatically

If we would like to add a view on our main view programmatically, we would use the following `UIView.AddSubview(UIView)` method:

```
this.View.AddSubview(this.subView);
```

The `AddSubview` method adds its parameter, which is of the `UIView` type, to the list of the caller's subviews and sets its `Superview` parameter to the caller. A view will not be displayed unless it is added to a parent view with the `AddSubview` method. Also, if a view already has a superview and it is added to another view with its `AddSubview` method, its `Superview` is changed to that of the new caller. What this means is that a view can have only one superview at a time.

 When adding a view as a subview with Interface Builder, it is not required to use the `AddSubview` method to display the subview. However, it is required to call the `AddSubview` method when adding views programmatically.

For removing a view from its superview programmatically, call its `RemoveFromSuperview` method. Calling this method on a view that has no superview does nothing. Care must be taken when we want to reuse the view we want to remove. We must keep a reference to it, or it might be released.

View content layout

Another important property of `UIView` is `ContentMode`. `ContentMode` accepts values of the `UIViewContentMode` enumeration type. This property sets how the `UIView` will display its content, usually an image. The default value of this property is `UIViewContentMode.ScaleToFill`. This scales the content to fit the exact view's size, stretching it if necessary. The available values of `UIViewContentMode` are explained in detail in the *Displaying Images* recipe later in this chapter.

See also

- ▶ The *Creating a custom view* recipe
- ▶ The *Creating the UI* recipe in *Chapter 1, Development Tools*
- ▶ The *Accessing the UI with Outlets* recipe in *Chapter 1, Development Tools*

Receiving user input with buttons

In this recipe, we will learn how to use buttons to receive and respond to user input.

Getting ready

We used buttons in *Chapter 1, Development Tools*, to discuss how to use Interface Builder to add controls to the user interface. In this recipe, we will describe the `UIButton` class in more detail. Open the `FirstViewApp` project, which we created in the previous recipe, in Xamarin Studio. Increase the height of the view, which we added, to cover the whole device screen in Interface Builder and save the document.

How to do it...

Perform the following steps:

1. We will programmatically add a button in our interface. This button will change our view's background color when tapped. Open the `FirstViewAppViewController.cs` file and enter the following code in the class:

```
UIButton buttonChangeColor;
private void CreateButton ()
{
  RectangleF viewFrame =
    this.subView.Frame;
  RectangleF buttonFrame = new
    RectangleF (10f, viewFrame.Bottom - 200f,
    viewFrame.Width - 20f, 50f);
  this.buttonChangeColor = UIButton.FromType
    (UIButtonType.System);
```

```
      this.buttonChangeColor.Frame = buttonFrame;
      this.buttonChangeColor.SetTitle ("Tap to change view
        color", UIControlState.Normal);
      this.buttonChangeColor.SetTitle ("Changing color...",
        UIControlState.Highlighted);
      this.buttonChangeColor.TouchUpInside +=
        this.ButtonChangeColor_TouchUpInside;
      this.subView.AddSubview (this.buttonChangeColor);
   }
   bool isYellow;
   private void ButtonChangeColor_TouchUpInside (object
     sender, EventArgs e)
   {
     if (this.isYellow) {
       this.subView.BackgroundColor = UIColor.LightGray;
       this.isYellow = false;
     } else {
       this.subView.BackgroundColor = UIColor.Yellow;
       this.isYellow = true;
     }
   }
}
```

2. In the `ViewDidLoad` method, add the following line:

    ```
    this.CreateButton ();
    ```

3. Compile and run the app on the simulator. When the button is tapped, the result should be similar to the following screenshot:

How it works...

In this recipe, we have added a button to the user interface. This button changes the background color of its superview. Furthermore, we have accomplished this without using Interface Builder at all.

Let's see now what the code does. We create the following field that will hold the button object:

```
// A button to change the view's background color
UIButton buttonChangeColor;
```

In the `CreateButton` method, we create the button and set some properties. The method is shown in the following code:

```
// Create the appropriate rectangles for the button's frame
RectangleF viewFrame = this.subView.Frame;
RectangleF buttonFrame = new RectangleF (10f, viewFrame.Bottom -
  200f, viewFrame.Width - 20f, 50f);
```

First, we assign the view's frame to a new variable named `viewFrame`. Then, we create a new `RectangleF` object named `buttonFrame`. This object will be assigned to the button's `Frame` property. Now that we have a frame for our button, we can initialize it as shown in the following code snippet:

```
// Create the button.
this.buttonChangeColor = UIButton.FromType (UIButtonType.System);
this.buttonChangeColor.Frame = buttonFrame;
```

The button is initialized with the `UIButton.FromType(UIButtonType)` static method. This method takes one parameter of the `UIButtonType` type and returns predefined types of buttons that are included in iOS SDK. The `UIButtonType.System` button enumeration value used here is the default type of button without any borders or background. After the `buttonChangeColor` object is initialized, we set its frame to the `RectangleF` value we created earlier.

Now that we have provided an initialization code for the button, we will set its titles (that's right, more than one) as shown in the following code:

```
// Set the button's titles
this.buttonChangeColor.SetTitle ("Tap to change view color",
  UIControlState.Normal);
this.buttonChangeColor.SetTitle ("Changing color...",
  UIControlState.Highlighted);
```

We call the `UIButton.SetTitle(string, UIControlState)` method twice. This method is responsible for setting the button's title for each given button state. The string parameter is the actual title that will be shown. The second parameter is an enumeration of the `UIControlState` type. This parameter indicates the different control states that apply to controls. These control states are as follows:

- ▶ **Normal**: This is the default idle state of an enabled control.
- ▶ **Highlighted**: This is the state of the control when a touch-up event occurs.
- ▶ **Disabled**: This is the state when the control is disabled and does not accept any events.
- ▶ **Selected**: This is the state when the control is selected. In most cases, this state does not apply. However, it is useful when a selection state is required, like in a `UISegmentedControl` object.
- ▶ **Application**: This is the additional control state value for an application's use.
- ▶ **Reserved**: This is for internal framework use.

So, with the `UIButton.SetTitle(string, UIControlState)` method, we have set the title that will be displayed when the button is in its default state and the title that will be displayed while the button is being tapped.

After this, we set the button's handler for the `TouchUpInside` event and add it as a subview to `subView` using the following code:

```
this.buttonChangeColor.TouchUpInside +=
  this.ButtonChangeColor_TouchUpInside;
// Display the button
this.subView.AddSubview (this.buttonChangeColor);
```

Inside the `buttonChangeColor_TouchUpInside` event, we change the background color of the view according to the Boolean field that we have declared, as shown in the following code:

```
if (this.isYellow) {
  this.subView.BackgroundColor = UIColor.DarkGray;
  this.isYellow = false;
} else {
  this.subView.BackgroundColor = UIColor.Yellow;
  this.isYellow = true;
}
```

This is done by setting the view's `BackgroundColor` property to the appropriate `UIColor` class instance we want, as shown in the preceding highlighted code. The `UIColor` object is a class with many different static methods and properties that allow us to create different colored objects.

When you compile and run the app on the simulator, notice the view's color change when you tap the button. Also notice how the button's title changes while the mouse cursor (or a finger on the device) is "touching" the button.

There's more...

In this recipe, we used the `UIButton.FromType(UIButtonType)` static method to initialize the button. A brief description of each of the enumeration flags of `UIButtonType` are as follows:

- ▶ **System**: This is the default type of button.
- ▶ **Custom**: This is a borderless transparent button. Use this flag when creating custom buttons with images as backgrounds. The button's title is not transparent.
- ▶ **RoundedRect**: This is the default type of button with rounded corners. As of iOS 7, this type of `UIButton` is deprecated. Use `UIButtonType.System` instead.
- ▶ **DetailDisclosure**: This is a round blue button that reveals additional information related to an item.
- ▶ **InfoLight**: This is a light-colored button with the letter (**i**) that represents information display.
- ▶ **InfoDark**: This is the same as InfoLight; it is shown with a dark color.
- ▶ **ContactAdd**: This is a round blue button with a white plus sign (**+**). Usually, this button is displayed to present contact information to add to an item.

Changing the appearance of buttons

For creating custom buttons with the `UIButtonType.Custom` type, use the `UIButton` class' `SetBackgroundImage` and `SetImage` methods. They both accept one `UIImage` and one `UIControlState` parameter so that different images for different control states can be set. When setting images for buttons, be sure to set the `UIButton.ContentMode` property accordingly, irrespective of whether creating a custom button or not.

The functionality provided by the `SetImage` and `SetBackgroundImage` methods can also be accomplished in the corresponding **Image** and **Background** fields in the **Attributes** tab of the **Inspector** pad in Interface Builder. Select the state for which to set the desired image(s) from the drop-down list box and set the path to the image file, as shown in the following screenshot:

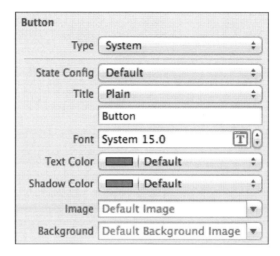

See also

▶ The *Adding and customizing views* recipe

▶ The *Displaying images* recipe

▶ The *Creating a custom view* recipe

▶ The *Styling views* recipe

▶ The *Creating the UI* recipe in *Chapter 1, Development Tools*

Displaying images

In this recipe, we will learn how to use the `UIImageView` class to display images on screen.

Getting ready

In this recipe, we will see how to bundle and display images in a project. An image file will be needed for display. The image file used here is named `Toroni.jpg`. Create a new iPhone **Single View Application** project in Xamarin Studio and name it `ImageViewerApp`.

How to do it...

The following are the steps for this recipe:

1. Open the `ImageViewerAppViewController.xib` file in Interface Builder.

2. Add a `UIImageView` object on its view. Connect the `UIImageView` object with an outlet named `imageDisplay`.

3. Save the document.

4. Back in Xamarin Studio, in the `ImageViewerAppViewController` class, enter the following code:

```
public override ViewDidLoad()
{
  base.ViewDidLoad();
  this.imageDisplay.ContentMode =
    UIViewContentMode.ScaleAspectFit;
  this.imageDisplay.Image = UIImage.FromFile("Toroni.jpg");
}
```

5. Right-click on the project in the **Solution** pad and navigate to **Add | Add Files...**. Select the image file you want to display and click on **Open**.

6. Right-click on the image file you have just added and navigate to **Build Action | BundleResource**.

7. Finally, compile and run the app on the simulator. The image you added to the project should be displayed on the screen, like in the following screenshot:

How it works...

The UIImageView class is basically a view customized for displaying images. When you add an image in a project, its **Build Action** must be set to **BundleResource** in the **Solution** pad; otherwise, the image will not be copied into the app bundle. Fortunately, Xamarin Studio is smart enough to handle this setting automatically for images.

The ContentMode property is very important when displaying images. It sets the way the UIView (UIImageView in this case) object will display the image. We have set it to UIViewContentMode.ScaleAspectFit so that it will be resized to fit the area of UIImageView, keeping the aspect ratio intact at the same time. If the ContentMode property was left at its default ScaleToFill value, the output would be something like the one shown in the following screenshot:

To set the image that UIImageView should display, we set its Image property with a UIImage object, as shown in the following code:

```
this.imageDisplay.Image = UIImage.FromFile("Toroni.jpg");
```

The `ContentMode` property accepts an enumeration type named `UIViewContentMode`. The values provided are as follows:

- `ScaleToFill`: This is the default value of the base `UIView` object. It scales the content to fit the size of the view, changing the aspect ratio as necessary.

- `ScaleAspectFit`: This scales the content to fit the size of the view, maintaining its aspect ratio. The remaining area of the view's content becomes transparent.

- `ScaleAspectFill`: This scales the content to fill the size of the view, maintaining its aspect ratio. Some part of the content may be left out.

- `Redraw`: When a view's bounds are changed, its content is not redrawn. This value causes the content to be redrawn. Drawing content is an expensive operation in terms of CPU cycles, so think twice before using this value with large content.

- `Center`: This places the content at the center of the view, keeping its aspect ratio.

- `Top`, `Bottom`, `Left`, `Right`, `TopLeft`, `TopRight`, `BottomLeft`, and `BottomRight`: These align the content in the view with the corresponding value.

There's more...

The `UIImage` class is the object that represents image information. The file formats it supports are listed in the following table:

File Format	File extension
Portable Network Graphics (PNG)	`.png`
Joint Photographic Experts Group (JPEG)	`.jpg`, `.jpeg`
Tagged Image File Format (TIFF)	`.tiff`, `.tif`
Graphic Interchange Format	`.gif`
Windows Bitmap Format	`.bmp`
Windows Icon Format	`.ico`
Windows Cursor	`.cur`
XWindow bitmap	`.xbm`

 Animated GIF image files are not supported by the `UIImageView` class. When an animated GIF is set to the `Image` property of `UIImageView`, only its first frame will be displayed as a static image.

Using images for different screen sizes

Creating images for backgrounds provides developers with the ability to produce rich and elegant user interfaces for their apps. The preferred image file format for creating backgrounds for views is PNG. However, since iPhone 4 was released, the screen resolution was increased. To support both screen resolutions in an app, the iOS SDK provides an easy solution. Just save the image in the higher resolution and add a `@2x` suffix to the file name just before the extension. For example, the name of a higher resolution version of a file named `Default.png` would be `Default@2x.png`. Also, no extra code is required to use both files. Just use the `UIImage.FromBundle(string)` static method, passing the file name without an extension. The following line of code would load the appropriate file, depending on the screen resolution:

```
this.imageDisplay = UIImage.FromBundle("Default");
```

iOS takes care of loading the appropriate file, depending on the device the app is running on.

 The preceding case only applies to PNG image files.

See also

▸ The *Adding and customizing views* recipe

▸ The *Selecting images and videos* recipe in *Chapter 7, Multimedia Resources*

Displaying and editing text

In this recipe, we will learn how to display simple text blocks with editing functionality.

Getting ready

In this recipe, we will discuss the usage of `UITextView` and how to display editable text with it. Create a new iPhone **Single View Application** project in Xamarin Studio and name it `TextViewApp`.

How to do it...

Perform the following steps:

1. Open `TextViewAppViewController.xib` in Interface Builder.

2. Add a `UIButton` near the top of its view and a `UITextView` below it. Connect both objects to their outlets.

3. Save the document.

4. Back in Xamarin Studio, enter the following `ViewDidLoad` method in the `TextViewAppViewController` class:

```
public override void ViewDidLoad ()
{
  base.ViewDidLoad ();
  this.buttonFinished.Enabled = false;
  this.buttonFinished.TouchUpInside += (sender, e) => {

    this.myTextView.ResignFirstResponder ();

  } ;
  this.myTextView.Delegate = new MyTextViewDelegate (this);
}
```

5. Add the following nested class:

```
private class MyTextViewDelegate : UITextViewDelegate
{

  public MyTextViewDelegate
    (TextView
    AppViewController parentController)
  {
    this.parentController = parentController;
  }
  private
    TextViewAppViewController parentController;

  public override void EditingStarted
    (UITextView textView)
  {
    this.parentController.buttonFinished.Enabled = true;
  }

  public override void EditingEnded
    (UITextView textView)
  {
    this.parentController.buttonFinished.Enabled = false;
  }

  public override void Changed
    (UITextView textView)
  {
    Console.WriteLine ("Text changed!");
  }

}
```

6. Compile and run the app on the simulator. Tap somewhere in the text view and the keyboard will appear. Type some text and then tap on the **Finished** button to hide the keyboard.

How it works...

The `UITextView` class provides an object that displays editable blocks of text. To respond to the events of our text view, we have implemented a class (shown in the following code) that inherits from `UITextViewDelegate`, which will act as the text view's delegate:

```
private class MyTextViewDelegate : UITextViewDelegate
{
  public MyTextViewDelegate
    (TextViewAppViewController parentController)
  {this.parentController = parentController;}
  private
    TextViewAppViewController parentController;
```

We declared a constructor that accepts a `TextViewAppViewController` object so that we can have the instance of our controller available to access our controls.

Then, we override three methods of the `UITextViewDelegate` class, as shown in the following code:

```
public override void EditingStarted (UITextView textView)
{
  this.parentController.buttonFinished.Enabled = true;
}

public override void EditingEnded (UITextView textView)
{
  this.parentController.buttonFinished.Enabled = false;
}

public override void Changed (UITextViewtextViewUITextView
  textView)
{
  Console.WriteLine ("Text changed!");
}
```

These methods are the handlers that will get called whenever a corresponding event is triggered. When tapping on the text view, the `EditingStarted` method gets called. We enable the **Finished** button in it. When we type some text in the text view, the `Changed` method gets called, and we can see the output of the `Console.WriteLine` method in Xamarin Studio's **Application Output** pad. Finally, when we tap on the **Finished** button, the keyboard hides, and the `EditingEnded` method gets called. This method allows us to disable the button.

In the `ViewDidLoad` method, we assign a handler to the `TouchUpInside` event of the button, as shown in the following code:

```
this.buttonFinished.TouchUpInside += (sender, e) => {
  this.myTextView.ResignFirstResponder ();
};
```

We call the text view's `ResignFirstResponder()` method in it so that when the button is tapped, the text view will lose focus, causing the keyboard to hide. Then, we assign a new instance of the delegate we created to the text view's `Delegate` property, passing the instance of the `TextViewAppViewController` object, as shown in the following code:

```
this.myTextView.Delegate = new MyTextViewDelegate (this);
```

There's more...

Delegates in Objective-C are somewhat different than those in C#. Although in both worlds, their most common usage is to provide access to some form of event notification mechanism, in Objective-C, this mechanism is a bit more complex. A C# delegate is much like a function pointer in C or C++ programming languages. It is an object that holds a reference to a method of a specific signature. On the other hand, an Objective-C delegate is a certain type of object that conforms to a specific `protocol`. It is basically an object that wraps one or more methods (and/or other members) that act as event handlers.

 An Objective-C protocol is similar to an interface in C#.

The concept of delegate objects might seem confusing at first, but it is not difficult to comprehend. Regarding the event notification mechanism, Xamarin.iOS simplifies things for .NET developers by providing events for most objects, including `UITextView` described here.

See also

▶ The *Using the keyboard* recipe

Using the keyboard

In this recipe, we will discuss some important aspects of the device's virtual keyboard usage.

Getting ready

In the previous recipe, we discussed how to edit text. In this recipe, we will discuss some of the things we can or even must do to use the keyboard effectively. Create a new iPhone **Single View Application** project in Xamarin Studio and name it `KeyboardApp`.

How to do it...

Perform the following steps:

1. Open the `KeyboardAppViewController.xib` file in Interface Builder.

2. Add a `UITextField` object in the bottom-half portion of the view and connect it to an outlet.

3. Save the document.

4. Back in Xamarin Studio, enter the following code in the `KeyboardAppViewController` class:

```
private NSObject kbdWillShow, kbdDidHide;
public override void ViewDidLoad()
{

  base.ViewDidLoad();

  this.emailField.KeyboardType =
    UIKeyboardType.EmailAddress;
  this.emailField.ReturnKeyType = UIReturnKeyType.Done;

  this.kbdWillShow =
    UIKeyboard.Notifications.ObserveWillShow((s, e) => {
    RectangleF kbdBounds = e.FrameEnd;
    RectangleF textFrame =
      this.emailField.Frame;
      textFrame.Y -= kbdBounds.Height;
  this.emailField.Frame = textFrame;
  } );
  this.kbdDidHide =
    UIKeyboard.Notifications.ObserveDidHide((s, e) => {
    RectangleF kbdBounds = e.FrameEnd;
    RectangleF textFrame =
      this.emailField.Frame;
    textFrame.Y += kbdBounds.Height;
    this.emailField.Frame = textFrame;
  } );


  this.emailField.ShouldReturn = delegate(UITextField
    textField) {
    return textField.ResignFirstResponder ();
  } ;


}
```

5. Compile and run the app on the simulator. Tap on the text field and watch it moving upwards to avoid being hidden from the keyboard. Tap the **Done** button on the keyboard and watch the text field returning to its original position when the keyboard hides.

How it works...

There are various types of keyboards in iOS. Since not all keys can be displayed at once due to the restricted screen size, it is a good practice to set the appropriate type of keyboard according to the text input we need the user to provide. In this project, we have set the keyboard to the **Email Address** type. We have also customized the type of **Return key** by setting it to **Done** in the following code:

```
this.emailField.KeyboardType = UIKeyboardType.EmailAddress;
this.emailField.ReturnKeyType = UIReturnKeyType.Done;
```

When the keyboard is displayed, it is the developer's responsibility to make sure it does not obstruct the essential UI elements. In this case, since we provide the user with the ability to enter some text input, we have to make sure that the text field is shown, so the user will be able to see what is being typed. For this, we add two observers in the default notification center using the following code:

```
// Add observers for the keyboard
this.kbdWillShow = UIKeyboard.Notifications.ObserveWillShow((s, e)
  => {
```

The notification center is iOS' mechanism for providing system-wide notifications. Normally, it can be accessed through the `NSNotificationCenter.DefaultCenter` static property. However, Xamarin.iOS provides some APIs that simplify things for us. In the example project for this recipe, you will find the usage of both APIs. In this recipe, we are using Xamarin's APIs.

By calling `UIKeyboard.Notifications.ObserveWillShow` and passing a handler to it, we subscribe to the notification center so that we get notified whenever the keyboard is about to be displayed. This handler is of the `EventHandler<UIKeyboardEventArgs>` type, and the `UIKeyboardEventArgs` parameter provides us with, among others, the frame of the keyboard after it has been shown (as shown in the following code):

```
// Get the keyboard's bounds
RectangleF kbdBounds = e.FrameEnd;
```

Then, we store the text field's frame in a variable using the following code:

```
// Get the text field's frame
RectangleF textFrame =
  this.emailField.Frame;
```

We reduce the frame's Y position using the following code value so that the text field will move upwards:

```
// Change the y position of the text field frame
textFrame.Y -= kbdBounds.Height;
```

When the new frame is set to emailField (as shown in the following code), it will move to the new position:

```
this.emailField.Frame = textFrame;
```

The second handler is needed for moving the text field back to its original position after the keyboard is closed. It is almost the same as the first handler, except for two differences. The UIKeyboard.Notifications.ObserveDidHide method is used. This method will trigger our handler after the keyboard is hidden. In this handler, we just make sure that we readjust the text field's position back to where it was.

The last few lines of code in the ViewDidLoad method set the ShouldReturn property of the UITextField class. This property accepts a delegate of the UITextFieldCondition type, as shown in the following code:

```
this.emailField.ShouldReturn = delegate(UITextField textField) {
   return textField.ResignFirstResponder ();
} ;
```

The handler we have added is called whenever the user taps the return key on the virtual keyboard. Here, we call the ResignFirstResponder method of UITextField, which will hide our keyboard.

There's more...

The two fields of the NSObject type in the class, which are assigned to the return values of the UIKeyboard.Notifications methods we used, hold information about the observers we added. For removing the two observers we have added here, add the following code:

```
NSNotificationCenter.DefaultCenter.RemoveObserver
   (this.kbdWillShow);
NSNotificationCenter.DefaultCenter.RemoveObserver
   (this.kbdDidHide);
```

Care must be taken when developing an app that uses the keyboard and supports multiple interface orientations. If, for example, the keyboard appears in portrait orientation and the user changes to landscape orientation, both the keyboard's bounds and the text field's frame will be different and must be adjusted accordingly.

See also

▶ The *Displaying and editing text* recipe

▶ The *Adjusting the UI orientation* recipe in *Chapter 9, Interacting with Device Hardware*

Displaying progress

In this recipe, we will discuss how to display the progress of known length.

Getting ready

In this recipe, we will talk about the `UIProgressView` control. This control provides a similar functionality to the ProgressBar control in .NET. Create a new iPhone **Single View Application** project in Xamarin Studio and name it `ProgressApp`.

How to do it...

The following are the steps for using the `UIProgressView` class. Note that in this recipe, we will add all the controls programmatically without the use of Interface Builder.

1. Add the following `using` directives in the `ProgressAppViewController` class file:

```
using System.Drawing;
using System.Threading;
using System.Threading.Tasks;
```

2. Add the following fields in the class:

```
UILabel labelStatus;
UIButton buttonStartProgress;
UIProgressView progressView;
float incrementBy = 0f;
```

3. Enter the following code in the `ViewDidLoad` override:

```
// Initialize the label
this.labelStatus = new UILabel (new RectangleF (60f, 60f,
  200f, 50f));
this.labelStatus.AdjustsFontSizeToFitWidth = true;
// Initialize the button
this.buttonStartProgress = UIButton.FromType
  (UIButtonType.System);
this.buttonStartProgress.Frame = new RectangleF (60f, 400f,
  200f, 40f);
```

```
    this.buttonStartProgress.SetTitle ("Tap to start
        progress!", UIControlState.Normal);
    this.buttonStartProgress.TouchUpInside += delegate {
        // Disable the button
        this.buttonStartProgress.Enabled = false;
        this.progressView.Progress = 0f;
        // Start a progress
        Task.Factory.StartNew(this.StartProgress);
    } ;

    // Initialize the progress view
    this.progressView = new UIProgressView (new RectangleF
        (60f, 200f, 200f, 50f));

    // Set the progress view's initial value
    this.progressView.Progress = 0f;

    // Set the progress increment value
    // for 10 items
    this.incrementBy = 1f / 10f;

    this.View.AddSubview(this.labelStatus);
    this.View.AddSubview(this.buttonStartProgress);
    this.View.AddSubview(this.progressView);
```

4. Add the following method in the class:

```
private void StartProgress ()
{
    float currentProgress = 0f;
    while (currentProgress < 1f)
    {
        Thread.Sleep(1000);
        this.InvokeOnMainThread(delegate {
            // Advance the progress
            this.progressView.Progress += this.incrementBy;
            currentProgress = this.progressView.Progress;
            // Set the label text
            this.labelStatus.Text = string.Format("Current value:
                { 0}", Math.Round((double)this.
                progressView.Progress, 2));
            if (currentProgress >= 1f)
            {
                this.labelStatus.Text = "Progress completed!";
                this.buttonStartProgress.Enabled = true;
            }//end if
```

```
        } );
      }//end while
  }
```

5. Compile and run the app on the simulator. Tap on the button and watch the progress bar fill.

How it works...

The current value of `UIProgressView` is represented by its `Progress` property. Its acceptable value range is always from 0 to 1. So, when we initialize it, we set it to 0 to make sure that the bar is not filled at all. This can be done using the following code:

```
this.progressView.Progress = 0f;
```

Since `UIProgressView` has a specific range, we need to assign the value we want it to be incremented by, depending on the number of items we need to process (in this case, 10) using the following code:

```
this.incrementBy = 1f / 10f;
```

In the button's `TouchUpInside` handler, we disable the button and start our progress through `Task` from `System.Threading.Tasks`, as shown in the following code:

```
this.buttonStartProgress.TouchUpInside += delegate {
  // Disable the button
  this.buttonStartProgress.Enabled = false;
  this.progressView.Progress = 0;
  // Start a progress
  Task.Factory.StartNew(this.StartProgress);
};
```

In the `StartProgress()` method, we start a loop that will process the work, which needs to be done. Since the work executes on a separate thread, when we want to make changes to the controls, it must be done on the main UI thread by calling the `InvokeOnMainThread` method, which accepts a parameter of the `NSAction` type. An `NSAction` type parameter can accept anonymous methods as well, as seen in the following code:

```
this.InvokeOnMainThread(delegate {
  // Advance the progress
  this.progressView.Progress += this.incrementBy;
  currentProgress = this.progressView.Progress;
  // Set the label text
  this.labelStatus.Text = string.Format("Current value: { 0}",
  Math.Round((double)this.progressView.Progress, 2));
  if (currentProgress >= 1f)
  {
```

```
        this.labelStatus.Text = "Progress completed!";
        this.buttonStartProgress.Enabled = true;
    }//end if
});
```

There's more...

The progress view supports two styles. `UIProgressViewStyle.Default` (the one that was used in this recipe) and `UIProgressViewStyle.Bar`. There is absolutely no functionality difference between the two styles, except for appearance. To change the style of the progress view, set its `Style` property to one of the previously mentioned values.

UIProgressView height

Setting the height of the progress view has no effect, as it is constant for the control. For creating a variable-height progress bar, the `UIProgressView` class must be subclassed.

See also

▸   The *Receiving user input with buttons* recipe

Displaying content larger than the screen

In this recipe, we will learn how to display content that extends beyond the screen's bounds.

Getting ready

In this recipe, we will discuss the `UIScrollView` control. Create a new iPhone **Single View Application** project and name it `ScrollApp`.

How to do it...

The following are the steps to create the project:

1. Open the `ScrollAppViewController.xib` file in Interface Builder.

2. Add a `UIScrollView` object on its view and connect it to an outlet. Save the document.

3. Back in Xamarin Studio, add the following code in the `ScrollAppViewController` class:

```
// Image view
UIImageView imgView;
public override void ViewDidLoad()
{
  base.ViewDidLoad();

  this.imgView = new UIImageView (UIImage.FromFile
    ("Kastoria.jpg"));
  this.scrollView.ContentSize = this.imgView.Image.Size;
  this.scrollView.ContentOffset = new PointF (200f, 50f);
  this.scrollView.PagingEnabled = true;
  this.scrollView.MinimumZoomScale = 0.25f;
  this.scrollView.MaximumZoomScale = 2f;
  this.scrollView.ViewForZoomingInScrollView =
    delegate(UIScrollView scroll) {
    return this.imgView;
  } ;
  this.scrollView.ZoomScale = 1f;

  this.scrollView.IndicatorStyle =
    UIScrollViewIndicatorStyle.White;
  this.scrollView.AddSubview (this.imgView);

}
```

4. Finally, add an image to the project and set its **Build Action** to **BundleResource**. An image larger than the screen size of 640 x 1136 pixels of iPhone 5S is preferable.

5. Compile and run the app on the simulator. Tap and drag the image to display different portions. By pressing *Alt* + left-mouse click, you can simulate the pinch zooming function.

How it works...

The `UIScrollView` is capable of managing content that expands beyond the screen size. The size of the content that the scroll view will display must be set in its `ContentSize` property, as shown in the following code:

```
this.scrollView.ContentSize = this.imgView.Image.Size;
```

The `ContentOffset` property shown in the following code defines the position of the content inside the scroll view's bounds:

```
this.scrollView.ContentOffset = new PointF (200f, 50f);
```

What this means is that the image's (x=200, y=50) point will be displayed at the origin (x=0, y=0) of `UIScrollView`. To provide a zooming functionality for the content, we first set the `MinimumZoomScale` and `MaximumZoomScale` properties, as shown in the following code:

```
this.scrollView.MinimumZoomScale = 0.25f;
this.scrollView.MaximumZoomScale = 2f;
```

The preceding code set the minimum and maximum zoom scale for the content. A value of 2 means that the content will be displayed double in size, while a value of 0.5 means that the content will be displayed at half its size.

For the actual zooming operation, we need to set the `ViewForZoomingInScrollView` property, as shown in the following code:

```
this.scrollView.ViewForZoomingInScrollView = delegate (UIScrollView
    scroll) {
    return this.imgView;
};
```

The `ViewForZoomingInScrollView` property accepts a `delegate` variable of the `UIScrollViewGetZoomView` type and returns `UIView`. Here, the image view that we created is returned, but another image view of a higher resolution can be used instead to provide better image quality when zooming. After the `delegate` variable is assigned, the initial zoom scale is set using the following code:

```
this.scrollView.ZoomScale = 1f;
```

Finally, the scroll view's indicator style is set, as shown in the following code:

```
this.scrollView.IndicatorStyle = UIScrollViewIndicatorStyle.White;
```

Indicators are the two lines that appear when scrolling or zooming: one vertical line on the right side and one horizontal line on the bottom side of the scroll view. These lines inform the user of the position of the content.

There's more...

To provide a more pleasing scrolling and zooming effect to the user, the `UIScrollView` exposes the `Bounce` property. By default, it is set to `true`, but we have the option to disable it by setting it to `false`. Bouncing the content gives immediate feedback to the user that the bounds of the content have been reached, in either a horizontal or vertical direction. Furthermore, the `AlwaysBounceHorizontal` and `AlwaysBounceVertical` properties can be set individually. Setting one or both of these properties will make the scroll view bounce the content in the respective direction always, even if the content is equal to or smaller than the scroll view's bounds. Hence, no actual scrolling is needed.

UIScrollView events

The `UIScrollView` class exposes some of the following very useful events:

- `Scrolled`: This occurs while the content is being scrolled
- `DecelerationStarted`: This occurs when the user has started scrolling the content
- `DecelerationEnded`: This occurs when the user has finished scrolling, and the content has stopped moving

 If a handler has been assigned to the `Scrolled` event, it will be triggered whenever the `ContentOffset` property is set.

See also

- The *Displaying images* recipe
- The *Displaying and editing text* recipe
- The *Navigating through the content divided into pages* recipe

Navigating through the content divided into pages

In this recipe, we will learn how to use the `UIPageControl` class to provide page navigation.

Getting ready

The `UIPageControl` provides a simple visual representation of multiple pages or screens in an iOS app, which is indicated by dots. The following screenshot shows an example of the page control indicating that content is divided into three pages:

The dot that corresponds to the current page is highlighted. It is usually combined with `UIScrollView`. Create a new iPhone **Single View Application** project in Xamarin Studio and name it `PageNavApp`. Add three image files in the project and set their **Build Action** to **BundleResource**.

How to do it...

The following are the steps to create this project:

1. Open the `PageNavAppViewController.xib` file in Interface Builder.

2. Add `UIPageControl` to the bottom of the view and `UIScrollView` above it. Resize the scroll view to take up all the remaining space of the view and save the document.

3. Back in Xamarin Studio, enter the following code in the `PageNavAppViewController` class:

```
UIImageView page1;
UIImageView page2;
UIImageView page3;
public override void ViewDidLoad()
{
  base.ViewDidLoad();
  this.scrollView.DecelerationEnded +=
    this.ScrollView_DecelerationEnded;
  this.pageControl.ValueChanged +=
    this.PageControl_ValueChanged;
  this.scrollView.Scrolled += delegate {
    Console.WriteLine ("Scrolled!");
  };

  this.scrollView.PagingEnabled = true;

  RectangleF pageFrame =
    this.scrollView.Frame;
  this.scrollView.ContentSize = new SizeF (pageFrame.Width
    * 3, pageFrame.Height);

  this.page1 = new UIImageView (pageFrame);
  this.page1.ContentMode = UIViewContentMode.ScaleAspectFit;
  this.page1.Image = UIImage.FromFile ("Parga01.jpg");

  pageFrame.X += this.scrollView.Frame.Width;
  this.page2 = new UIImageView (pageFrame);
  this.page2.ContentMode =
    UIViewContentMode.ScaleAspectFit;
  this.page2.Image = UIImage.FromFile ("Parga02.jpg");

  pageFrame.X += this.scrollView.Frame.Width;
  this.page3 = new UIImageView (pageFrame);
  this.page3.ContentMode =
    UIViewContentMode.ScaleAspectFit;
  this.page3.Image = UIImage.FromFile ("Parga03.jpg");
```

```
    this.scrollView.AddSubview (this.page1);
    this.scrollView.AddSubview (this.page2);
    this.scrollView.AddSubview (this.page3);

}
```

4. Add the following methods in the class:

```
private void scrollView_DecelerationEnded (object sender,
  EventArgs e)
{
  float x1 = this.page1.Frame.X;
  float x2 = this.page2.Frame.X;

  float x = this.scrollView.ContentOffset.X;

  if (x == x1)
  {
    this.pageControl.CurrentPage = 0;
  }  else if (x == x2)
  {
    this.pageControl.CurrentPage = 1;
  }  else
  {
    this.pageControl.CurrentPage = 2;

  }

}

private void pageControl_ValueChanged (object sender,
  EventArgs e)
{
  PointF contentOffset =
    this.scrollView.ContentOffset;

  switch (this.pageControl.CurrentPage)
  {
    case 0:
    contentOffset.X = this.page1.Frame.X;
    this.scrollView.SetContentOffset (contentOffset, true);
    break;

    case 1:
    contentOffset.X = this.page2.Frame.X;
    this.scrollView.SetContentOffset (contentOffset, true);
    break;
```

```
case 2:
contentOffset.X = this.page3.Frame.X;
this.scrollView.SetContentOffset (contentOffset, true);
break;

default:
// do nothing
break;
}

}
```

5. Compile and run the app on the simulator. Scroll sideways on the scroll view to change the page. Likewise, tap or scroll on the page control to change the page.

How it works...

The first thing that we need to do is set the `UIScrollView.PagingEnabled` property to true, as shown in the following code:

```
this.scrollView.PagingEnabled = true;
```

This property instructs the scroll view to stop scrolling at multiples of the scroll view's bounds, hence providing paging functionality. After this, the image views that will be displayed on different pages are prepared. Here, we take care of adjusting each image view's frame so that they will be positioned next to each other, using the following code:

```
this.page1 = new UIImageView (pageFrame);

// Frame for 2nd page
pageFrame.X += this.scrollView.Frame.Width;

// Frame for 3rd page
pageFrame.X += this.scrollView.Frame.Width;
```

We have attached handlers for two events. The first one is the `UIScrollView.DecelerationEnded` event, which will adjust the page control's current page when the user scrolls the scroll view. The current page is determined by the scroll view's `ContentOffset` property, as shown in the following code:

```
float x = this.scrollView.ContentOffset.X;
if (x == x1) {
  // First page
  this.pageControl.CurrentPage = 0;
// etc.
```

The second event to which we attach a handler is the `UIPageControl.ValueChanged` event. In this handler, we make sure that the content is scrolled when the user taps or drags on the page control. The scrolling action is performed when the `ContentOffset` property is set to the desired image view's `Frame.X` property using the `UIScrollView.SetContentOffset(PointF, bool)` method, as shown in the following code:

```
case 0:
  // Scroll to first page
  contentOffset.X = this.page1.Frame.X;
    this.scrollView.SetContentOffset (contentOffset, true);
  break;
// etc.
```

The second parameter of the `SetContentOffset` method instructs the scroll view to animate while scrolling.

There's more...

In this recipe, different `UIImageView` objects have been used. Any kind of `UIView` object can be used according to the type of content we want to display.

Proper usage of UIPageControl

Users expect that scrolling to other pages will occur when tapping or dragging on the page control. It is not a good practice to use it for displaying page indexing only.

See also

▸   The *Displaying images* recipe
▸   The *Displaying content larger than the screen* recipe

Displaying alerts

The `UIAlertView` class provides us with the ability to display alert messages to the user. In this recipe, we will discuss how to use this class and respond to user input.

Getting ready

For this recipe, create an iPhone **Single View Application** project in Xamarin Studio and name it `AlertViewApp`. Open the `AlertViewAppViewController.xib` file in Xcode and add a button on its view. Don't forget to connect it to an outlet.

How to do it...

Perform the following steps to implement the `UIAlertView` in the app:

1. In Xamarin Studio, open the `AlertViewAppViewController.cs` file and add the following method:

```
private void ShowAlert(string title, string message)
{
  // Create the alert
  UIAlertView alertView = new
    UIAlertView();
  alertView.Title = title;
  alertView.Message = message;
  // Add buttons
  alertView.AddButton("OK");
  alertView.AddButton("Cancel");
  // Add event handler
  alertView.Dismissed += (sender, e) => {
    if (e.ButtonIndex == 0)
    {
      this.btnShowAlert.SetTitle("OK!",
        UIControlState.Normal);
    } else
    {
      this.btnShowAlert.SetTitle("Cancelled!",
        UIControlState.Normal);
    }//end if else
  };
  // Display it
  alertView.Show();
}//end void ShowAlert
```

2. In the `ViewDidLoad` method, add the following line of code:

```
this.btnShowAlert.TouchUpInside += (sender, e) => this.
ShowAlert("Alert Message", "Tap OK or Cancel");
```

3. Compile and run the app in the simulator.

4. Tap the button on the view. The alert should be displayed, as shown in the following screenshot:

5. Tap either **OK** or **Cancel**. The **Show alert** button's title will change according to the alert button that was tapped.

How it works...

The `UIAlertView` is a modal control. This means that once it is presented, the user is required to take an action for it to disappear. After creating the instance, we assign the title and the message that will be displayed through the `Title` and `Message` properties, respectively, as shown in the following code:

```
alertView.Title = title;
alertView.Message = message;
```

We then add the buttons we want to display through the `AddButton` method, which accepts a `string` parameter for the button's title, as shown in the following code:

```
// Add buttons
alertView.AddButton("OK");
alertView.AddButton("Cancel");
```

We can practically add as many buttons as we want; however, it would be good to avoid adding more than three or four buttons. If there is a need for more options, it would be best to show a new view to the user with these options, instead of using an alert view.

After adding the buttons, we need an event handler (as shown in the following code) that will inform us of the user's action on the alert view:

```
// Add event handler
alertView.Dismissed += (sender, e) => {
  if (e.ButtonIndex == 0)
  {
    this.btnShowAlert.SetTitle("OK!", UIControlState.Normal);
  } else
  {
    this.btnShowAlert.SetTitle("Cancelled!",
      UIControlState.Normal);
  }
};
```

For this functionality, we use the `Dismissed` event that is triggered whenever the alert view is hidden. This occurs when any of its buttons are tapped. In the event handler, we can determine which button was tapped through the passed `ButtonIndex` property of `UIButtonEventArgs`. It is pretty clear which index corresponds to which button. The first button we added will have an index of `0`, the second button will have an index of `1`, and so on.

Finally, to display the alert view, we call its `Show` method using the following code:

```
// Display it
alertView.Show();
```

There's more...

`UIAlertView` also supports text input. We can implement it by setting its `AlertViewStyle` property before displaying it. The `AlertViewStyle` property accepts the following values:

▶ `UIAlertViewStyle.Default`: This alert view will not contain text input

▶ `UIAlertViewStyle.SecureTextInput`: This alert view will contain a text field for password input, which obscures the typed text

- ▸ `UIAlertViewStyle.PlainTextInput`: In this, only one simple text field will be included

- ▸ `UIAlertViewStyle.LoginAndPasswordInput`: Using this property, two text fields will be displayed, one plain and one secure, for entering the login credentials

To access any of the mentioned text fields, we call the `GetTextField` method, passing the appropriate index, as shown in the following code:

```
// Get the text that was entered in the second text field
string password = alertView.GetTextField(1).Text;
```

Of course, we can also modify the text fields themselves. For example, if we want to disable obscuring the characters of the password text field, we can add the following line of code:

```
alertView.GetTextField(1).SecureTextEntry = false;
```

See also

- ▸ The *Receiving user input with buttons* recipe
- ▸ The *Displaying and editing text* recipe

Creating a custom view

In this recipe, we will learn how to override the `UIView` class and/or classes that derive from it to create custom views.

Getting ready

So far, we have discussed many of the available views to create iOS apps. There will be many cases, however, we will need to implement our own custom views. In this recipe, we will see how to create a custom view and use it.

 Creating custom views is very useful when we want to capture touches or implement other custom behavior such as drawing.

Create a new iPhone **Single View Application** project in Xamarin Studio and name it `CustomViewApp`.

How to do it...

The following are the steps to complete this recipe:

1. Add a new C# class file in the project and name it `MyView`.

2. Implement it with the following code:

```csharp
using System;
using MonoTouch.UIKit;
using MonoTouch.Foundation;
using System.Drawing;

namespace CustomViewApp
{
  [Register("MyView")]
  public class MyView : UIView
  {

    private UILabel labelStatus;

    public MyView (IntPtr handle) : base(handle)
    {
      this.Initialize ();
    }

    public MyView (RectangleF frame) :
      base(frame)
    {
      this.Initialize ();
    }

    private void Initialize ()
    {

      this.BackgroundColor = UIColor.LightGray;

      this.labelStatus = new
        UILabel (new RectangleF (0f, 400f,
        this.Frame.Width, 60f));
      this.labelStatus.TextAlignment =
        UITextAlignment.Center;
      this.labelStatus.BackgroundColor = UIColor.DarkGray;
      this.AddSubview (this.labelStatus);

    }
```

```
public override void
  TouchesMoved (NSSet touches, UIEventevtUIEvent evt)
{
  base.TouchesMoved (touches, evt);

  UITouch touch = (UITouch)touches.AnyObject;

  PointF touchLocation =
    touch.LocationInView (this);

  this.labelStatus.Text = String.Format ("X: {0} - Y:
    {1}", touchLocation.X, touchLocation.Y);

}
}
}
```

3. Open the `CustomViewAppViewController.xib` file in Interface Builder and add a `UIView` object on the main view.

4. Set its **Class** field in the **Identity Inspector** to `MyView`.

5. Save the document.

6. Compile and run the app on the simulator. Tap and drag the view and watch the touch coordinates being displayed in the label at the bottom of the screen.

How it works...

The first thing to note when creating custom views is to derive them from the `UIView` class and decorate them with the `RegisterAttribute`, as shown in the following code:

```
[Register ("MyView")]
public class MyView : UIView
```

The `RegisterAttribute` basically exposes our class to the Objective-C world. Note that the name we pass as its parameter must be the same name we enter in the **Class** field in the **Identity Inspector**. It is important to create the following constructor:

```
public MyView (IntPtr handle) : base(handle) {}
```

This constructor overrides the base class' `UIView(IntPtr)`. This constructor is always being called when a view is initialized through the native code. If we do not override it, an exception will occur upon the initialization of the object. The other constructor that is used in this example is just provided as guidance on what might be used if the view was initialized programmatically:

```
public MyView (RectangleF frame) : base(frame) {}
```

Both these constructors call the `Initialize()` method that performs the initialization we need, such as creating the label that will be used and setting the background colors.

Then, the `TouchesMoved` method is overridden. This is the method that is executed when the user drags a finger on the view. Inside the method, we retrieve the `UITouch` object from the method's NSSet parameter, using the following code:

```
UITouch touch = (UITouch)touches.AnyObject;
```

 An `NSSet` object is a collection of data that are not in particular order. It is similar to an array. Its `AnyObject` parameter returns an object from the collection.

The `UITouch` object contains information about user touches. We retrieve the touch's current location from the `UITouch` object, using the following code:

```
PointF touchLocation = touch.LocationInView
  (this);
```

The `UITouch` object's `LocationInView` method accepts a parameter of the `UIView` type, which declares in which view's coordinate system will the location be calculated. In this case, we are interested in the coordinates of `MyView`.

There's more...

If we would like to initialize the custom view we created programmatically, we would enter the following code:

```
MyView myView = new MyView(new RectangleF(0f, 0f,
  320f, 480f));
```

See also

▸ The *Adding and customizing views* recipe

▸ The *Loading a view with a view controller* recipe in *Chapter 3, User Interface – View Controllers*

Styling views

iOS provides a set of APIs through the **UIAppearance** protocol that allows us to adjust the appearance of the views once, without having to explicitly modify the styling properties on every instance of each view. This is particularly useful if, say, we want a specific view to have the same appearance throughout the app.

Apart from setting the styling properties of a view globally, we can also define the appearance of this view to be different under certain circumstances. Read on to find out how to accomplish this.

Getting ready

We will work on the existing `CustomViewApp` project we created in the preceding recipe. Open the project in Xamarin Studio.

 The downloadable code contains a separate project for this recipe. It is named `CustomViewApp2`.

How to do it...

Perform the following steps to complete this recipe:

1. Open the `CustomViewAppViewController.xib` file in Xcode.

2. Resize the `MyView` object, which we created earlier, to make some room at the top.

3. Add a `UILabel` above the `MyView` object. Make sure that the label is added on the main view and not on `MyView`.

4. Connect both objects to their respective outlets.

5. Back in Xamarin Studio, add the following code in the `ViewDidLoad` method of `CustomViewAppViewController`:

```
UILabel.Appearance.BackgroundColor = UIColor.Blue;
var labelStyle =
   UILabel.AppearanceWhenContainedIn(typeof(MyView));
labelStyle.BackgroundColor = UIColor.Green;
```

6. Compile and run the app on the simulator. The output should be similar to the one shown in the following screenshot:

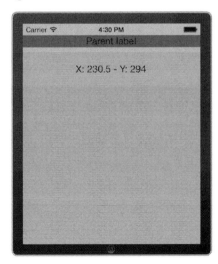

How it works...

The `UIAppearance` class is basically a proxy to the specific properties of each control. In Xamarin.iOS, we can access each control's proxy through its static `Appearance` property. The changes we make to this object's properties will reflect on the instances of the object throughout the app. In this case, we set the `BackgroundColor` attribute of all `UILabel` instances to blue using the following code:

```
UILabel.Appearance.BackgroundColor = UIColor.Blue;
```

However, we can provide different behavior for specific instances of `UILabel`. For example, we want the labels that are contained in `MyView` objects to have a green background. We accomplish this by calling the static `AppearanceWhenContainedIn` method, as shown in the following code:

```
var labelStyle =
   UILabel.AppearanceWhenContainedIn(typeof(MyView));
```

We pass the types of objects for which we want to set the specific style. In this case, passing `typeof(MyView)` instructs the appearance proxy to make sure that we are referring to objects that are only contained in `MyView` objects. We then set the value we want to the object that was returned from this method, as shown in the following code:

```
labelStyle.BackgroundColor = UIColor.Green;
```

There's more...

Through the `AppearanceWhenContainedIn` method, we can target a more specific set of styling. For example, consider the following line of code:

```
var labelStyle =
   UILabel.AppearanceWhenContainedIn(typeof(AnotherView),
   typeof(MyView));
```

This would return a styling object that acts as a proxy for all instances of `UILabel`, which are part of `MyView`, only when `MyView` is included in `AnotherView` objects.

Limitations of UIAppearance

The `UIAppearance` protocol has some limitations, which are as follows:

▶ Only specific properties can be set. For example, we cannot set the `Frame` of a view globally. Each set of properties that can be changed for a control can be accessed through its appearance proxy. If a control property is not in the appearance proxy, we cannot modify it for all instances of that particular control.

> ▶ For modifying the appearance of a custom view (in this case, `MyView`), using the following line of code will yield an unwanted result:

```
MyView.Appearance.BackgroundColor = UIColor.Yellow;
```

That is, all instances of `UIView` will have a yellow background. This is because C# cannot override the static methods in derived classes. To overcome this issue, we use the `GetAppearance<T>` static method on the derived class instead, as shown in the following code:

```
MyView.GetAppearance<MyView>().BackgroundColor = UIColor.Yellow;
// We can also call GetAppearance on the base class:
//UIView.GetAppearance<MyView>().BackgroundColor = UIColor.Yellow;
```

See also

> ▶ The *Creating a custom view recipe*
>
> ▶ The *Creating a custom view controller* recipe in *Chapter 3, User Interface – View Controllers*

3
User Interface – View Controllers

In this chapter, we will cover the following recipes:

- ▶ Loading a view with a view controller
- ▶ Navigating through different view controllers
- ▶ Providing controllers in tabs
- ▶ Modal view controllers
- ▶ Creating a custom view controller
- ▶ Using view controllers efficiently
- ▶ iPad view controllers
- ▶ UI flow design with storyboards
- ▶ Unwinding in storyboards

Introduction

So far, we have discussed views and how to use them. In most cases of real world app scenarios, views alone are not enough. Apple provides another base class, the `UIViewController` class, which is responsible for managing views. A view controller can respond to device notifications, such as when the device rotates, or can provide different ways to display and dismiss multiple views or even other view controllers. There are a number of view controllers available for us to use. In this chapter, we will discuss the most important ones.

These view controllers are as follows:

- ▸ **UIViewController**: This is the base class of all view controllers.

- ▸ **UINavigationController**: This is the view controller that provides various ways of navigating through different view controllers.

- ▸ **UITabBarController**: This is a view controller that displays multiple view controllers in a tab-like interface.

- ▸ **iPad-specific view controllers**: These are the view controllers that only apply to the iPad device.

Furthermore, we will learn how to create our own custom view controllers, and we will create an app whose user interface will be created with storyboard files.

Loading a view with a view controller

In this recipe, we will learn how to use the `UIViewController` class to manage views.

Getting ready

Create a new iPhone **Empty Project** in Xamarin Studio and name it `ViewControllerApp`.

How to do it...

Perform the following steps to load a view with a view controller:

1. Add a new file to the project.

2. Right-click on the project in the **Solution** pad and go to **Add | New File...**.

3. In the dialog that will appear, select **iPhone View Controller** from the **iOS** section. Name it `MainViewController` and click on the **New** button. Xamarin Studio will create a new XIB file and will automatically open the `MainViewController.cs` source file. This file contains a class that overrides the `UIViewController` class, and we can implement any code related to our view controller in it.

4. Open the `MainViewController.xib` file in Interface Builder.

5. Add `UILabel` on the view.

6. Create and connect an outlet for it inside the `MainViewController` class and name it `myLabel`.

7. Enter the text `View in controller!` in the label.

8. Save the XIB document.

9. In Xamarin Studio, enter the following code in the `FinishedLaunching` method of the `AppDelegate` class, right after the window initialization line:

```
MainViewController mainController =
    new MainViewController ();
window.RootViewController = mainController;
```

10. Compile and run the app on the simulator.

How it works...

When we add a new `iPhone View Controller` file in a project, in this case `MainViewController`, Xamarin Studio basically creates and adds the following three files:

▶ `MainViewController.xib`: This is the XIB file that contains the controller.

▶ `MainViewController.cs`: This is the C# source file that implements the class of our controller.

▶ `MainViewController.designer.cs`: This is the autogenerated source file that reflects the changes we make to the controller in Interface Builder.

Notice that we do not need to add an outlet for the view as this is taken care of by Xamarin Studio. We initialize the controller through its class, as follows:

```
MainViewController mainController = new MainViewController ();
```

Then, we assign the controller to the `window.RootViewController` property, as follows:

```
window.RootViewController = mainController.
```

Our view controller is now the root view controller of our app's window, and it is the first one that will be shown when the app starts.

There's more...

The project we have just created only shows how we can add a controller with a view. Notice that we created the outlet for the label inside the `MainViewController` class, which acts as the file's owner object in the XIB file. To provide some functionality for the `MainViewController` class, add the following method in the `MainViewController` class in the `MainViewController.cs` file:

```
public override void ViewDidLoad ()
{
    this.myLabel.Text = "View loaded!";
}
```

This method overrides the `UIViewController.ViewDidLoad()` method, which is executed after the controller has loaded its view.

UIViewController methods to override

The `UIViewController` class contains a number of methods that allow us to manage the view controller's life cycle. These methods are called by the system on the view controller, and we can override them to add our own implementation. Some of these methods are as follows:

- ▶ `ViewWillAppear`: This method is called when the controller's view is about to appear.

- ▶ `ViewDidAppear`: This method is called when the controller's view has been displayed.

- ▶ `ViewWillDisappear`: This method is called when the controller's view is about to disappear, for example, when another controller will be displayed.

- ▶ `ViewDidDisappear`: This method is called when the view has disappeared.

See also

- ▶ The *Navigating through different view controllers* recipe
- ▶ The *Creating an iOS project with Xamarin Studio* and *Accessing the UI with Outlets* recipes from *Chapter 1, Development Tools*

Navigating through different view controllers

In this recipe, we will learn how to use the `UINavigationController` class to navigate among multiple view controllers.

Getting ready

The `UINavigationController` class is a controller that provides hierarchical navigation functionality with multiple view controllers. Create a new iPhone **Empty Project** in Xamarin Studio and name it `NavigationControllerApp`.

How to do it...

Perform the following steps to create navigation among multiple view controllers:

1. Add three new iPhone view controllers in the project and name them `MainController`, `ViewController1`, and `ViewController2`.

2. Open the `AppDelegate.cs` file and add the following code in the `FinishedLaunching` method:

```
MainController mainController = new MainController();
mainController.Title = "Main View";
UINavigationController navController =
   new UINavigationController(mainController);
window.RootViewController = navController;
```

3. Open `MainController.xib` in Interface Builder and add two buttons with their corresponding outlets. Set their titles to `First View` and `Second View`, respectively.

4. Add the following code in the `ViewDidLoad` method of the `MainController` class:

```
this.buttonFirstView.TouchUpInside += (sender, e) => {

        ViewController1 v1 = new ViewController1();
        v1.Title = "First View";
        this.NavigationController.PushViewController(v1, true);

    } ;
    this.buttonSecondView.TouchUpInside += (sender, e) => {

        ViewController2 v2 = new ViewController2();
        v2.Title = "Second View";
        this.NavigationController.PushViewController(v2, true);

    };
```

5. Add a button in each of the `ViewController1` and `ViewController2` controllers in Interface Builder with the title `Pop to root`. Then, add the following code in both of these controllers' `ViewDidLoad` methods:

```
this.buttonPop.TouchUpInside += (sender, e) => {
   this.NavigationController.PopToRootViewController(true);
};
```

6. Run the app on the simulator.

7. Click on the buttons and see how the user interface navigates from one controller to another.

How it works...

The `UINavigationController` class preserves a stack of controllers. The `UIViewController` class has a property named `NavigationController`. In normal situations, this property returns null. However, if the controller is pushed into a navigation controller's stack, it returns the instance of the navigation controller. In this case, all of our controllers' `NavigationController` property will return the instance of our navigation controller. So this way, at any point in the hierarchy of controllers, access to the navigation controller is provided. To push a view controller to the navigation stack, we call the `UINavigationController.PushViewController(UIViewController, bool)` method, using the following line of code:

```
this.NavigationController.PushViewController (v1, true);
```

Notice that the `MainController` class is the topmost or root controller in the navigation stack. A navigation controller must have at least one view controller that will act as its root controller. We can provide it upon initialization of the navigation controller, as follows:

```
UINavigationController navController =
  new UINavigationController(mainController);
```

To return to the root controller, we call the `PopToRootViewController(bool)` method inside the current controller, as follows:

```
this.NavigationController.PopToRootViewController (true);
```

The boolean parameters in both methods are used for animating the transition between the view controllers. Setting it to `false` will result in the controllers instantly snapping onto the screen, which in most cases does not provide a very good user experience.

There's more...

In this simple example, we provided backward navigation to the root controller with buttons. Notice that there is an arrow-shaped button at the top bar, as shown in the following screenshot:

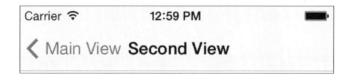

This top bar is called the navigation bar and is of the `UINavigationBar` type. The arrow-shaped button is called the back button and is of the `UIBarButtonItem` type. The back button, when it exists, always navigates to the previous controller in the navigation stack. If the previous controller in the stack has its `Title` property set, the back button will display that title. If it does not have a title, the back button will be titled `Back`.

Managing navigation bar buttons

To change, add, and hide the buttons of the navigation bar, we can use the following methods of our currently displayed view controller's `NavigationItem` property:

- ▶ `SetLeftBarButtonItem`: This method adds a custom button on the left-hand side of the navigation bar, replacing the default back button.

- ▶ `SetRightBarButtonItem`: This method adds a custom button on the right-hand side of the navigation bar.

- ▶ `SetHidesBackButton`: This method sets the visibility of the default back button.

To remove or hide the custom buttons on the left or right-hand side of the navigation bar, call the appropriate methods passing null instead of a `UIBarButtonItem` object.

See also

- ▶ The *Modal view controllers* and *Using view controllers efficiently* recipes
- ▶ The *Animating views* recipe in *Chapter 11, Graphics and Animation*

Providing controllers in tabs

In this recipe, we will learn how to display multiple view controllers in a tabbed interface.

Getting ready

The `UITabBarController` class provides a way to display different view controllers on the same hierarchy level divided into a tab-like interface. Create a new iPhone **Empty Project** in Xamarin Studio and name it `TabControllerApp`.

How to do it...

Perform the following steps to provide controllers in tabs:

1. Add two iPhone view controllers to the project. Name them `MainController` and `SettingsController`.

2. Add the following code to the `ViewDidLoad` method of `MainController`:

   ```
   this.View.BackgroundColor = UIColor.Blue;
   ```

3. Add the following code to the `ViewDidLoad` method of `SettingsController`:

   ```
   this.View.BackgroundColor = UIColor.Yellow;
   ```

4. Add the following code to the `FinishedLaunching` method of the `AppDelegate` class:

```
MainController mainController = new MainController();
SettingsController settingsController = new SettingsController();
UITabBarController tabController = new UITabBarController();
tabController.SetViewControllers(new UIViewController[] {
    mainController,
    settingsController
}, true);
tabController.TabBar.Items[0].Title = "Main";
tabController.TabBar.Items[1].Title = "Settings";
window.RootViewController = tabController;
```

5. Run the app on the simulator. Click on each of the tabs at the bottom. The interface should be similar to the following screenshot when `MainController` is selected:

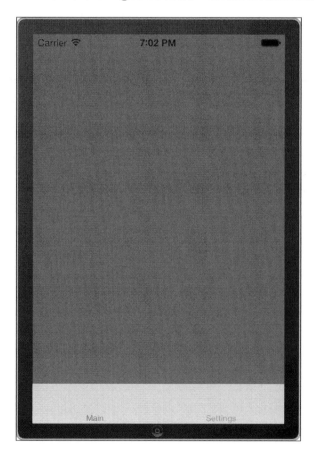

How it works...

The `UITabBarController` class displays one tab for each of the controllers it manages. That tab is of the `UITabBarItem` type that can accept both text and images. We set the controllers it will display through its `SetViewControllers` property, as follows:

```
tabController.SetViewControllers(new UIViewController[] {
  mainController,
  settingsController
}, true);
```

After we have added the controllers, we can access its tab bar items through the `TabBar` property. In this case, we set the tab's `Title` attribute:

```
tabController.TabBar.Items[0].Title = "Main";
```

Each `UIViewController` contains a `TabController` property. Similar to the `NavigationController` property, when the controller is part of a tab controller, the property will return the instance of that tab controller.

There's more...

The controller can accept as many controllers as we want but if we add six or more, four will be displayed with their tabs, while a fifth predefined **More** tab will represent all the remaining controllers. This is to keep the interface easily accessible to the user by keeping the tabs to a specific size suitable for human fingers. When we add more than six controllers in a tab bar controller interface, by default, the object provides an **Edit** button on top in the **More** tab that allows the user to rearrange the order of controllers. If we want to exclude some controllers from this functionality, we have to remove it from the `CustomizableViewControllers` array.

Useful UITabBarController properties

Some more useful properties of the `UITabBarController` class are as follows:

- ▶ `ViewControllers`: This is an array containing all the controllers that the tab controller holds.
- ▶ `SelectedIndex`: This is the zero-based index of the selected tab. Setting this property to the desired index programmatically selects the corresponding controller.
- ▶ `SelectedViewController`: This is the currently selected controller.

Determining tab selection

To determine when the user has selected a tab on a tab controller, we can subscribe to its `ViewControllerSelected` event:

```
tabController.ViewControllerSelected += (sender, e) => {
  // Do something with e.ViewController.
};
```

See also

▸   The *Using view controllers efficiently* recipe

Modal view controllers

In this recipe, we will discuss how to display view controllers modally.

Getting ready

A modal view controller is any controller that is presented above other views or controllers. The concept is similar to displaying a Windows Form as a dialog, which takes control of the interface and does not allow access to other windows of the application unless it is dismissed. Create a new iPhone **Empty Project** in Xamarin Studio and name it `ModalControllerApp`.

How to do it...

Perform the following steps:

1.   Add two view controllers to the project and name them `MainController` and `ModalController`.

2.   Open the `MainController.xib` file in Interface Builder and add a button on its view with the title `Present`. Create and connect the appropriate outlet for the button.

3.   In the `MainController` class, add the following code in the `ViewDidLoad` method:

```
this.buttonPresent.TouchUpInside += async (s, e) => {
  ModalController modalController = new ModalController();
  await this.PresentViewControllerAsync(modalController, true);
};
```

4.   Open the `ModalController.xib` file. Add a button on its view with the title `Dismiss` and create the appropriate outlet for it.

5.   Set its view background color to something other than white. Save the document and enter the following code in the `ViewDidLoad` method of `ModalController`:

```
this.buttonDismiss.TouchUpInside += async (s, e) => {
  await this.DismissViewControllerAsync (true);
};
```

6.   Finally, add code to display the main controller in the `FinishedLaunching` method:

```
MainController mainController = new MainController();
window.RootViewController = mainController;
```

7. Compile and run the app on the simulator. Click on the **Present** button and watch the modal controller present itself on top of the main controller. Click on the **Dismiss** button to hide it.

How it works...

Each controller object has two methods that handle presenting and dismissing controllers modally. In our example, we call the `PresentViewControllerAsync(UIViewController, bool)` method to present a controller, as follows:

```
this.buttonPresent.TouchUpInside += async (s, e) => {
    ModalController modal = new ModalController ();
    await this.PresentViewControllerAsync (modal, true);
};
```

Its first parameter represents the controller we want to display modally, and the second parameter determines if we want the presentation to be animated. To dismiss the controller, we call its `DismissViewControllerAsync(bool)` method, as follows:

```
await this.DismissViewControllerAsync (true);
```

It accepts only one parameter that toggles the animation for the dismissal.

In this example, we use `async/await` and the methods with the `Async` suffix to present and dismiss a controller modally. These methods are included in Xamarin.iOS for convenience. We can also use `PresentViewController` and `DismissViewController`; both accept another parameter of the `NSAction` type that represents the callback of the completion. However, no need to get into all that "trouble", right?

There's more...

We can define the transition style for a modal view controller presentation with the controller's `ModalTransitionStyle` property. Enter the following line of code before presenting the modal controller:

```
modalController.ModalTransitionStyle =
    UIModalTransitionStyle.FlipHorizontal;
```

The main controller will flip to present the modal controller, giving the impression it is attached behind it.

Accessing a modal controller

Each controller that presents another controller modally provides access to its "child" controller through the `ModalController` property. If you need to access the modal controller through this property, make sure to do it before the `DismissViewControllerAsync` method is called.

How many modal controllers?

In theory, we can present an unlimited number of modal controllers. Of course, there are two restrictions on this, which are as follows:

▶ **Memory is not unlimited**: View controllers consume memory, so the more view controllers we present, the worst performance we get.

▶ **Bad user experience**: Presenting many controllers modally might confuse the user.

In general, it is advised to not present more than one consecutive controller modally.

See also

▶ The *Navigating through different view controllers* and *Providing controllers in tabs* recipes

Creating a custom view controller

In this recipe, we will learn how to create a subclass of `UIViewController` and use it to derive view controllers that were created in Interface Builder.

Getting ready

In this recipe, we will create a custom view controller that will act as a base controller, providing common functionality among its inheritors. Create a new iPhone **Empty Project** in Xamarin Studio and name it `CustomControllerApp`.

How to do it...

Perform the following steps:

1. Right-click on the project in the **Solution** pad and go to **Add | New File...**.

2. In the dialog that appears, navigate to **General | Empty Class**. Name the file `BaseController` and click on the **New** button.

3. Open the `BaseController.cs` file that was just created and modify it to match the following code:

```
using System;
using MonoTouch.UIKit;
using MonoTouch.Foundation;
using System.Drawing;

namespace CustomControllerApp {
public class BaseController : UIViewController {
```

```
//Constructor
public BaseController (string nibName,
   NSBundle bundle) : base(nibName, bundle) {}

public override void TouchesMoved (NSSet touches, UIEventevt)
{
   base.TouchesMoved (touches, evt);
   // Capture the position of touches
   UITouch touch = touches.AnyObject as UITouch;
   if (null != touch) {
      PointF locationInView = touch.LocationInView (this.View);
      Console.WriteLine ("Touch coordinates: {0}",
         locationInView);
   }
}
```

4. Now, add an iPhone view controller to the project and name it `DerivedController`. Change the class it inherits from `UIViewController` to `BaseController` in its class definition: `public partial class DerivedController : BaseController`.

5. Set the derived controller to be the root view controller of the main window (in `AppDelegate.cs`):

```
DerivedController derivedController =
   new DerivedController();
window.RootViewController = derivedController;
```

6. Compile and run the app on the simulator. Click-and-drag the mouse pointer on the white surface and watch Xamarin Studio's application output pad displaying the current position of the pointer on the simulator's screen.

How it works...

What we have done here is that we have created a base controller class that can be used in multiple Xamarin.iOS projects. The functionality we have added to this controller is to respond to user touches. Any controller that inherits it will inherit the same functionality. The code we have added to create the `BaseController` class is fairly simple. To make this work, we have added the following constructor to the class:

```
public BaseController (string nibName,
   NSBundle bundle) : base(nibName, bundle) {}
```

This is the base constructor that will get called when we initialize the `DerivedController` class with the new keyword, `this.derivedController = new DerivedController();`, through our derived object's `DerivedController()` constructor. So, what this practically means is that we can normally use inheritance with controllers that are loaded from XIB files.

There's more...

We can also create base controllers from XIB files. However, if the XIB files contain outlets, we need to make sure to populate these outlets in our derived classes; otherwise, they will not be available in our derived controllers. For example, if we have an outlet for a button named `btnStart` in the base XIB file, we would have to create the following property in our derived class:

```
[Outlet("btnStart")]
public UIButton BtnStart {
  get { return base.btnStart; }
  set { base.btnStart = value; }
}
```

The `Outlet` attribute tells the runtime that the specific property is an outlet. Not only that, it also helps Xamarin Studio in creating the Xcode project when we are using the derived class in a XIB.

See also

> ▸ The *Loading a view with a view controller, Using view controllers efficiently*, and *UI flow design with storyboards recipes*

> ▸ The *Adding and customizing views* recipe in *Chapter 2, User Interface – Views*

Using view controllers efficiently

iOS is very strict about memory usage. If an app uses too much memory, iOS will issue memory warnings. If we do not respond to these memory warnings accordingly by releasing resources that are not needed, it is very likely that iOS will terminate the app.

Getting ready

Let's see what we can do to avoid this situation. Create a new project in Xamarin Studio and name it `EfficientControllerApp`.

How to do it...

Perform the following steps to complete this recipe:

1. Add a view controller to the project and name it `MainController`.

2. Enter the following code in the `DidReceiveMemoryWarning` method of the `MainController` class:

   ```
   Console.WriteLine("Main controller
     received memory warning!");
   ```

3. Make the controller the root view controller of the app in `AppDelegate.cs` as follows:

   ```
   MainController mainController = new MainController();
   window.RootViewController = mainController;
   ```

4. Compile and run the app on the simulator.

5. With iOS Simulator window active, navigate to **Hardware | Simulate Memory Warning** on the menu bar, as shown in the following screenshot:

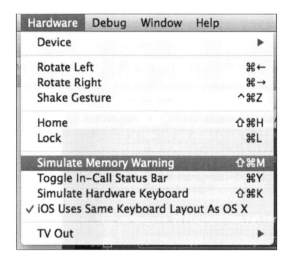

6. Check the **Application Output** pad in Xamarin Studio. You should see an output similar to the following:

   ```
   2013-12-04 08:09:47.695 EfficientControllerApp[1383:80b] Received
   memory warning.
   2013-12-04 08:09:47.709 EfficientControllerApp[1383:80b] Main
   controller received memory warning!
   ```

How it works...

This project does not provide any useful functionality. Its main purpose is to show how to get notified on memory warnings issued by iOS.

When a memory warning is issued, the `DidReceiveMemoryWarning` method will be called on all instantiated view controllers that are currently in memory. When this method is called, we should make sure we release the resources that are not currently required. This way, we are making more memory available to the system.

iOS Simulator provides the option of simulating memory warnings so that we can test how our app will behave when memory is low. On a real device, we cannot force the system to issue memory warnings on demand. Note that although we can practically simulate an unlimited number of memory warnings on the simulator, the app will never be terminated. On the other hand, on the device, the app will be terminated after two or three memory warnings (the actual number varies according to memory usage), so we need to take this into account.

There's more...

View controllers are not the only object that can receive memory warnings. We can capture memory warning notifications by overriding the `UIApplicationDelegate.ReceiveMemoryWarning(UIApplication)` method inside the `AppDelegate` class, as follows:

```
public override void ReceiveMemoryWarning(UIApplication application)
{  //...    }
```

See also

▶ The *Creating a custom view controller* recipe

▶ The *Interface Builder* recipe in *Chapter 1, Development Tools*

iPad view controllers

All the controllers we have worked with so far can be used in both iPhone and iPad applications. There are, however, two controllers that are only available to the iPad. These are the `UISplitViewController` and `UIPopoverController` classes. In this recipe, we will create an iPad project that uses the `UISplitViewController` class.

Getting ready

Create a new iPad **Empty Project** and name it `SplitControllerApp`.

How to do it...

Perform the following steps to complete this recipe:

1. Add two iPad view controllers to the project and name them `FirstController` and `SecondController`. Set the background colors of their views to different colors, for example, blue for `FirstController` and yellow for `SecondController`.

2. Open `SecondController.xib` in Interface Builder and add `UIToolbar` close to the top of its view. Connect the toolbar to an outlet named `myToolbar`.

3. By default, the properties that represent the outlets are created as private by Xamarin Studio. Add the following property in the `SecondController` class to expose the toolbar outlet:

```
public UIToolbar MyToolbar {
  get { return this.myToolbar; }
}
```

4. Add the following class to the project:

```
public class SplitControllerDelegate :
  UISplitViewControllerDelegate
  {
    public SplitControllerDelegate (SecondController controller)
    {
      this.secondController = controller;
    }
    private SecondController secondController;
    public override void WillHideViewController
      (UISplitViewController svc,
      UIViewController aViewController,
      UIBarButtonItem barButtonItem, UIPopoverController pc)
    {
      barButtonItem.Title = "First";
      this.secondController.MyToolbar.SetItems (new
        UIBarButtonItem[] { barButtonItem }, true);
    }
    public override void WillShowViewController
      (UISplitViewController svc,
      UIViewController aViewController,
      UIBarButtonItem button)
    {
      this.secondController.MyToolbar.SetItems (new
        UIBarButtonItem[0], true);
    }
  }
```

5. Add the following code in the `FinishedLaunching` method of the `AppDelegate` class:

```
FirstController firstController = new FirstController();

SecondController secondController = new SecondController();

UISplitViewController splitController =
  new UISplitViewController();

splitController.ViewControllers = new UIViewController[] {

    firstController,

    secondController

};

splitController.Delegate =
  new SplitControllerDelegate(secondController);

window.RootViewController = splitController;
```

6. Compile and run the app on the simulator.

7. Click on the **First** button on the toolbar. `FirstController` should slide in from the side. The result is similar to the following screenshot:

How it works...

The `UISplitViewController` class helps to take full advantage of the iPad's larger screen. It provides a way of displaying two different views simultaneously on the same screen area. It does this by displaying one controller in fullscreen in the portrait orientation and a secondary controller whenever is needed, in a smaller size.

To provide access to both controllers in our project to the user, we have implemented a class that inherits from `UISplitViewControllerDelegate` and assigned it to our split controller inside the `FinishedLaunching` method. The `Delegate` object we created overrides two methods. In the first method, we assign a button to the toolbar, as follows:

```
public override void WillHideViewController
  (UISplitViewController svc, UIViewController aViewController,
  UIBarButtonItem barButtonItem, UIPopoverController pc)
{
  barButtonItem.Title = "First";
  this.secondController.MyToolbar.SetItems (new
    UIBarButtonItem[] { barButtonItem }, true);
}
```

The `WillHideViewController` method is executed whenever `UISplitViewController` changes orientation from landscape to portrait and its smaller controller is about to be hidden. So to display it, we provide a button on the fullscreen controller's toolbar. When we click on that button, the other controller will slide in from the side. When the orientation changes from portrait to landscape, the smaller controller appears beside the larger controller automatically. So, we no longer need the button on the toolbar; hence, we override the `WillShowViewController` method to remove it. We do this by assigning an empty `UIBarButtonItem[]` array, as follows:

```
public override void WillShowViewController (UISplitViewController
svc, UIViewController aViewController, UIBarButtonItem button)
{
  this.secondController.Toolbar.SetItems (new UIBarButtonItem[0],
    true);
}
```

There's more...

To rotate the simulator to (and from) the landscape orientation, press *Cmd* and the left arrow key (or the right arrow key) with the app running on iOS Simulator. The following screenshot shows iOS Simulator rotated in landscape orientation. No other action was taken to make both controllers appear at the same time, as the split controller handles this for us:

iPad-specific controller usage

Although all other controllers are available to both the iPhone and iPad, an exception will occur if a UISplitViewController method is used in an app that runs on an iPhone.

See also

> ▸ The *Adjusting UI orientation* recipe in *Chapter 9, Interacting with Device Hardware*

UI flow design with storyboards

Back when iOS 5 was released, Apple introduced **storyboards**. A storyboard is a new type of user interface file that accepts multiple view controllers, but it also holds information about how all these controllers relate to each other in the hierarchy of an application. Storyboards are very helpful when designing the screens of an application, as they are more efficient than loading different controllers from individual XIB files; they also keep a group of view controllers together in a single file.

Getting ready

Create a new iPhone **Empty Project** in Xamarin Studio and name it StoryboardApp.

 Xamarin Studio includes a number of project templates for storyboard applications. We will, however, use an empty iPhone project because it will help us to better comprehend how storyboards work.

How to do it...

Here are the steps to complete this recipe:

1. Add two new C# classes (not view controllers) to the project and name them FirstController and SecondController.

2. Derive both classes from UIViewController and decorate them with the Register attribute. Make sure that you pass a different name for each controller in the attribute, as follows:

   ❑ The FirstController class:
   ```
   [Register("FirstController")]
   public class FirstController : UIViewController
   { //..
   ```

   ❑ The SecondController class:
   ```
   [Register("SecondController")]
   public class SecondController : UIViewController
   { //..
   ```

3. Add the IntPtr constructor of UIViewController in both classes:
   ```
   public FirstController(IntPtr handle) : base(handle)
   {}
   ```

4. Add an `Empty iPhone Storyboard` file to the project and name it `MainStoryboard`.

5. Open the `MainStoryboard.storyboard` file that was created in Interface Builder. Just like opening XIBs, double-click on the file in Xamarin Studio.

6. Drag `UINavigationController` on the empty canvas. By default, Xcode adds a table view when adding navigation controllers. Select it and delete it by pressing the *Backspace* key; we only need the navigation controller.

7. Add two `UIViewController` objects to the canvas. By selecting each view controller individually, set their **Class** field in the **Identity Inspector** window to the classes we created in the preceding steps. The following screenshot shows the **Class** field of the first controller set to **FirstController**:

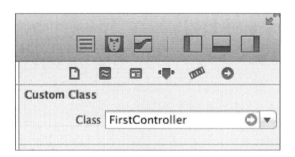

8. We now need to connect the controllers. Just like adding an outlet, press *Ctrl* and drag from the navigation controller to `FirstController`. In the context menu that will appear when you release the button, select **root view**.

9. Add `UIButton` on `FirstController`. Press *Ctrl* and drag from the button to `SecondController`. Select **push** in the context menu that will appear. No need to connect the button to an outlet.

10. Back in Xamarin Studio, add the following code in the `FinishedLaunching` method:

```
UIStoryboard storyboard = UIStoryboard.FromName("MainStoryboard",
    NSBundle.MainBundle);
UINavigationController navController =
    (UINavigationController)storyboard.
    InstantiateInitialViewController();
window.RootViewController = navController;
```

11. Compile and run the app on the simulator. Clicking on the button will push the second controller into display.

How it works...

As you see, we managed to create the user interface for the application with minimal code. Inside storyboard files, we need to connect each element with each other, according to how we want the screen hierarchy to appear. We first set `FirstController` as a root view controller to the navigation controller. Then, we assigned a relationship to the button with the `SecondController` class. So, when the button is clicked, the `SecondController` class will be pushed into the navigation controller's stack, just as if we were calling the `UINavigationController.PushViewController` method. This relationship is called **segue**. In a storyboard file, we can individually select segues and set their properties. For example, we can set an identifier string or change its behavior from **push** to **modal**.

In the `FinishedLaunching` method, we first instantiate a `UIStoryboard` instance through the static `UIStoryboard.FromName` method, as follows:

```
UIStoryboard storyboard = UIStoryboard.FromName("MainStoryboard",
    NSBundle.MainBundle);
```

We then call the `InstantiateInitialViewController` method to get the initial controller of the storyboard, as follows. In this case, the initial controller is `UINavigationController`:

```
UINavigationController navController =
    (UINavigationController)storyboard.
    InstantiateInitialViewController();
```

Note that we need to cast the return value to the correct type of controller, as its return type is `NSObject`.

There's more...

We can also initiate segues programmatically. To do this, we first need to select the segue in Xcode and set an identifier for it through the **Attributes** inspector tab. Then, we can trigger it through code by calling the `PerformSegue` method of the `UIViewController` instance it belongs to, as follows:

```
this.PerformSegue("MyPushSegue", null);
```

Passing data

With storyboards, the system is instantiating the view controllers we need. We can have access to the view controller that will be displayed through a segue by overriding the PrepareForSegue method on the controller that is the owner, or source of the segue, as follows:

```
public override void PrepareForSegue (UIStoryboardSegue segue,
  NSObject sender)

{

    base.PrepareForSegue (segue, sender);


    if (segue.Identifier == "MyPushSegue")

    {

      SecondController secondController =

        (SecondController)segue.DestinationViewController;

      // Create a public method or property in SecondController

      // for passing data to it.

    }//end if

}
```

As you can see, there is also a UIStoryboardSegue class which provides us with the necessary information.

The PrepareForSegue method is called after the involving view controllers have been instantiated and before the segue starts. So, by determining which segue triggered the preparation method through the Identifier property, we retrieve the controller that the segue will display through the DestinationViewController property.

 The PrepareForSegue method will be called regardless if the segue was triggered programmatically through the PerformSegue method or was just set to a button in the storyboard file.

See also

▶ The *Interface Builder* recipe in *Chapter 1, Development Tools*

Unwinding in storyboards

Another very useful feature of storyboards is **unwinding**. Unwinding is a process similar to that of a segue, but instead of presenting the next view controller, it reverses to a previous view controller in a storyboard. The great thing about it is that it allows us to go back to any view controller, not just the one that is right before the current controller we are in. This recipe will show how to use unwinding.

Getting ready

For this recipe, we will need the project StoryboardApp we created in the previous recipe. Open it in Xamarin Studio.

How to do it...

Perform the following steps to implement unwinding:

1. Add a new class to the project and name it ModalController.

2. Make the class a custom view controller, similar to FirstController and SecondController in the project, as follows:

   ```
   [Register("ModalController")]
   public class ModalController : UIViewController
   {
     public ModalController (IntPtr handle) : base(handle)
     {
     }
   }
   ```

3. Add the following method in the FirstController class:

   ```
   [Action("unwindFromModalController:")]
   public void UnwindFromModalController(UIStoryboardSegue segue)
   {
   }
   ```

4. Open the MainStoryboard.storyboard file in Xcode and add another UIViewController. Set this controller's **Class** to **ModalController**.

5. Add **UIButton** to SecondController and set its title to Show modal.

6. Press *Ctrl* and drag from the button to ModalController. Set this segue to **modal**.

7. Add another button, this time on ModalController. Set its title to Unwind to first.

8. Press *Ctrl* and drag from the button to the **Exit** item on the controller's dock, as shown in the following screenshot:

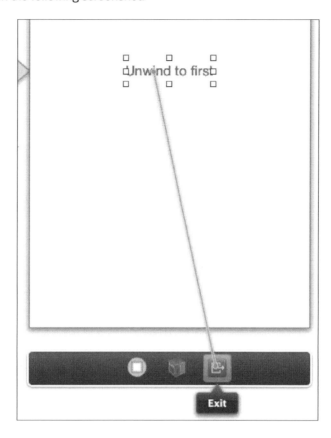

9. Select **unwindFromModalController** in the context menu that will appear.
10. Compile and run the app on the simulator. Flow through the screens until you reach the modal controller and click on the **Unwind to first** button. The user interface will flow back to the first controller.

How it works...

By using unwinding or **unwind segues**, we can get back to any controller in the hierarchy. The basic requirement is to add a method decorated with the `Action` attribute to the controller you want to unwind to, as follows:

```
[Action("unwindFromModalController:")]
public void UnwindFromModalController(UIStoryboardSegue segue) {}
```

The attribute will basically expose the method as an action to Xcode so that when the storyboard file is opened, we will be able to add the unwind segue. This is how the action **unwindFromModalController** appeared when we dragged to the **Exit** item. It doesn't matter if the action is inside another class Xcode is smart enough to search all classes in the storyboard.

 The **Exit** item in the dock of every view controller is responsible for creating unwind segues. It represents the exit of a view controller, which is determined by how the controller was displayed.

There's more...

We can have access to the controller that initiated the unwind segue through the UIStoryboardSegue object that is passed to the unwind action, as follows:

```
//..
ModalControllermodalController =
    (ModalController)segue.SourceViewController;
```

Where is the unwind segue in the storyboard?

When we create unwind segues, there is no apparent change in Xcode's appearance or an indication that we created something, like when we create segues. After creating the unwind, we can find it by expanding the document outline, as shown in the following screenshot:

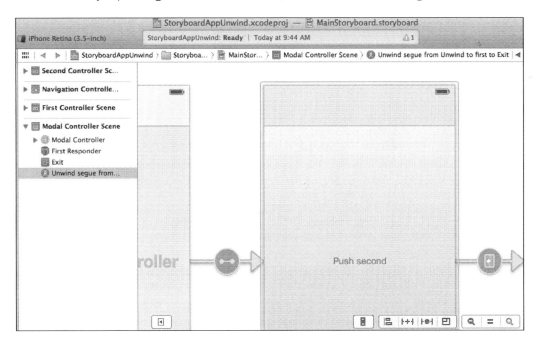

See also

▶ The *Navigating through different view controllers* and *Modal view controllers* recipes

4

Data Management

In this chapter, we will cover the following topics:

- ▶ Creating files
- ▶ Using a SQLite database
- ▶ Preparing for iCloud support
- ▶ iCloud key/value data storage

Introduction

Almost every application needs to have permanent data storage on the filesystem. In this chapter, we will discuss different ways of storing data. We will see how to create a **SQLite database** and manage data with it from within an iPhone application. Also, we will learn how to use an already existing database in a project.

 SQLite (`http://www.sqlite.org`) is a self-contained transactional database system. Each database is saved in a standalone file and there is no database server. In iOS, SQLite support is native.

Following SQLite, we will have a look at **iCloud storage** and how to incorporate it in our apps.

Creating files

In this recipe, we will learn how to create files on the filesystem of iOS devices.

Getting ready

Create a new iPhone **Single View Application** in Xamarin Studio and name it
`FileCreationApp`.

How to do it...

Follow the ensuing steps to complete this recipe:

1. Open the `FileCreationAppViewController.xib` file in Interface Builder.

2. Add a button and a label on its view.

3. Back in Xamarin Studio, enter the following code in the `ViewDidLoad` method of the controller class:

```
string filePath = Path.Combine (Environment.GetFolderPath
  (Environment.SpecialFolder.Personal),
  "MyFile.txt");
using (StreamWriter sw = new StreamWriter (filePath))
{
  sw.WriteLine ("Some text in file!");
}
this.btnShow.TouchUpInside += (s, e) => {
  using (StreamReader sr = new StreamReader (filePath))
  {
    this.labelStatus.Text = sr.ReadToEnd ();
  }
};
```

4. Compile and run the app on the simulator. Tap the button to fill the label with the contents of the file.

How it works...

As one can see from the preceding code, we can use standard classes from the `System.IO` namespace, just like in desktop applications. We will set a path for the file we want to save. We will do this in the following line of code:

```
string filePath = Path.Combine
(Environment.GetFolderPath(Environment.SpecialFolder.
  Personal), "MyFile.txt");
```

In iOS, we do not have access to the whole filesystem, not even inside the application bundle. An exception will occur if we try to write inside a folder we do not have access to. So we use the `static Environment.GetFolderPath(SpecialFolder)` method and retrieve the `Personal` special folder, that corresponds to our app's `Documents` folder. Note the use of `Path.Combine(string, string)` that combines two strings and returns a path. After that, we create a new instance of the `StreamWriter` class as follows:

```
using (StreamWriter sw = new StreamWriter (filePath))
{
  sw.WriteLine ("Some text in file!");
}
```

We write some text in the file with its `WriteLine(string)` method. To retrieve the text from the file, we create a new instance of the `StreamReader` class and read the text with its `ReadLine` method using the following code:

```
using (StreamReader sr = new StreamReader (filePath))
{
  this.labelMessage.Text = sr.ReadToEnd ();
}
```

There's more...

Practically, every available class in the `System.IO` namespace will work on Xamarin.iOS, as long as we have access to the target folder.

The Documents folder

An app bundle's `Documents` folder is relevant to the app alone. If the app is uninstalled from the device, its contents are also removed. Files created in this folder are automatically backed up to iCloud, unless we explicitly request that a particular file is excluded. This can be done by skipping the backup attribute of the file. For example, if we wanted to exclude the `MyFile.txt` file that we created, we would have to add the following code:

```
NSError error = NSFileManager.SetSkipBackupAttribute(filePath,
  true);
if (null == error) {
  // Success
}
```

If the file does not exist when we call this method, the `error` object will contain the appropriate error information.

If we would like to include a file to iCloud backup, we would just have to call the preceding method, passing `false` as the second argument.

It is important that we consider skipping the backup attribute for large files. Apple will reject apps that contain large files to be backed up to iCloud.

iCloud backup is the automatic procedure of iOS backup feature. It is primarily used for restoring a device from iCloud. Other than excluding or including files from iCloud backups, we have no other access to it. It is also different from iCloud storage, which we have access to and will be discussing later in this chapter.

The Caches folder

The `Caches` folder (`Library/Caches/`) can be used for storing application-specific data that can be easily recreated by the application. Files in this folder are not backed up to iCloud and can be deleted by the system, if there is need for more space.

We can get the full path of the `Caches` folder in an iOS app, through the `Environment.SpecialFolder.InternetCache` value, as shown in the following code:

```
string cachesFolder =
    Environment.GetFolderPath(Environment.SpecialFolder.
    InternetCache);
```

See also

▶ The *iCloud key/value data storage* recipe

Using a SQLite database

In this recipe, we will learn how to create a SQLite database file. We will create a table, insert some data into it, and then query the table to display the data on screen.

Getting ready

Create a new iPhone **Single View Application** in Xamarin Studio and name it `SQLiteApp`. Add three buttons and a label on the view controller. Do not forget to connect them to the outlets.

How to do it...

Perform the following steps:

1. Add references to the assemblies `Mono.Data.Sqlite` and `System.Data`. The following screenshot shows how to add a reference to the project:

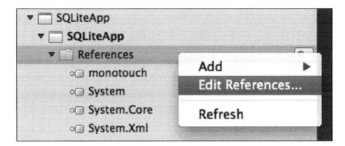

2. For creating the database and the table, enter the following method in the `SQLiteAppViewController` class:

```
private void CreateSQLiteDatabase (string databaseFile)
{
  try
  {
    if (!File.Exists (databaseFile))
    {
      SqliteConnection.CreateFile (databaseFile);
      using (SqliteConnection sqlCon = new SqliteConnection
        (String.Format ("Data Source = {0};",
        databaseFile)))
      {
        sqlCon.Open ();
        using (SqliteCommand sqlCom = new SqliteCommand
          (sqlCon))
        {
          sqlCom.CommandText = "CREATE TABLE Customers (ID
            INTEGER PRIMARY KEY, FirstName VARCHAR(20),
            LastName VARCHAR(20))";
          sqlCom.ExecuteNonQuery ();
```

```
        }
        sqlCon.Close ();
      }
      this.lblStatus.Text = "Database created!";
    } else {
      this.lblStatus.Text = "Database already exists!";
    }
  } catch (Exception ex) {
    this.lblStatus.Text = String.Format ("Sqlite error:
      {0}", ex.Message);
  }
}
```

3. Add the following method for inserting data to the database:

```
private void InsertData(string databaseFile) {
  try {
    if (File.Exists(databaseFile)) {
      using (SqliteConnection sqlCon = new
        SqliteConnection(String.Format("Data Source = {
        0};", databaseFile))) {
        sqlCon.Open();
        using (SqliteCommand sqlCom = new
          SqliteCommand(sqlCon)) {
          sqlCom.CommandText = "INSERT INTO Customers
            (FirstName, LastName) VALUES ('Dimitris',
            'Tavlikos')";
          sqlCom.ExecuteNonQuery();
          }
        sqlCon.Close();
      }
      this.lblStatus.Text = "Inserted 1 row.";
    }  else {
      this.lblStatus.Text = "Database file does not
        exist!";
    }
  }  catch (Exception ex) {
    this.lblStatus.Text = String.Format("Sqlite error: {
      0}", ex.Message);
  }
}
```

4. Add the following method for querying the data from the database:

```
private void QueryData(string databaseFile) {
  try {
    if (!File.Exists(databaseFile)) {
```

```
        using (SqliteConnection sqlCon = new
          SqliteConnection(String.Format("Data Source = {
            0};", databaseFile))) {
            sqlCon.Open();
          using (SqliteCommand sqlCom = new
            SqliteCommand(sqlCon)) {
            sqlCom.CommandText = "SELECT * FROM Customers
              WHERE FirstName='Dimitris'";
            using (SqliteDataReader dbReader =
              sqlCom.ExecuteReader()) {
              while (dbReader.Read()) {
                this.lblStatus.Text = String.Format("First
                  name: { 0}\ nLast name: { 1}",
                  dbReader["FirstName"],
                  dbReader["LastName"]);
              }
            }
          }
        }
      } else {
        this.lblStatus.Text = "Database file does not
          exist!";
      }
    } catch (Exception ex) {
      this.lblStatus.Text = String.Format("Sqlite error: {
        0}", ex.Message);
    }
  }
}
```

5. Add the following code in the `ViewDidLoad` method:

```
string sqlitePath = Path.Combine (Environment.GetFolderPath
  (Environment.SpecialFolder.Personal), "MyDB.db3");
this.btnCreate.TouchUpInside += (s, e) =>
  this.CreateSQLiteDatabase (sqlitePath);
this.btnInsert.TouchUpInside += (s, e) =>
  this.InsertData(sqlitePath);
this.btnQuery.TouchUpInside += (s, e) =>
  this.QueryData(sqlitePath);
```

6. Compile and run the app on the simulator. Tap each button in sequence, to create, insert, and query the data from the database.

How it works...

iOS provides native support for SQLite databases. We can access SQLite databases with Mono's `Mono.Data.Sqlite` namespace:

```
using Mono.Data.Sqlite;
```

Inside the `CreateSQLiteDatabase` method, we first check if the file already exists using the following code so as to avoid destroying any data:

```
if (!File.Exists (databaseFile))
```

Then we can continue with the creation of the database. We first create the file with the `SqliteConnection.CreateFile(string)` static method using the following code:

```
SqliteConnection.CreateFile (databaseFile);
```

We connect to the newly created file by initializing a `SqliteConnection` object and calling its `Open()` method. The connection string for a SQLite database is `Data Source =` followed by the filename of the database, as shown in the following code:

```
using (SqliteConnection sqlCon = new SqliteConnection
   (String.Format ("Data Source = {0};", databaseFile)))
   sqlCon.Open ();
```

To create a table in the database, a `SqliteCommand` object is initialized. We pass a standard SQL string to its `CommandText` property and call the `ExecuteNonQuery()` method to execute the SQL as shown in the following code:

```
sqlCom.CommandText = "CREATE TABLE Customers (ID INTEGER PRIMARY KEY,
FirstName VARCHAR(20), LastName VARCHAR(20))";
sqlCom.ExecuteNonQuery ();
```

To insert data to the database, we use the following code in the `InsertData` method:

```
sqlCom.CommandText = "INSERT INTO Customers (FirstName, LastName)
   VALUES ('Dimitris', 'Tavlikos')";
sqlCom.ExecuteNonQuery();
```

Finally, we query the data through a `SELECT` statement and retrieve it with the help of `SqliteDataReader`, as shown in the following code:

```
sqlCom.CommandText = "SELECT * FROM Customers WHERE
   FirstName='Dimitris'";
using (SqliteDataReader dbReader = sqlCom.ExecuteReader()) {
   while (dbReader.Read()) {
     this.lblStatus.Text = String.Format("First name: {0}\nLast
       name: {1}", dbReader["FirstName"], dbReader["LastName"]);
   }
}
```

Note the usage of a `try-catch` block. It is provided to display a message to the user if something goes wrong with the creation of the database.

SQL table creation

In this recipe, we have created a simple table for our database with the name `Customers`. It contains three fields. The `FirstName` and `LastName` parameters are of type `VARCHAR(20)` while `ID` is of type `INTEGER` and is also the `PRIMARY KEY` of the table.

Apart from using SQL commands to create tables, we can create a SQLite database with various commercial or free GUI tools. A simple search on the internet will yield various results.

See also

▶   The *Creating files* recipe

▶   The *Displaying data in a table* recipe in *Chapter 5, Displaying Data*

Preparing for iCloud support

With the release of iOS 5, Apple introduced iCloud. iCloud is a service that provides cloud storage to iOS users, in a variety of configurations. For app development, we can use iCloud storage to save information that can be shared among different instances of our app running on different devices under the same user account. In this recipe, we will learn how to prepare an app to provide iCloud storage support.

Getting ready

Create a new iPhone **Single View Application** in Xamarin Studio and name it `KeyValueApp`. For this recipe, an App ID with iCloud enabled needs to exist on the developer account. Refer to *Chapter 14, Deploying*, for more information on how to create an App ID.

How to do it...

Perform the following steps:

1.   Double-click on the `Entitlements.plist` file to open it in Xamarin Studio.

2.   Check the **Enable iCloud** checkbox.

3.   If it asks you to choose an account, select your Apple developer account from the list.

4. After enabling iCloud, the **Use key-value store** checkbox should appear. Enable it. The **Entitlements.plist** file settings should now look like the following screenshot:

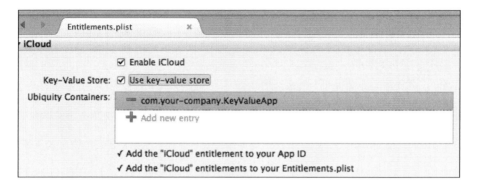

5. In the project options, under **iPhone Bundle Signing**, select **Entitlements.plist** for the **Custom entitlements** field. It is important to perform this step, despite the fact that the field might already be set.

How it works...

Enabling iCloud support is simply a matter of setting the appropriate setting for our project. By checking the **Enable iCloud** and **Use key-value store** checkboxes, Xamarin Studio adds the necessary keys in the **Entitlements.plist** file, that will allow the app to use iCloud storage.

There's more...

Although we can run iCloud-enabled apps on the simulator, the iCloud functionality will not work.

See also

▸ The *Creating profiles* recipe in *Chapter 14, Deploying*

iCloud key/value storage

In this recipe, we will learn how to save and retrieve small amounts of data that are suitable for storing app settings or anything that would be useful to be shared among different devices.

 Apps can only store up to a total of 1 MB of data with key/value store, in up to 1024 keys. So it cannot be used to back up files or similar functionality.

Getting ready

We will need two devices under the same iCloud account to actually see iCloud storage in action. On one device we will save some data, and on the second device we will load the data. If only one device is available, it is not an issue as it will work flawlessly because the data will just be loaded from local storage, instead of iCloud.

How to do it...

The following are the steps to complete the recipe:

1. Create a new iPhone **Single View Application** in Xamarin Studio and enable it for iCloud, as shown in the previous recipe. Name the project `KeyValueApp`.

2. Add two buttons and one label on the view controller.

3. Add the following code in the view controller's `ViewDidLoad` method:

```
this.btnSave.TouchUpInside += (s, e) => {
  NSUbiquitousKeyValueStore kvStore =
    NSUbiquitousKeyValueStore.DefaultStore;
  kvStore.SetString("LastSavedSearch", "How to implement
    iCloud");
  kvStore.Synchronize();
  this.lblStatus.Text = "Saved!";
};
this.btnLoad.TouchUpInside += (s, e) => {
  NSUbiquitousKeyValueStore kvStore =
    NSUbiquitousKeyValueStore.DefaultStore;
  this.lblStatus.Text = string.Format("Last saved search is: {0}",
kvStore.GetString("LastSavedSearch"));
};
```

4. Compile and run the app on the device. Tap the **Save** button to save the key and value to iCloud.

5. Tap the **Load** button to display the data on the label.

6. If there is access to a second device, run the app on it and tap the **Load** button. The data will be retrieved from iCloud and displayed on the screen of the second device.

How it works...

To save key/value pairs to iCloud, we use the `NSUbiquitousKeyValueStore` class, which is responsible for handling the data. We retrieve the default key value store through the `DefaultStore` static property and call its `Save` method, as shown in the following code:

```
NSUbiquitousKeyValueStore kvStore =
  NSUbiquitousKeyValueStore.DefaultStore;
kvStore.Save("LastSavedSearch", "How to implement iCloud ");
```

Calling the `Save` method pushes the data in a queue for being saved locally and then uploaded to iCloud. The `Synchronize` method syncs the key/value store and can basically be used to speed up the process of syncing the data. However, calling the method does not mean that the data will be synced right away. iOS is responsible for when the data will be synced and we have no control over it. However, iCloud is designed to provide a seamless syncing experience, so the delays are usually unnoticeable:

```
kvStore.Synchronize();
```

To load the data from iCloud, we simply call the `GetString` method, passing the key for which to retrieve the data using the following code:

```
kvStore.GetString("LastSavesSearch");
```

There's more...

iCloud key/value store only accepts a specific set of values, which are of the following types:

- `double`
- `bool`
- `long`
- `NSObject[]`
- `NSDictionary`
- `NSData`
- `string`

Getting notified on key/value store changes

We can also get notified of when a key/value pair or set of pairs have been changed on another device. To do this, we need to add a notification observer, as shown in the following code:

```
NSObject coudObserver =
  NSUbiquitousKeyValueStore.Notifications.
  ObserveDidChangeExternally((s, e) => {
  if (e.ChangeReason == NSUbiquitousKeyValueStoreChangeReason.
    ServerChange) {
    e.ChangeKeys.Foreach(k => Console.WriteLine("Key changed:
      {0}", k));
  }
};
```

The `NSUbiquitousKeyValueStoreChangeReason` enumeration contains the following values:

- ▶ **ServerChange**: It shows if a value was changed on another device or not.
- ▶ **QuotaViolationChange**: The quota limit was reached. Some key/value pairs need to be removed.
- ▶ **InitialSyncChange**: A key/value pair was discarded as the initial iCloud setup on the device has not been completed.
- ▶ **AccountChange**: The user has changed the iCloud account on the device. The whole key/value store is replaced with the one from the new iCloud account.

See also

- ▶ The *Preparing for iCloud support* recipe
- ▶ The *Creating profiles* recipe in *Chapter 14, Deploying*

5
Displaying Data

In this chapter, we will cover the following topics:

- ► Providing lists
- ► Displaying data in a table
- ► Customizing rows
- ► Editing a table
- ► Table indexing
- ► Searching through the data
- ► Creating a simple web browser
- ► Displaying data in a grid
- ► Customizing the grid

Introduction

In the previous chapter, we discussed some of the available options for data management in an iOS app. In this chapter, we will discuss the various ways of displaying data to the user.

Specifically, we will focus on how to use the following controls:

- ► **UIPickerView**: This control provides functionality that is similar to a list box.
- ► **UITableView**: This is a very customizable view for displaying data. It is one of the most used controls in iOS apps.
- ► **UISearchBar and UISearchDisplayController**: This is a combination of controls that provides an easy-to-use interface for searching through data.
- ► **UIWebView**: This brings web-browser functionality to apps.
- ► **UICollectionView**: This displays data in a customizable grid.

Furthermore, we will learn how to provide indexing in tables to make large volumes of data easily accessible to the user.

Providing lists

In this recipe, we will learn how to use the `UIPickerView` class.

Getting ready

The `UIPickerView` class provides us with a control whose functionality is similar to that of a list box. It is specifically designed for human fingers that touch the screen. Its main difference from a common list box is that each column can have its own number of rows. To get started, create a new iPhone **Single View Application** project and name it `PickerViewApp`.

How to do it...

Perform the following steps:

1. Open the `PickerViewAppViewController.xib` file in Interface Builder. Add `UILabel` and `UIPickerView` on the main view and save the document.

2. Back in Xamarin Studio, create a nested class in the `PickerViewAppViewController` class that inherits from UIPickerViewModel using the following code:

   ```
   private class PickerModel : UIPickerViewModel
   ```

3. Add the following constructor and fields in the nested class:

   ```
   public PickerModel (PickerViewAppViewController controller) {
     this.parentController = controller;
     this.transportList = new List<string>() { "On foot", "Bi
       cycle", "Motorcycle", "Car", "Bus" };
     this.distanceList = new List<string>() { "0.5",      "1",
       "5", "10", "100" };
     this.unitList = new List<string>() { "mi", "km" };
     this.transportSelected = this.transportList [0];
     this.distanceSelected = this.distanceList [0];
     this.unitSelected = this.unitList [0];
   }
   private PickerViewAppViewController parentController;
   private List<string> transportList;
   private List<string> distanceList;
   private List<string> unitList;
   string transportSelected;
   string distanceSelected;
   string unitSelected;
   ```

4. You will now need to override four methods from the `UIPickerViewModel` class, as shown in the following code:

```
public override int GetComponentCount (UIPickerView picker) {
   return 3;
}
public override int GetRowsInComponent (UIPickerView picker,
   int component) {
   switch (component) {
   case 0:
     return this.transportList.Count;
   case 1:
     return this.distanceList.Count;
   default:
     return this.unitList.Count;
   }
}
public override string GetTitle (UIPickerView picker, int
   row, int component) {
   switch (component) {
   case 0:
     return this.transportList[row];
   case 1:
     return this.distanceList[row];
   default:
     return this.unitList[row];
   }
}
public override void Selected (UIPickerView picker, int
   row, int component) {
   switch (component) {
     case 0:
       this.transportSelected = this.transportList[row];
     break;
     case 1:
       this.distanceSelected = this.distanceList[row];
     break;
     default:
       this.unitSelected = this.unitList[row];
     break;
   }
   this.parentController.lblStatus.Text =
     String.Format("Transport: {0}\nDistance: {1}{2}",
     this.transportSelected, this.distanceSelected,
     this.unitSelected);
}
```

5. Finally, set the model object we created to the picker view's `Model` property inside the controller's `ViewDidLoad` method, as shown in the following code:

```
this.pickerView.Model = new PickerModel (this);
```

6. Compile and run the app on the simulator. Drag through the items in the picker view and watch the label's content change according to your selection. The following screenshot shows how it should look:

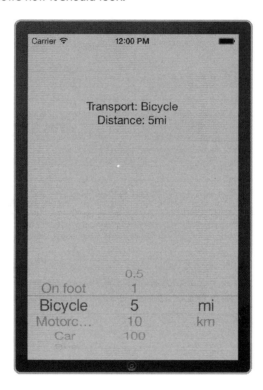

How it works...

The `UIPickerViewModel` class does not exist in Objective-C. Xamarin.iOS provides this class as a wrapper around the `UIPickerViewDataSource` and `UIPickerViewDelegate` native protocols, and contains both of these classes' methods for us to override. This is extremely helpful since we only have to implement and assign one class instead of two for our picker view. Both of these protocols are available as `C#` classes in Xamarin.iOS at the same time.

Inside the constructor, we initialize the lists that will hold the data to be displayed in the picker. The following four methods we need to override are responsible for displaying the data:

- ▶ `int GetComponentCount (UIPickerView picker)`: This returns the number of columns we want the picker view to display

- ▶ `int GetRowsInComponent (UIPickerView picker, int component)`: This returns the number of rows each component will display

- ▶ `string GetTitle (UIPickerView picker, int row, int component)`: This is the text of each row

- ▶ `void Selected (UIPickerView picker, int row, int component)`: This is the action to be taken when the user selects an item from any component/row combination in the picker view

We use the lists we have assigned in the constructor to display the data. For example, the `GetTitle` method is implemented as shown in the following code:

```
switch (component)
{
case 0:
  return this.transportList[row];
case 1:
  return this.distanceList[row];
default:
  return this.unitList[row];
}
```

There's more...

We can programmatically select the initial selection of the picker view by calling the `Select (int, int, bool)` method. The first two parameters reflect the row and component index, respectively, while the `bool` parameter toggles the selection animation. The only thing to remember with this method is to call it after we have assigned the picker's `Model` property. An exception will occur otherwise.

More UIPickerView customization

Apart from the options presented earlier, we also have the option of setting the width of each component. To do this, we override the `GetComponentWidth (UIPickerView, int)` method, which returns a float that represents the width for each component.

We can also set custom views as items in the picker view, instead of plain text. This can be done by overriding the `GetView (UIPickerView, int, int, UIView)` method and returning the view we want to be displayed on each position in the `UIPickerView` control.

Date and time selection

There is a control named `UIDatePicker` that is similar to `UIPickerView` and is specifically customized to display and select the date and time values. Note that although its user interface is the same as the picker view, it does not inherit the `UIPickerView` class. It just uses an instance of it as a subview.

See also

 ▸ The *Displaying data in a table* recipe

Displaying data in a table

In this recipe, we will learn how to use the `UITableView` class to display data. This class, along with the `UITableViewCell` object, provides an interface for displaying data on the screen in multiple rows, but on a single column.

Getting ready

To get started, create a new project in Xamarin Studio and name it `TableViewApp`. In this recipe, we will not use the XIB files. We will create our user interface in code.

How to do it...

Perform the following steps:

1. Add a new class to the project and name it `TableController`. Derive the class from `UITableViewController` using the following code:

   ```
   public class TableController : UITableViewController
   ```

2. Create the following nested class inside the `TableController` class:

   ```
   private class TableSource : UITableViewSource
   {
     public TableSource ()
     {
       this.cellID = "cellIdentifier";
       this.tableData = new Dictionary<int, string> () {
         {0, "Music"},
         {1, "Videos"},
         {2, "Images"}
       };
   ```

```
    }
    private readonly string cellID;
    private Dictionary<int, string> tableData;
    public override int RowsInSection (UITableView tableview,
      int section)
    {
      return this.tableData.Count;
    }
    public override UITableViewCell GetCell (UITableView
      tableView, NSIndexPath indexPath)
    {
      int rowIndex = indexPath.Row;
      UITableViewCell cell = tableView.DequeueReusableCell
        (this.cellID);
      if (null == cell)
      {
        cell = new UITableViewCell
          (UITableViewCellStyle.Default, this.cellID);
      }
      cell.TextLabel.Text = this.tableData[rowIndex];
      return cell;
    }
  }
```

3. Override the controller's `ViewDidLoad` method and add the following line of code:

```
this.TableView.Source = new TableSource ();
```

4. Add the following code in the `FinishedLaunching` method to display the table controller:

```
TableController tableController = new TableController();
UINavigationController navController = new
  UINavigationController(tableController);
window.RootViewController = navController;
```

5. Compile and run the application on the simulator. The result should be similar to the one shown in the following screenshot:

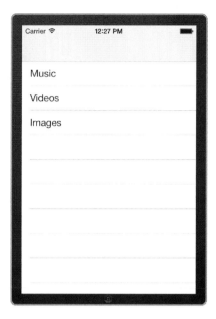

How it works...

The nested class we created acts as the data source of `UITableView`. The class created in the following code inherits from the Xamarin.iOS `UITableViewSource` class:

```
private class TableSource : UITableViewSource
```

 Like `UIPickerView`, in the example discussed in the previous recipe, the `UITableViewSource` class does not exist in Objective-C. It is merely a wrapper object offered by Xamarin.iOS around the `UITableViewDelegate` and `UITableViewSource` protocols.

In its constructor, we initialize two variables (as shown in the following code): `string`, which will act as the cells' identifier, and a generic `Dictionary` variable for our data source:

```
this.cellID = "cellIdentifier";
this.tableData = new Dictionary<int, string> () {
    {0, "Music"},
    {1, "Videos"},
    {2, "Images"}
};
```

To make the `TableSource` class work, we need to override two methods. The first method, named `RowsInSection`, returns the number of rows that the table shall display. In the following code, we return the number of items in our data source object:

```
return this.tableData.Count;
```

The second method, `GetCell`, returns the `UITableViewCell` object that will be displayed in the table.

 The `UITableViewCell` class represents a single row and manages its content in `UITableView`.

To be more efficient, the table view creates its cell objects when they are needed. For this reason, we need to get `UITableViewCell` (that was used earlier) from the table through its `DequeueReusableCell` method, as shown in the following code:

```
UITableViewCell cell = tableView.DequeueReusableCell
    (this.cellID);
```

If no cells exist for the particular cell identifier, the method returns `null`. Hence, we create the cell that will be used, using the following code:

```
cell = new UITableViewCell (UITableViewCellStyle.Default,
    this.cellID);
```

Then, we assign the text that the particular cell will display and return using the following code:

```
cell.TextLabel.Text = this.tableData[rowIndex];
return cell;
```

By default, the `UITableViewCell` class contains two labels that can be used to display text. The main label can be accessed through the `TextLabel` property and the secondary label through the `DetailTextLabel` property. Note that when using a cell with the `Default` style, the `DetailTextLabel` property cannot be used and will return `null`.

There's more...

To provide functionality when the user selects a particular row, we need to override the `RowSelected` property in the class that acts as a `UITableViewSource`. By default, when the user taps on a row, the cell is highlighted with a light gray color to indicate the selection. To deselect the row, we use the `UITableView.DeselectRow(NSIndexPath, bool)` method, as shown in the following code:

```
public override void RowSelected (UITableView tableView, NSIndexPath
indexPath)
{
    tableView.DeselectRow (indexPath, true);
}
```

The UITableView styles

UITableView can be created with two different styles. The default style is Plain. The other style that can be used is the Grouped style. This style is being used in many iOS native apps such as the *Settings* app.

Also, UITableView supports the display of data divided into different sections. We must explicitly return the number of rows each section will have in the RowsInSection override if we want to use different sections.

The UITableViewCell styles

A table cell can have four different cell styles, which are represented by the UITableViewCellStyle enumeration. Its values are listed as follows:

- ▶ **Default**: This is the default cell style. Only the TextLabel property can be used to display text.
- ▶ **Subtitle**: This is a style that provides DetailTextLabel as a subtitle to TextLabel.
- ▶ **Value1**: This is a style that displays both TextLabel and DetailTextLabel text in the same size, with a different color, and aligned to the sides of the cell.
- ▶ **Value2**: This is a style that displays the TextLabel text smaller than the DetailTextLabel text. This style is used in the native *Contacts* app, in the contact details screen.

See also

- ▶ The *Providing lists* recipe
- ▶ The *Customizing rows* recipe
- ▶ The *Navigating through different view controllers* recipe in *Chapter 3, User Interface – View Controllers*

Customizing rows

In this recipe, we will create a table view that uses our own custom subclass of UITableViewCell to display data.

Getting ready

Create a new project in Xamarin Studio in the same manner in which the project in the earlier recipe was created. Name it CustomRowsApp.

How to do it...

Perform the following steps:

1. Add a new class to the project and name it `CustomCell`.

2. Implement the class with the following code:

```
[Register("CustomCell")]
public partial class CustomCell : UITableViewCell {
    public const string CELLID = "CustomCell";
    public CustomCell (IntPtr handle)  : base(handle) {}
    [Outlet("lblTitle")]
    public UILabel LabelTitle { get; private set; }
    [Outlet("imgView")]
    public UIImageView ImgView { get; private set; }
}
```

3. Add a new **Empty iPhone Interface Definition** to the project and name it `CustomCell`. Don't worry about the name conflicting with the class we created earlier, as this is an XIB file. Open the file in Interface Builder.

4. Add `UITableViewCell` on the canvas. The following screenshot shows a selected `UITableViewCell` in the object browser in Xcode:

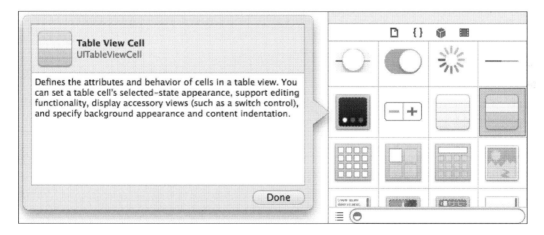

5. Set the **Class** field of the table cell to `CustomCell` in the **Identity** inspector.

6. Set the **Identifier** field of the cell to `CustomCell` in the **Attributes** inspector.

7. Add a `UIImageView` and a `UILabel` on the cell and connect them to their outlets. Save the document.

8. Add the `TableController.cs` file we created in the previous recipe, *Displaying data in a table*, to the project. Change its namespace from `TableViewApp` to `CustomRowsApp`.

9. Change the `TableSource` class' `GetCell` method to the following code:

```
public override UITableViewCell GetCell (UITableView
  tableView, NSIndexPath indexPath) {
  int rowIndex = indexPath.Row;
  CustomCell cell =
    (CustomCell)tableView.DequeueReusableCell(
    CustomCell.CELLID);
  cell.LabelTitle.Text = this.tableData[rowIndex];
  return cell;
}
```

10. Add the following code in the `ViewDidLoad` method of `TableController`:

```
this.TableView.RegisterNibForCellReuse
  (UINib.FromName("CustomCell", NSBundle.MainBundle),
  CustomCell.CellID);
```

11. Finally, make sure that `TableController` is presented in the `FinishedLaunching` method, as shown in the following code:

```
TableController tableController = new TableController();
UINavigationController navController = new
  UINavigationController();
window.RootViewController = navController;
```

How it works...

Just like creating a custom view, we are able to create our own custom cells to present data with a `UITableView`. The main difference lies in the fact that the table view reuses the instances of its cells so that it is more efficient when we want to display multiple rows.

To make our table view "aware" of our custom cell, we call the `RegisterNibForCellReuse` method using the following code:

```
this.TableView.RegisterNibForCellReuse
  (UINib.FromName("CustomCell", NSBundle.MainBundle),
  CustomCell.CellID);
```

This way, when we call the `DequeueReusable` cell method in `GetCell`, the system will automatically create a cell instance for us or get one that was created earlier. Hence, there is no need for us to check if the cell is null or not:

```
CustomCell cell = (CustomCell)tableView.DequeueReusableCell(
  CustomCell.CELLID);
```

Did you notice something common in the two method calls discussed earlier? They both need an identifier string for the cell. The `CustomCell.CELLID` constant has the same value we entered in the **Identifier** field of the cell in Xcode: `CustomCell`. In this case, it is the same as the class name of our cell, as it keeps things tidy if we were to have different custom cells to present. However, basically, the identifier for a cell can be whatever we want it to be.

There's more...

We can create as many custom cells as we need. As discussed earlier, we need to make sure that we set a unique identifier for each of the cell classes we are going to use. Also, if the custom cells we create have different heights, we need to make sure we override the `GetHeightForRow` method in our `UITableViewSource` implementation using the following code:

```
public override float GetHeightForRow (UITableView tableView,
  NSIndexPath indexPath) {
  return 44f; // Or whatever height we want the particular row to
  have.
}
```

For greater efficiency, it's good to have the heights of the rows calculated beforehand and not calculate them inside `GetHeightForRow`.

Useful properties of the UITableViewCell class

Apart from adding text in the default labels, the `UITableViewCell` contains some other properties whose values we can set to add more default items in a cell. These properties are are follows:

▶ `ImageView`: This accepts a `UIImageView` parameter. We can use it to display an image in a cell, on its left-hand side.

▶ `AccessoryView`: This accepts any instance of `UIView`. Its position defaults to the right of the cell, in the place of the cell's accessory, which is located on the right-hand side of the cell.

▶ `Accessory`: This accepts values of the `UITableViewCellAccessory` type. It provides predefined views for the cell's accessory, such as `DetailDisclosureButton` or `Checkmark`.

UINib class

The `UINib` class is responsible for loading NIB files at runtime. We instantiate a `UINib` instance through its `FromName` static method, passing the name of the NIB file we want to load without its extension, as shown in the following code:

```
UINib nib = UINib.FromName("CustomCell", NSBundle.MainBundle);
```

Adding content programmatically

We can add views to a table cell programmatically. However, we should not add them to the cell directly, but to its `ContentView`, using the following code:

```
// Inside our custom cell class:
this.ContentView.AddSubview(myView);
```

See also

▸ The *Displaying data in a table* recipe

▸ The *Editing a table* recipe

▸ The *Creating a custom view* recipe in *Chapter 2, User Interface – Views*

Editing a table

In this recipe, we will discuss how to insert and delete rows at runtime from a `UITableView`, providing the user with the appropriate user interface interaction.

Getting ready

Open the `CustomRowsApp` project we created in the previous recipe, *Customizing rows*.

How to do it...

Perform the following steps:

1. Remove the `tableData` field from the `TableSource` class and replace it with the following property:

   ```
   public List<string> TableData { get; private set; }
   ```

2. Initialize the list in the constructor using the following code:

   ```
   this.TableData = new List<string>() { "Music", "Videos",
      "Images" };
   ```

3. In the `TableSource` class, override the `CommitEditingStyle` method and implement it with the following code:

   ```
   public override void CommitEditingStyle (UITableView
      tableView, UITableViewCellEditingStyle editingStyle,
      NSIndexPath indexPath) {
      if (editingStyle == UITableViewCellEditingStyle.Delete) {
        this.tableData.RemoveAt(indexPath.Row);
        tableView.DeleteRows(new NSIndexPath[] { indexPath },
          UITableViewRowAnimation.Automatic);
   ```

```
  }
}
```

4. In the `TableController` class, add a `UIBarButtonItem` using the following code:

```
UIBarButtonItem btnAdd;
public override ViewDidLoad() {
  // ... existing code here.
  this.btnAdd = new UIBarButtonItem(
    UIBarButtonSystemItem.Add, (s, e) => {
    TableSource tableSource =
      (TableSource)this.TableView.Source;
    int itemCount = tableSource.TableData.Count;
    tableSource.TableData.Add(string.Format("Inserted item:
      {0}", itemCount));
    this.TableView.InsertRows(new NSIndexPath[] {
      NSIndexPath.FromRowSection(itemCount, 0)
    }, UITableViewRowAnimation.Automatic);
  };
  this.NavigationItem.SetRightBarButtonItem(this.btnAdd,
    false);
}
```

5. Compile and run the app on the simulator. Tap the plus button to add new rows to the table and swipe on an item from right to left to delete items. The following screenshot shows the table after having added one item and swiped on another one:

 To swipe an item on the simulator, click-and-drag the cursor sideways.

How it works...

The `CommitEditingStyleForRow` method is called whenever an editing action is about to take place. In our implementation, we check if the editing action is about deleting an item, and if it is, we remove the row. To do this, we first remove the corresponding item from our data source and then call the `DeleteRows` method of the table view:

```
this.tableData.RemoveAt(indexPath.Row);
tableView.DeleteRows(new NSIndexPath[] { indexPath },
   UITableViewRowAnimation.Automatic);
```

Similarly, when we want to add a row to the table, we first add the item we want to our data source and then call the `InsertRows` method, as follows:

```
tableSource.TableData.Add(string.Format("Inserted item: {0}",
   itemCount));
this.TableView.InsertRows(new NSIndexPath[] {
   NSIndexPath.FromRowSection(itemCount, 0)
}, UITableViewRowAnimation.Automatic);
```

There's more...

The `UITableView` also supports an editing mode. We can activate/deactivate the editing mode of a table view by calling the `SetEditing` method, passing `true` or `false`, respectively, an example of which is shown in the following code:

```
this.TableView.SetEditing(true, true);
```

The second parameter determines whether we want the table view to transition to/from the editing mode with an animation.

When a table view is in the editing mode, each row has a red minus sign on its left-hand side. If the user taps the sign, the **Delete** button will appear on the right-hand side of the row, just as it appears when they swipe the row.

Enabling editing modes for individual rows

We can also enable a specific editing mode or even disable it for individual rows. To do this, we need to override the `EditingStyleForRow` method in our `UITableViewSource` subclass, as shown in the following code:

```
public override UITableViewCellEditingStyle
   EditingStyleForRow(UITableView tableView,
   NSIndexPath indexPath) {
   // To disable the editing style of a row:
   // return UITableViewCellEditingStyle.None;
   return UITableViewCellEditingStyle.Delete;
}
```

See also

▸ The *Displaying data in a table* recipe

Table indexing

In this recipe, we will learn how to provide an index in a table, allowing the user to quickly browse through the rows of `UITableView`.

Getting ready

Create a new project in Xamarin Studio and name it `TableIndexApp`. Add a `UITableViewController`, as shown in the previous tasks in this chapter, and implement the `TableSource` class.

How to do it...

Perform the following step:

1. In the table source class, override and implement the following methods:

```
public override int NumberOfSections (UITableView
  tableView)
{
  return this.tableData.Count;
}
public override string TitleForHeader (UITableView
  tableView, int section)
{
  return Convert.ToString (this.tableData[section][0]);
}
public override string[] SectionIndexTitles (UITableView
  tableView)
{
  return this.tableData.Select (s => Convert.ToString
  (s[0])).Distinct ().ToArray ();
}
```

How it works...

The table source created in this recipe contains many different sections. For simplicity, each section contains one row. The `NumberOfSections` method returns the total number of sections that the table will display.

To set a title for each section, we must override the `TitleForHeader` method, as shown in the following code:

```
public override string TitleForHeader (UITableView tableView, int
section)
{
  return Convert.ToString (this.tableData[section][0]);
}
```

This implementation returns the first letter of each string in the data source. To provide the index, we override the `SectionIndexTitles` method, as shown in the following code:

```
public override string[] SectionIndexTitles (UITableView
  tableView)
{
  return this.tableData.Select (s => Convert.ToString
  (s[0])).Distinct ().ToArray ();
}
```

Here, it returns the first letter of each item in the data source. The result of this project will be similar to one shown in the following screenshot:

When the user touches the screen anywhere on the index, the table view will scroll to that specific section.

There's more...

Indexing should be applied to tables with a **Plain** style. Applying an index on tables with a **Grouped** style set is not advisable, because the index will not be easily distinguished.

A good example of a native iOS app with an index on a table can be found in the native *Contacts* app.

See also

▸   The *Displaying data in a table* recipe

Searching through the data

In this recipe, we will learn how to provide search functionality for the content in a table view.

Getting ready

Create a new project in Xamarin Studio and name it `SearchTableApp`. Add `UIViewController` and name it `SearchController`.

How to do it...

Perform the following steps:

1.   Open the `SearchController.xib` file in Interface Builder. Add **Search Bar and Search Display Controller** in `UITableView`. The following screenshot shows the `UISearchDisplayController` object selected in the object browser:

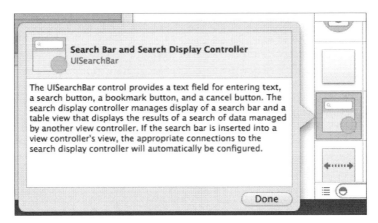

Note that after this action, some outlets are created and connected automatically. We need most of them, so we leave them as they are.

2. Add `UITableView` and connect it to an outlet. Save the document.

3. Back in Xamarin Studio, create a `UITableViewSource` subclass that will act as the data source for the table view. Refer to the *Displaying data in a table* recipe in this chapter for information on how to do this. This time, make sure that the `List<string>` variable, which will hold the data, is a member of the `SearchController` class.

4. Add another `List<string>` variable in the `SearchController` class using the following code:

```
private List<string> filterDataList;
```

5. Implement a subclass that will act as a delegate object for the search display controller, as shown in the following code:

```
private class SearchDelegate : UISearchDisplayDelegate
{
  public SearchDelegate (TableController controller)
  {
    this.parentController = controller;
  }
  private TableController parentController;
  public override bool ShouldReloadForSearchString
    (UISearchDisplayController controller, string
    forSearchString)
  {
    this.parentController.filterDataList =
      this.parentController.tableData
      .Where (s => s.ToLower ().Contains
        (forSearchString.ToLower ()))
        .ToList ();
    this.parentController.filterDataList.Sort
      (delegate(string firstStr, string secondStr) {
        return firstStr.CompareTo (secondStr);
      });
    return true;
  }
}
```

6. Add the following code in the `ViewDidLoad` method and assign the source and delegate objects in it:

```
this.TableView.Source = new TableSource (this);
this.SearchDisplayController.SearchResultsSource = new
   TableSource(this);
this.SearchDisplayController.Delegate = new
   SearchDelegate(this);
```

7. Compile and run the app on the simulator. Tap the search bar and start typing into it. It will automatically search the table and show the results.

You can find the complete code in the `SearchTableApp` project. The result will be the common iOS search bar above the table, similar to the following screenshot:

How it works...

The `UISearchDisplayController` class provides a convenient way of searching through data. It contains `UISearchBar` which accepts input from the user, and `UITableView` which is used to display the results. After we add a search controller in a view controller, we can access it through that controller's `SearchDisplayController` property. To trigger the results table, we must implement `UISearchDisplayDelegate` and override its `ShouldReloadForSearchString` (which returns a Boolean value) using the following code:

```
private class SearchDelegate : UISearchDisplayDelegate
```

Inside the `ShouldReloadForSearchString` method override, we search our data source, saving the filtered results in a new data source according to its `forSearchString` parameter:

```
this.parentController.filterDataList =
  this.parentController.tableData
  .Where (s => s.ToLower ().Contains (forSearchString.ToLower ()))
  .ToList ();
```

We then sort the results alphabetically and return `true` so that the search controller's table will reload its data, as shown in the following code:

```
this.parentController.filterDataList.Sort (delegate(string
  firstStr, string secondStr) {
  return firstStr.CompareTo (secondStr);
});
return true;
```

The search controller's table view also needs a source object. In this example, we set it to the same object we created for our table, as shown in the following code:

```
this.TableView.Source = new TableSource (this);
this.SearchDisplayController.SearchResultsSource = new
  TableSource(this);
```

As we are using instances of the same object, we need to modify some things in it to display data according to which table calls it. So, for example, the `RowsInSection` method looks like the following code:

```
public override int RowsInSection (UITableView tableview, int
  section)
{
  if (tableview.Equals (this.parentController.TableView))
  {
    return this.parentController.tableData.Count;
  } else
  {
    return this.parentController.filterDataList.Count;
  }
}
```

In this way, we return the number of rows according to which table calls the method. Similarly, we need to set each cell's text label inside the `GetCell` method, as shown in the following code:

```
if (tableView.Equals (this.parentController.TableView))
{
  cell.TextLabel.Text =
    this.parentController.tableData[rowIndex];
```

```
} else
{
  cell.TextLabel.Text =
    this.parentController.filterDataList[rowIndex];
}
```

There's more...

When the user taps on the search bar, the keyboard appears, making the search controller active. To deactivate it, we can hook on the search bar's `SearchButtonClicked` event. This event will get triggered when the user taps on the keyboard's **Search** button:

```
this.SearchDisplayController.SearchBar.SearchButtonClicked +=
  (s, e) => {
  this.SearchDisplayController.SetActive(false, true);
};
```

The `SetActive` method is what we can use to enable or disable the search controller.

See also

▸   The *Displaying data in a table* recipe

▸   The *Table indexing* recipe

Creating a simple web browser

In this recipe, we will discuss displaying online content with the `UIWebView` class.

Getting ready

Create a new **Single View Application** project in Xamarin Studio and name it `WebBrowserApp`.

How to do it...

Perform the following steps:

1. Open the `WebBrowserAppViewController.xib` file in Interface Builder and add a `UIWebView` object on the main view. Create and connect an outlet for it with the name `webView`. Save the document.

2. Override the `ViewDidAppear` method in the `WebBrowserAppViewController` class, as shown in the following code:

```
public override void ViewDidAppear (bool animated)
{
  NSUrl url = new NSUrl ("http://software.tavlikos.com");
  NSUrlRequest urlRequest = new NSUrlRequest (url);
  this.webView.LoadRequest (urlRequest);
}
```

3. Compile and run the app on the simulator. Watch the website load on the screen!

How it works...

The `UIWebView` class is iOS SDK's web browser control. To load web content, we just have to call its `LoadRequest` method, which accepts a parameter of the `NSUrlRequest` type. The `NSUrlRequest` object contains the URL we want it to load, as shown in the following code:

```
NSUrl url = new NSUrl ("http://software.tavlikos.com");
```

There's more...

The `UIWebView` class contains some very useful events, which are as follows:

- `LoadStarted`: This is triggered when the control has started loading content
- `LoadFinished`: This is triggered when the content finished loading successfully
- `LoadError`: This is triggered when the loading of the content failed

Scaling the content

Another important feature of the `UIWebView` is the automatic scaling of content. It can be activated by setting its `ScalePageToFit` property to `true`.

UIWebView supported files

Apart from web pages, the `UIWebView` control can be used to display local content with the following types of files:

- Excel (`.xls`)
- Keynote (`.key.zip`)
- Numbers (`.numbers.zip`)
- Pages (`.pages.zip`)
- PDF (`.pdf`)
- Powerpoint (`.ppt`)

- ▶ Word (.doc)
- ▶ Rich Text Format (.rtf)
- ▶ Rich Text Format Directory (.rtfd.zip)
- ▶ Keynote (.key)
- ▶ Numbers (.numbers)
- ▶ Pages (.pages)

Displaying data in a grid

In this recipe, we will discuss using the UICollectionView object to display data in a grid-like layout. The UICollectionView class was introduced in iOS 6, and is a very useful control that was missed by iOS developers. Prior to UICollectionView, the only way to display data in a grid was to create a custom control, which was not a very easy task.

Getting ready

Create a new project in Xamarin Studio and name it CollectionViewApp. We will also need something to display, so add an image to the project.

How to do it...

Perform the following steps:

1. Open the CollectionViewAppViewController.xib file in Interface Builder and add a UICollectionView on its main view. The following screenshot shows the object in the object browser:

2. Back in Xamarin Studio, add the following class:

```
public class ImageCell : UICollectionViewCell {
  public const string CELLID = "ImageCell";
  public ImageCell(IntPtr handle) : base(handle) {
    this.Initialize();
  }
  public UIImageView ImageView { get; private set; }
  private void Initialize() {
    this.ImageView = new
      UIImageView(this.ContentView.Bounds);
    this.ContentView.AddSubview(this.ImageView);
  }
}
```

3. Add the following nested class in the controller:

```
private class CollectionSource : UICollectionViewSource {
  public CollectionSource(CollectionViewAppViewController
    parentController) {
    this.parentController = parentController;
  }
  private CollectionViewAppViewController parentController;
  public override int GetItemsCount(UICollectionView
    collectionView, int section) {
    return this.parentController.collectionData.Count;
  }
  public override UICollectionViewCell
    GetCell(UICollectionView collectionView, NSIndexPath
    indexPath) {
    ImageCell cell = (ImageCell)collectionView.
      DeqeueReusableCell((NSString)ImageCell.Cell,
      indexPath);
    cell.ImageView.Image = this.parentController.
      collectionData[indexPath.Row];
    return cell;
  }
}
```

4. Add the following code in the controller:

```
private List<UIImage> collectionData;
public override ViewDidLoad() {
  base.ViewDidLoad();
  this.collectionData = new List<UIImage>();
  for (int i = 0; i < 30; i++) {
    this.collectionData.Add(UIImage.FromBundle("shapes"));
  }
```

```
    this.collectionView.RegisterClassForCell(
      typeof(ImageCell), (NSString)ImageCell.CELLID);
    this.collectionView.Source = new CollectionSource(this);
}
```

5. Compile and run the app on the simulator. The result should be similar to the one shown in the following screenshot:

How it works...

The `UICollectionView` class is used in a manner that is similar to `UITableView`. The main difference is that instead of showing the data in a single column, it does so in a grid arrangement. The `UICollectionViewSource` class is overridden to provide the data source of the collection view, as shown in the following code:

```
private class CollectionSource : UICollectionViewSource {
```

Just like table views in `UITableViewSource`, we need to provide the number of items in the grid and the object for single items, in this case, `UICollectionViewCell`, as shown in the following code:

```
public override int GetItemsCount(UICollectionView collectionView,
    int section) {
    return this.parentController.collectionData.Count;
}
public override UICollectionViewCell GetCell(UICollectionView
    collectionView, NSIndexPath indexPath) {
    ImageCell cell = (ImageCell)collectionView.
      DeqeueReusableCell((NSString)ImageCell.Cell, indexPath);
    cell.ImageView.Image = this.parentController.
      collectionData[indexPath.Row];
    return cell;
}
```

Note that unlike `UITableViewCell`, the `UICollectionViewCell` class doesn't offer much for us to use. So, we have to override it to create our own cell for the collection, as shown in the following code:

```
public class ImageCell : UICollectionViewCell
```

As we are using a custom cell, we have to let the collection view know about it through the `RegisterClassForCell` method, using the following code:

```
this.collectionView.RegisterClassForCell(typeof(ImageCell),
    (NSString)ImageCell.CELLID);
```

There's more...

Apart from showing individual items with the `UICollectionViewCell` class, the `UICollectionView` supports the display of supplementary views of the `UICollectionReusableView` type. These views basically represent either the header or the footer of the sections in the collection view.

To provide supplementary views, we need to create our own subclass using the following code:

```
public class CollectionHeader : UICollectionReusableView
```

We then need to override the following method in the collection source (this method will return the supplementary view that we want):

```
public override UICollectionReusableView
    GetViewForSupplementaryElement(UICollectionView collectionView,
    NSString elementKind, NSIndexPath indexPath) {
```

```
CollectionHeader header =
    (CollectionHeader)collectionView.
    DequeueReusableSupplementaryView(
    UICollectionElementKindSection.Header, viewIdentifier,
    indexPath);
    return header;
}
```

The elementKind parameter is the NSString representation of the UICollectionElementKindSection enumeration, which contains two values: Footer and Header.

Finally, we need to call the RegisterClassForSupplementaryView method to register our custom class with the collection view, using the following code:

```
this.collectionView.RegisterClassForSupplementaryView(typeof(Colle
    ctionHeader), UICollectionElementKindSection.Header,
    viewIdentifier);
```

More information on UICollectionView

A good tutorial on UICollectionView can be found at Xamarin's website: http://docs.
xamarin.com/guides/ios/user_interface/introduction_to_collection_
views/.

See also

▸ The *Displaying data in a table* recipe
▸ The *Customizing rows* recipe

Customizing the grid

In this recipe, we will learn how to customize the display of the collection view.

Getting ready

In this recipe, we will work on the CollectionViewApp project we created in the *Displaying data in a grid* recipe. Open the project in Xamarin Studio.

How to do it...

Perform the following steps:

1. In the `ViewDidLoad` method of the controller, add the following code:

```
UICollectionViewFlowLayout flowLayout = new
    UICollectionViewFlowLayout();
flowLayout.MinimumLineSpacing = 20f;
flowLayout.MinimumInteritemSpacing = 4f;
flowLayout.SectionInset = new UIEdgeInset(4f, 4f, 4f, 4f);
flowLayout.ItemSize = new SizeF(20f, 20f);
this.collectionView.CollectionViewLayout = flowLayout;
```

2. Compile and run the app on the simulator. The result should be similar to the one shown in the following screenshot:

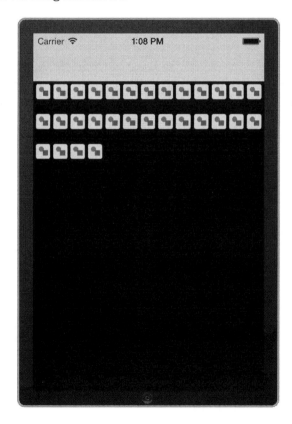

How it works...

The collection view's layout can be customized through the `UICollectionViewLayout` class. `UICollectionViewFlowLayout` is a subclass of this class and offers a simple layout that we can use.

By setting specific properties, we define how the cells will be arranged by the collection view. The following list describes the properties we are setting in this project:

- `MinimumLineSpacing`: This is the smallest distance between rows in the grid
- `MinimumInteritemSpacing`: This is the smallest distance between individual items in the grid
- `SectionInset`: This is the area around each section in the collection view that should be left blank
- `ItemSize`: This is the size of each item in the collection view

The following image shows what each property corresponds to in the collection view:

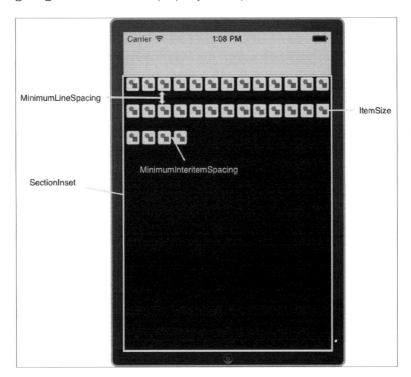

There's more...

Setting the `ItemSize` parameter of the collection layout object will adjust the size of all the items in the collection view. We can set the size for every cell individually by providing the following method in the `CollectionSource` subclass:

```
[Export("collectionView:layout:sizeForItemAtIndexPath:")]
public SizeF GetSizeForItem(UICollectionView collectionView,
  UICollectionViewLayout layout, NSIndexPath indexPath) {
  if (indexPath.Item > 11 && indexPath.Item < 19) {
    return new SizeF(40f, 40f);
  } else {
    return new SizeF(20f, 20f);
  }
}
```

Adding the preceding method to our own `CollectionSource` subclass would give the result shown in the following screenshot:

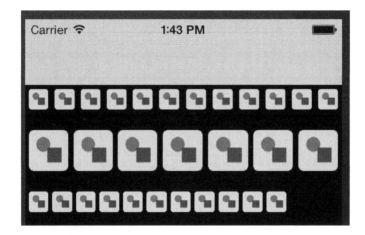

See also

▸   The *Displaying data in a grid* recipe

6
Web Services

In this chapter, we will cover the following topics:

- ▶ Consuming web services
- ▶ Consuming REST services
- ▶ Communicating with native APIs
- ▶ Using WCF services

Introduction

Providing online information to the user is a crucial part of mobile development. In this chapter, we will discuss developing apps that communicate with web services to provide information. We will see how to consume and invoke web services based on SOAP. We will also discuss on how to use REST web services and how to parse the popular JSON data format from a web server. Last but not least, we will take a look at how to use the native iOS APIs for communication and also how to use WCF services.

All examples in this chapter use **XSP**, a lightweight web server that is shipped with the Mono Framework; so, there is no need to have a live web service up and running online or locally to make use of the provided code.

Consuming web services

In this recipe, we will learn how to use a SOAP web service in a Xamarin.iOS project.

Getting ready

Create a new **Single View Application** project in Xamarin Studio and name it `WebServiceApp`. This chapter's code contains a web service project named `MTWebService`. This is the web service that will be used.

To use the `MTWebService` web service, we need a web server. Mono Framework provides us with the XSP lightweight web server for testing purposes. Open a terminal and type the following command to get to the web service's directory, replacing `<code_directory>` with the path the downloaded code is in:

```
cd <code_directory>/CH06_code/MTWebService/MTWebService
```

Run the XSP web server by typing `xsp4` in the prompt. You will see an output that is similar to the following:

```
xsp4

Listening on address: 0.0.0.0

Root directory:
/Users/dtavlikos/projects/CH06_code/MTWebService/MTWebService

Listening on port: 8080 (non-secure)

Hit Return to stop the server.
```

The web server is now up and running.

How to do it...

Perform the following steps to complete this recipe:

1. We need to add a reference to the web service in our project. Right-click on the project in the **Solution** pad and navigate to **Add | Add Web Reference**. In the dialog box that will be shown, add `http://localhost:8080/MTTestWebService.asmx?wsdl` in the **Web Service Url** field and click on the **Jump to** button.

2. Select **.NET 2.0 Web Services** in the **Framework** combo box.

3. Set the **Reference** field to `mtWebService`.

4. With all the settings properly entered, the dialog box should look similar to the following screenshot. Click on the **OK** button to add the web reference:

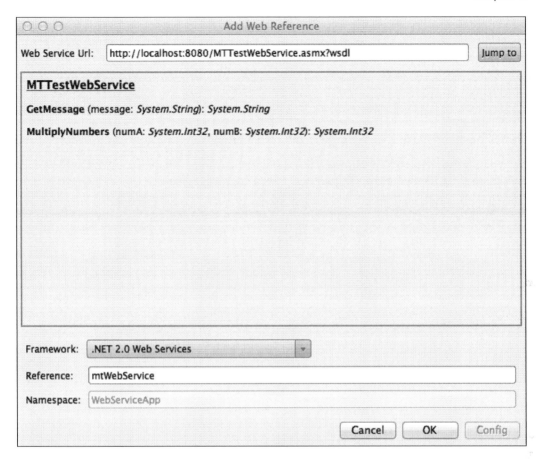

5. Add a button and label to `WebServiceAppViewController`.

6. In the `ViewDidLoad` method of the controller, add the following code:

```
this.btnFetch.TouchUpInside += (s, e) => {
  using (MTTestWebService webService =
    new MTTestWebService())
  {
    this.lblOutput.Text =
      webService.GetMessage ("Hello Web Service!");
  }
};
```

7. Add the following `using` directive to the `WebServiceAppViewController.cs` file:

```
using WebServiceApp.mtWebService;
```

8. Compile and run the app on the simulator. Click on the **Fetch** button and the output should be displayed on the screen.

How it works...

Xamarin.iOS apps can consume web services just like a .NET desktop application. The XSP lightweight web server is installed when installing the Mono Framework by default, which is a requirement for the Xamarin installation. When running the `xsp4` command in the terminal without any parameters, it sets its base directory to the current directory by default and starts listening on the `8080` port. If the web server is started, the web service description can be viewed by entering `http://localhost:8080/MTTestWebService.asmx` in a browser.

Xamarin Studio reads the **WSDL** information from the provided URL and creates the necessary proxy that will allow us to use the web service in the project.

We then set the **Framework** value to **.NET 2.0 Web Services** and provide a **Reference** name, which will reflect the namespace of the web reference. To make use of the web service within our code, we instantiate it and then just call the method we are interested in:

```
this.lblOutput.Text =
  webService.GetMessage ("Hello Web Service!");
```

There's more...

Apart from using a local hosted web service, there are also numerous sample web services on the Internet. A simple search will yield many results.

Invoking web service methods asynchronously

The created proxy also contains methods based on Begin/End and the event to invoke the web service asynchronously. The following example shows us how to use the event-based methods:

```
MTTestWebService webService = new MTTestWebService();
webService.GetMessageCompleted += (sender, args) =>
  this.InvokeOnMainThread(() => this.lblOutput.Text =
  args.Result);
webService.GetMessageAsync("Hello Web Service!");
```

Note the `InvokeOnMainThread` call inside the event handler; it is being called on a separate thread. So, if we want to access the main thread in it, we need to wrap our calls with `InvokeOnMainThread`.

The XSP shutdown

To shut down the XSP web server, just click on the *Return* key in the terminal where it was executed from.

See also

▶ The *Communicating with native APIs* recipe

Consuming REST services

In this recipe, we will discuss how to properly use and consume REST services with Xamarin.iOS.

Getting ready

Create a new **Single View Application** in Xamarin Studio and name it `ForecastApp`. In this recipe, we will use the **Open Meteo Foundation** REST API. The use of this API is subject to the terms of use stated in this page: `http://openmeteofoundation.org/terms-of-use`.

How to do it...

Perform the following steps to complete this recipe:

1. Add a label and a button on `ForecastAppViewController`. Make sure that the label's **Lines** property is set to at least three lines.

2. Add the following code in the controller's `ViewDidLoad` method:

```
this.btnForecast.TouchUpInside += async (sender, e) => {

    HttpClient client = new HttpClient();
    string jsonResponse = await
        client.GetStringAsync("http://api.ometfn.net/
        0.1/forecast/eu12/46.5,6.32/now.json");
    JsonValue jsonObj = JsonValue.Parse(jsonResponse);
    JsonArray tempArray = (JsonArray)jsonObj["temp"];
    double temp = (double)tempArray[0];
    JsonArray windSpeedArray =
        (JsonArray)jsonObj["wind_10m_ground_speed"];
    double windSpeed = (double)windSpeedArray[0];
    this.lblOutput.Text =
        string.Format("Temperature: {0}\nWind speed: {1}",
        temp, windSpeed);
};
```

3. Add the `System.Net.Http` and `System.Json` references to the project. Don't forget to include the corresponding `using` directives to the `ForecastAppViewcontroller.cs` file.

4. Compile and run the app on the simulator. Click on the **Get Forecast** button to display the current temperature and wind speed on the screen.

How it works...

In this recipe, we created an app that uses a REST API to get the current forecast for a location. We are using the `async`/`await` pattern that allows us to connect and retrieve the data asynchronously. This helps us make sure that our app will not freeze while it is connected to retrieve the data.

As it all happens when we click on the button, its `TouchUpInside` handler method needs to be marked `async`, as follows:

```
this.btnForecast.TouchUpInside += async (sender, e) => {
//..
```

We then use the `HttpClient` class, which is part of the `System.Net.Http` namespace that provides us with asynchronous methods to connect to endpoints, as follows:

```
HttpClient client = new HttpClient();
  string jsonResponse =
    await client.GetStringAsync("http://api.ometfn.net/
    0.1/forecast/eu12/46.5,6.32/now.json");
```

We pass the endpoint to the `GetStringAsync` method, and we get back a JSON response string.

After retrieving the response, we need to parse it to extract the information we need from it. We do this by using the `System.Json` namespace. This namespace contains a set of simple classes that allow us to parse JSON strings, as follows:

```
JsonValue jsonObj = JsonValue.Parse(jsonResponse);
```

The temperature is contained in the JSON response under the temp key that contains an array, albeit with a single item, as follows:

```
JsonArray tempArray = (JsonArray)jsonObj["temp"];
double temp = (double)tempArray[0];
```

After we read the information we need from the JSON response, we display it as follows:

```
this.lblOutput.Text =
    string.Format("Temperature: {0}\nWind speed: {1}", temp,
    windSpeed);
```

The `System.Json` namespace is very helpful for parsing simple JSON strings. However, things could get very complicated if we have to parse large and more complex objects. There are a number of open source libraries we can download and use in our Xamarin.iOS projects. The most popular are as follows:

▶ **Xamarin port of NewtonSoft Json.NET from Andrew Young**: Even if this is outdated, it is fully functional for Xamarin projects. You can find the page at `https://github.com/ayoung/Newtonsoft.Json`.

▶ **ServiceStack.Text**: You can find the page at `https://github.com/ServiceStack/ServiceStack.Text`.

See also

▶ The *Consuming web services* recipe

Communicating with native APIs

In this recipe, we will discuss using native iOS APIs to connect and consume REST services.

Getting ready

For this recipe, we will work on the `ForecastApp` we created in the previous recipe, *Consuming REST services*. Open the project in Xamarin Studio.

How to do it...

Perform the following steps:

1. Comment out the code in the `ViewDidLoad` method and add the following code:

```
this.btnForecast.TouchUpInside += (sender, e) => {
  NSUrlRequest request = new NSUrlRequest(new
    NSUrl("http://api.ometfn.net/0.1/forecast/eu12/
    46.5,6.32/now.json"));
  NSUrlConnection connection = new NSUrlConnection(request,
    new ConnectionDelegate((response) => {
    JsonValue jsonObj = JsonValue.Parse(response);
    JsonArray tempArray = (JsonArray)jsonObj["temp"];
    double temp = (double)tempArray[0];
    JsonArray windSpeedArray =
      (JsonArray)jsonObj["wind_10m_ground_speed"];
    double windSpeed = (double)windSpeedArray[0];
```

```
      this.lblOutput.Text =
        string.Format("Temperature: { 0}\ nWind speed: { 1}",
        temp, windSpeed);
      }));
    connection.Start();
  };
```

2. Add the following class to the project:

```
public class ConnectionDelegate : NSURLConnectionDelegate {
  private Action<string> finishedCallback;
  private StringBuilder responseData;
  public ConnectionDelegate(Action<string> callback) {
    this.finishedCallback = callback;
    this.responseData = new StringBuilder();
  }
  public override void ReceivedData(NSUrlConnection
    connection, NSData data) {
    if (null != data) {
      this.responseData.Append(data.ToString());
    }
  }
  public override FinishedLoading(NSUrlConnection
    connection) {
    if (null != this.finishedCallback) {
      this.finishedCallback(this.responseData.ToString());
    }
    this.responseData.Clear();
  }
}
```

3. Compile and run the app on the simulator. Click on the **Get Forecast** button to fetch and display the forecast data.

How it works...

The NSUrlConnection class is the native iOS class that provides basic connectivity functionality. We initialize it by passing NSUrlRequest and a delegate object, as follows:

```
NSUrlRequest request = new NSUrlRequest(new
  NSUrl("http://api.ometfn.net/0.1/forecast/eu12/
  46.5,6.32/now.json"));
  NSUrlConnection connection = new NSUrlConnection(request,
    new ConnectionDelegate((response) => {
```

The `ConnectionDelegate` class that we created acts as the delegate object of our `NSUrlConnection`. Inside the class, we need to override the `ReceivedData` method to fill our internal buffer with the data received from the service, as follows:

```
public override void ReceivedData(NSUrlConnection connection, NSData
data) {
```

Similarly to reading data from the `Stream` object of `HttpWebResponse`, the `ReceivedData` method will be called as soon as new data becomes available. Inside `ReceivedData`, we make sure we append the data to our buffer. When all the data has been received and the response is finished, the `FinishedLoading` method will be called, as follows:

```
public override void FinishedLoading(NSUrlConnection connection) {
```

After initializing the `NSUrlConnection` instance, we call its `Start` method to initiate the connection, as follows:

```
connection.Start();
```

There's more...

If something goes wrong with the connection, the `FailedWithError` method of `NSUrlConnectionDelegate` will be called. We can override it to get information on the error that occurred, as follows:

```
public override void FailedWithError(NSUrlConnection connection,
NSError error) {
  if (null != error) {
    Console.WriteLine("Connection error: {0}",
      error.LocalizedDescription);
  }
}
```

Synchronous NSUrlConnection

Using the `NSUrlConnection` class with a delegate object means that the connection will take place asynchronously on the thread that it was started from. If we wanted to start a synchronous connection, we can use the `SendSynchronousRequest` static method, as follows:

```
NSUrlResponse response;
NSError error;
NSData data = NSUrlConnection.SendSyncrhonousRequest(request,
  out response, out error);
// do something with data
```

Usability

As you might have already noticed, using `NSUrlConnection` is a bit more complicated than plain old Mono BCL classes. In general, using BCL classes is the best practice for most scenarios, as it helps us maintain a multi-platform code base, among other things.

There are some cases, however, where the native APIs are very useful and are the only available solution. For example, iOS supports certain connectivity features in the background, which are only possible with the native APIs.

See also

▸ The *Consuming REST services* recipe

▸ The *Updating data in the background* recipe in *Chapter 12, Multitasking*

Using WCF services

In this recipe, we will learn how to consume WCF services with Xamarin.iOS.

 The WCF service support is only available in business and enterprise licenses of Xamarin.

Getting ready

For this project, we will need a running WCF service. A WCF service can be found in the code download of this chapter. To start the service, open a terminal and go to the project's directory. Start the service by running the `start_wcfservice.sh` shell script, as follows:

```
cd <code_directory>/CH06_code/WcfService/WcfService
./start_wcfservice.sh
```

After the service is started, create a new **Single View Application** in Xamarin Studio and name it `WcfServiceApp`. A machine running on Windows will also be needed.

How to do it...

Perform the following steps:

1. Add the references to the `System.Runtime.Serialization` and `System.ServiceModel` namespaces of the project and their corresponding `using` directives in the `WcfServiceAppViewController.cs` file.

2. Xamarin.iOS does not provide full support for WCF services. To generate a proxy for the client, we will need to use the `slsvcutil` tool on a Windows machine. Run the following command in the command prompt under Windows:

```
"c:\Program Files\Microsoft
SDKs\Silverlight\v3.0\Tools\slsvcutil /noconfig
http://192.168.0.113:8080/WcfService.svc?wsdl"
```

This command will produce a C# source file named `service.cs`. Add this file to the Xamarin.iOS project. Replace the IP address in the following highlighted code with your own to make it work correctly.

3. Add a label and a button on the view of `WcfServiceAppViewController`. Add the following code in the `ViewDidLoad` method:

```
this.btnFetchData.TouchUpInside += (sender, e) => {
  WcfTestServiceClient client =
    new WcfTestServiceClient (new BasicHttpBinding (),
    new EndpointAddress
    ("http://192.168.0.113:8080/WcfTestService.svc"));
  client.GetBookInfoCompleted +=
    WcfTestServiceClient_GetBookInfoCompleted;
  client.GetBookInfoAsync ();
  UIApplication.SharedApplication.
    NetworkActivityIndicatorVisible = true;
};
```

4. Finally, add the following method:

```
private void WcfTestServiceClient_GetBookInfoCompleted
  (object sender, GetBookInfoCompletedEventArgs e)
{
  this.InvokeOnMainThread (delegate {
    UIApplication.SharedApplication.
      NetworkActivityIndicatorVisible = false;
    this.lblResponse.Text = String.Format ("Book title:
      {0}\nAuthor: {1}", e.Result.Title, e.Result.Name);
  } );
}
```

5. Compile and run the app on the simulator. Click on the button and watch the data returned from the service get populated in the label.

How it works...

Xamarin.iOS relies on Mono Framework's support for WCF services, which is not complete. Although, the fact that WCF services can be used in iOS apps makes Xamarin.iOS more appealing to .NET developers.

However, there is no tool to create the client proxy on a Mac, and Xamarin Studio can not create a proper proxy either; so, we will need to have access to a Windows machine to do this with the Silverlight Service Model Proxy Generation Tool (`SLsvcUtil.exe`). The source file that this tool generates allows us to consume the WCF service in our project.

It is important to use Silverlight Version 3.0 `slsvcutil` to create the client proxy.

Apart from Mono Framework's support, there is another limitation, that is, the dynamic code generation is not allowed on iOS. This makes any code that relies on the `System.Reflection.Emit` namespace unusable. In fact, the `System.Reflection.Emit` namespace is not available at all in Xamarin.iOS.

After copying the produced file on Mac, we add it to the project, and we are ready to use the WCF service. The preceding highlighted code shows us how to instantiate the service object. Note that the default constructor of the service object cannot be used, as Xamarin.iOS does not support the `System.Configuration` namespace.

> The actual communication occurs by calling the method's asynchronous implementation after setting a handler to its corresponding completion event. Note that in this case, there is no alternative to using synchronous invocations or the `BeginInvoke` and `EndInvoke` pattern:
>
> ```
> client.GetBookInfoCompleted +=
>     WcfTestServiceClient_GetBookInfoCompleted;
> client.GetBookInfoAsync ();
> ```
>
> The result returned from the service can be retrieved through the specified `EventArgs` derivative's `Result` property:
>
> ```
> this.labelResult.Text = String.Format ("Book
> title:
>   {0}\nAuthor: {1}", e.Result.Title,
> e.Result.Name);
> ```

There's more...

When debugging a project that consumes WCF services, remember to set the address of the machine the service is running on, instead of localhost or 127.0.0.1. This is because when we run the app on the device, the app will fail to connect to the service.

More information on Xamarin Studio's WCF support

There is an option of adding a WCF web reference through Xamarin Studio in the **Add Web References** window shown in the *Consuming web services* recipe. However, it is not yet complete and the proxy it generates will not work.

WCF service creation

The object returned from the `WcfService` service and the actual service itself was created completely on a Mac as a Xamarin Studio project. As there is no WCF project template, the **Empty Project** template was used.

See also

- ▶ The *Consuming web services* recipe

7
Multimedia Resources

In this chapter, we will cover the following topics:

- ▶ Selecting images and videos
- ▶ Capturing media with the camera
- ▶ Playing videos
- ▶ Playing music and sounds
- ▶ Recording with the microphone
- ▶ Managing album items directly

Introduction

One of the most important features of today's smartphones and tablets is their ability to capture and manage multimedia resources. Be it photos, videos, or audio, an app targeted at these devices that can handle multimedia effectively is very important.

In this chapter, we will see how to manage media stored on the device. We will also learn how to use the device's multimedia capturing devices (a camera and microphone) to capture content and create an app that will provide a rich experience to the user.

More specifically, we will discuss the following topics:

- ▶ `UIImagePickerController`: This is a controller that provides access to the saved photos and videos on the device through a user interface, but also a camera interface for capturing photos through the device's camera hardware.
- ▶ `MPMoviePlayerController`: This is a controller that allows us to play and stream video files.
- ▶ `MPMediaPickerController`: This is the default user interface to access the saved content managed by the native iPod app.

- ▶ `MPMusicPlayerController`: This is the object that is responsible for playing the iPod content.

- ▶ `AVAudioPlayer`: This is the class that allows us to play sound files.

- ▶ `AVAudioRecorder`: This is the class that allows us to use the microphone to record audio.

- ▶ `ALAssetsLibrary`: This is the class that provides access to the device's available assets and their metadata.

Selecting images and videos

In this recipe, we will learn how to provide the user with the ability to import images and videos from the device album.

Getting ready

Create a new **Single View Application** in Xamarin Studio and name it `ImagePickerApp`. For this recipe, we will need some images to be stored in the simulator's photo albums.

An easy way to add images to the simulator is by navigating to a web page with Safari. Long-tapping (click + hold) on any image in Safari will show us an action sheet with a **Save** option. Tapping the option saves the image to the photo albums.

How to do it...

Perform the following steps:

1. Open the `ImagePickerAppViewController.xib` file in Interface Builder and add `UIImageView` and `UIButton` to it.

2. Enter the following code in the `ViewDidLoad` method:

```
this.imagePicker = new UIImagePickerController();
this.imagePicker.FinishedPickingMedia +=
  this.ImagePicker_FinishedPickingMedia;
this.imagePicker.Canceled += this.ImagePicker_Cancelled;
this.imagePicker.SourceType =
  UIImagePickerControllerSourceType.PhotoLibrary;
this.btnSelect.TouchUpInside += async (s, e) => {
  await this.PresentViewControllerAsync(this.imagePicker,
    true);
};
```

3. Implement the handler methods for the `FinishedPickingMedia` and `Canceled` events as shown in the following code:

```
private async void ImagePicker_FinishedPickingMedia (object
    sender, UIImagePickerMediaPickedEventArgs e)
{
    UIImage pickedImage =
        e.Info[UIImagePickerController.OriginalImage] as
        UIImage;
    this.imageView.Image = pickedImage;
    await this.imagePicker.DismissViewControllerAsync(true);
}
private async void ImagePicker_Cancelled (object sender,
    EventArgs e)
{
    await this.imagePicker.DismissViewControllerAsync(true);
}
```

4. Compile and run the app on the simulator. Tap on the button you added in the initial steps to present the image picker and select an image by tapping on its thumbnail. The image will be displayed in the image view. The `UIImagePickerController` is shown in the following screenshot:

 Just before the first time `UIImagePickerController` is shown in an app, iOS will display an alert, asking the user for permission to access the photo albums. Handling this situation is described in the *Managing album items directly* recipe later in this chapter.

How it works...

`UIImagePickerController` is a special view controller that iOS provides to select images and videos that are saved on the device album or even to capture new media from the camera.

After initializing the image picker object, we need to subscribe to its `FinishedPickingMedia` event, which provides us with the media that the user has selected. In the handler we assign to it, we get the selected image:

```
UIImage pickedImage =
    e.Info[UIImagePickerController.OriginalImage] as UIImage;
```

The `Info` property returns an `NSDictionary` object that contains various kinds of information about the picked media. We retrieve the image, passing the `UIImagePickerController.OriginalImage` constant as key. As the values of the dictionary are of the `NSObject` type, we cast the return value to `UIImage`. After we assign the image to the `UIImageView` to be displayed, we dismiss the controller by using the following code:

```
await this.imagePicker.DismissViewControllerAsync(true);
```

The `Canceled` event is triggered when the user taps on the controller's **Cancel** button. We must subscribe to it to dismiss the controller, because it will not be dismissed automatically when the user taps on the **Cancel** button.

There's more...

We can define the source of the images/videos the image picker will read from through its `SourceType` property. In this example, we use `UIImagePickerController.PhotoLibrary` because the simulator does not support the camera hardware.

Picking videos

`UIImagePickerController` displays only images by default. To support videos, its `MediaType` property must be set. It accepts a `string[]` parameter, with the specified media names as shown in the following code:

```
this.imagePicker.MediaTypes = new string[] { "public.image",
    "public.movie" };
```

To determine the media type the user has picked, we check the `MediaType` key of the dictionary in the `FinishedPickingMedia` handler. If it is a video, we get its URL with the `MediaUrl` key, as shown in the following code:

```
if (e.Info[UIImagePickerController.MediaType].ToString() ==
    "public.movie")
```

```
{
  NSUrl mediaUrl = e.Info[UIImagePickerController.MediaURL] as
    NSUrl;
  // Do something useful with the media url.
}
```

See also

▶ The *Capturing media with the camera* recipe

▶ The *Managing album items directly* recipe

Capturing media with the camera

In this recipe, we will learn how to use the device camera to capture the media.

Getting ready

Open the `ImagePickerApp` project that we created in the previous recipe.

The camera functionality is not available on iOS Simulator. This example can only run on the device. Refer to *Chapter 14, Deploying,* for more information.

How to do it...

Perform the following steps:

1. In the ViewDidLoad method of the controller class, replace `this.imagePicker.SourceType = UIImagePickerControllerSourceType.PhotoLibrary;` with the following code block:

    ```
    if (UIImagePickerController.
      IsSourceTypeAvailable(UIImagePicker
        ControllerSourceType.Camera))
    {
      this.imagePicker.SourceType =
        UIImagePickerControllerSourceType.Camera;
    } else
    {
      this.imagePicker.SourceType =
        UIImagePickerControllerSourceType.PhotoLibrary;
    }
    ```

2. In the `FinishedPickingMedia` handler, add the following code before the dismissal of the image picker:

```
pickedImage.SaveToPhotosAlbum((s, error) => {
  if (null != error)
  {
    Console.WriteLine("Image not saved! Message: {0}",
      error.LocalizedDescription);
  }
} );
```

3. Compile and run the app on the device. Tap the button to open the camera and take a picture. The picture will be saved to the device album.

How it works...

Before presenting the camera viewfinder, we have to make sure that the device that the app is running on actually has the appropriate hardware. We do this by calling the static `IsSourceTypeAvailable` method of the `UIImagePickerController` class as follows:

```
if (UIImagePickerController.
  IsSourceTypeAvailable(UIImagePicker
  ControllerSourceType.Camera))
```

If this returns `true`, we set the source type to `Camera` by using the following code:

```
this.imagePicker.SourceType =
  UIImagePickerControllerSourceType.Camera;
```

This will cause the image picker controller to start the camera device instead of loading the device albums.

When the user takes a photo (or video) through our application, it is not automatically saved on the device. To save it, we use the `SaveToPhotosAlbum` method of the `UIImage` class. This method accepts a delegate of the `UIImage.SaveStatus` type, which will report an error if something goes wrong:

```
if (null != error)
{
  Console.WriteLine("Image not saved! Message: {0}",
    error.LocalizedDescription);
}
```

There's more...

The camera view can also be customized. To disable the default camera controls, set the `ShowsCameraControls` property to `false`. Then, pass a custom view with the controls you want to the `CameraOverlayView` property. To trigger the shutter of the camera, call the `TakePicture` method.

Image editing

The camera supports a simple editing function after capturing an image. This editing function allows the user to select a specific part of the image and even zoom to a specific area. To present the editing controls, set the `AllowsEditing` property to `true`. The edited image can be retrieved from the dictionary in the `FinishedPickingMedia` handler, passing the `UIImagePickerController.EditedImage` key. The editing interface is shown in the following screenshot:

See also

▸ The *Selecting images and videos* recipe

Playing videos

In this recipe, we will learn how to display a video player interface and play video files.

Getting ready

Create a new **Single View Application** in Xamarin Studio and name it `PlayVideoApp`.

How to do it...

Perform the following steps:

1. Add a button to the main view of the controller.

2. Add a video file to the project and set its **Build Action** to **Content**.

3. Add the following code to the `ViewDidLoad` method of the controller class:

```
this.moviePlayer = new
  MPMoviePlayerController(NSUrl.FromFilename("video.mov"));
this.moviePlayer.View.Frame = new RectangleF(0f, 20f,
  this.View.Frame.Width, 320f);
this.View.AddSubview(this.moviePlayer.View);
this.playbackStateChanged =
  MPMoviePlaybackController.Notifications.
  ObservePlaybackStateDidChange(this.MoviePlayer_
  PlaybackStateChanged);
this.finishedPlaying =
  MPMoviePlaybackController.Notifications.
  ObservePlaybackDidFinish(this.MoviePlayer_FinishedPlayback);
this.btnPlayVideo.TouchUpInside += delegate {
  this.moviePlayer.Play();
} ;
```

4. Enter the following methods in the `MainController` class:

```
private void MoviePlayer_PlaybackStateChanged(object
  sender, NSNotificationEventArgs e)
{
  Console.WriteLine("Movie player load state changed: {0}",
    this.moviePlayer.PlaybackState);
}
private void MoviePlayer_FinishedPlayback(object sender,
  NSNotificationEventArgs e)
{
  Console.WriteLine("Movie player finished playing.");
}
```

5. Compile and run the app on the simulator. Tap on the button and the video will load and start playing. Watch the messages displayed in the **Application Output** pad in Xamarin Studio. The following screenshot shows us the video that is playing on the simulator:

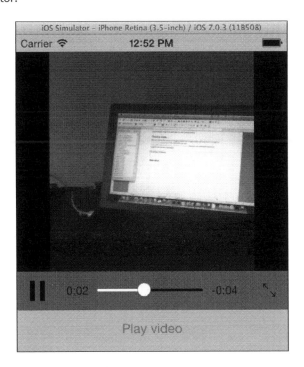

How it works...

The MPMoviePlayerController controller plays video files stored locally or streamed from the network. We initialize the controller with the constructor that accepts an NSUrl parameter, as shown in the following code:

```
this.moviePlayer = new
    MPMoviePlayerController(NSUrl.FromFilename("video.mov"));
```

The NSUrl class is the standard iOS class for URLs.

After creating the instance, we define a frame for its view and add it to our view by using the following code:

```
this.moviePlayer.View.Frame = new RectangleF(0f, 20f,
    this.View.Frame.Width, 320f);
this.View.AddSubview(this.moviePlayer.View);
```

The highlighted code in the preceding section adds observers to the default notification center so that we will be notified when the state of the playback changes or finishes. Then, we call its `Play` method and the `MPMoviePlayerController` controller's view is displayed, and the video starts playing.

Inside the `MoviePlayer_PlaybackStateChanged` method, we output the `PlaybackState` property by using the following code:

```
Console.WriteLine("Movie player load state changed: {0}",
    this.moviePlayer.PlaybackState);
```

This property informs us about the status of the playback, for example, `Paused`, `Playing`, `SeekingForward`, and `SeekingBackward`.

There's more...

Apart from the ones used in this example, we can add observers for more notifications of an `MPMoviePlayerController` controller, some of which are as follows:

- ▶ `DidEnterFullscreenNotification`: This notifies us that the user has tapped the fullscreen control and the controller has entered the fullscreen mode

- ▶ `DidExitFullscreenNotification`: It notifies that the controller has left fullscreen mode

- ▶ `DurationAvailableNotification`: This notifies us that the controller has received information on the duration of the video

- ▶ `LoadStateDidChangeNotification`: This is useful for network playback; it is triggered when the controller has finished preloading the media in the buffer

- ▶ `NaturalSizeAvailableNotification`: This is triggered when the dimensions of the movie frame are made available. The size can be retrieved through the player's `NaturalSize` property

- ▶ `NowPlayingMovieDidChangeNotification`: This is triggered when the video content of the player has changed. The current content is available through its `ContentUrl` property

Wireless streaming

Starting from iOS Version 4.3, `MPMoviePlayerController` can be used to stream video to Apple's AirPlay-enabled devices. To enable wireless streaming, set the `MPMoviePlayerController` instance's `AllowsAirPlay` property to `true`. When `controller` is displayed, it will present an interface that will allow the user to select the devices it detects.

See also

- ▶ The *Playing music and sounds* recipe

Playing music and sounds

In this recipe, we will learn how to play both simple audio files and songs stored on the device.

Getting ready

Create a new **Single View Application** in Xamarin Studio and name it `PlayMusicApp`.

 This example will not work on the simulator. You will also need at least one song stored on the device's iTunes library.

How to do it...

Perform the following steps:

1. Add three buttons to the view of the controller.

2. Add the following using directive in the `PlayMusicAppViewController.cs` file:

   ```
   using MonoTouch.MediaPlayer;
   ```

3. Add the following two fields in the class:

   ```
   private MPMusicPlayerController musicPlayer;
   private MPMediaPickerController mediaPicker;
   ```

4. Add the following code in the `ViewDidLoad` method:

   ```
   this.mediaPicker = new
     MPMediaPickerController(MPMediaType.Music);
   this.mediaPicker.ItemsPicked += MediaPicker_ItemsPicked;
   this.mediaPicker.DidCancel += MediaPicker_DidCancel;
   this.musicPlayer =
     MPMusicPlayerController.ApplicationMusicPlayer;
   this.btnSelect.TouchUpInside += async (s, e) => {
     await this.PresentViewControllerAsync(this.mediaPicker,
       true);
   } ;
   this.btnPlay.TouchUpInside += (s, e) => {
     this.musicPlayer.Play();
   } ;
   this.btnStop.TouchUpInside += (s, e) => {
     this.musicPlayer.Stop();
   } ;
   ```

5. Add the following methods in the class:

```
private async void MediaPicker_ItemsPicked (object sender,
  ItemsPickedEventArgs e)
{
  this.musicPlayer.SetQueue(e.MediaItemCollection);
  await this.DismissViewControllerAsync(true);
}
private async void MediaPicker_DidCancel (object sender,
  EventArgs e)
{
  await this.mediaPicker.DismissViewControllerAsync(true);
}
```

6. Compile and run the app on the device. Tap the **Select songs** button and select one or more songs.

How it works...

The `MPMediaPickerController` controller provides the same user interface as the native *Music* app for selecting songs. The `MPMusicPlayerController` controller is responsible for playing the songs stored on the device.

We first initialize the media picker, passing the type of media we want it to look for in its constructor by using the following code:

```
this.mediaPicker = new
  MPMediaPickerController(MPMediaType.Music);
```

After this, we subscribe to its `ItemsPicked` and `DidCancel` events so that we can capture the feedback from the user by using the following code:

```
this.mediaPicker.ItemsPicked += MediaPicker_ItemsPicked;
this.mediaPicker.DidCancel += MediaPicker_DidCancel;
```

The highlighted code in the preceding section shows us how to initialize the music player object. The option demonstrated here, `MPMusicPlayerController.ApplicationMusicPlayer`, creates an instance that is specific only to the app. The other option that is available, `MPMusicPlayerController.iPodMusicPlayer`, creates an instance that allows the media to be played even if the app is in the background, similar to the native *Music* app.

In the `MediaPicker_ItemsPicked` handler, we set the songs that were picked by the user to the music player through its `SetQueue` method, as shown in the following code:

```
this.musicPlayer.SetQueue(e.MediaItemCollection);
```

After this, we dismiss the modal media picker controller. Playing and stopping songs is achieved through the `Play()` and `Stop()` methods of `MPMusicPlayerController`, respectively.

There's more...

`MPMusicPlayerController` holds information on the item that is being played currently. This information can be accessed through its `NowPlayingItem` property. It is of the `MPMediaItem` type and holds various types of information of the media that is being played currently. The following example outputs the title of the song that is being played:

```
Console.WriteLine(this.musicPlayerController.NowPlayingItem.Va
    lueForProperty(MPMediaItem.TitleProperty));
```

Playing sound files

The `MPMusicPlayerController` controller is an object that is specifically designed to manage and play items and playlists stored on the device's music library.

To play simple sound files, Xamarin.iOS provides another wrapper to the iOS's class, `AVAudioPlayer`. The following code is an example of its most simple usage:

```
using MonoTouch.AVFoundation;
//...
AVAudioPlayer audioPlayer = AVAudioPlayer.FromUrl(new
    NSUrl("path/to/sound file"));
audioPlayer.Play();
```

See also

► The *Playing videos* recipe

Recording with the microphone

In this recipe, we will learn how to use the device's microphone to record sounds.

Getting ready

Create a new project in Xamarin Studio and name it `RecordSoundApp`.

 This example will not work on the simulator.

How to do it...

Perform the following steps:

1. Add two buttons and a label to the view of the controller.

2. Enter the following `using` directives in the `RecordSoundAppViewController.cs` file:

```
using System.IO;
using MonoTouch.AVFoundation;
using MonoTouch.AudioToolbox;
```

3. Override the `ViewDidLoad` method and add the following code to it:

```
NSUrl soundFileUrl = null;
NSError error = null;
AVAudioSession session = AVAudioSession.SharedInstance();
session.SetCategory(AVAudioSession.CategoryPlayAndRecord,
    out error);
session.SetActive(true, out error);
bool grantedPermission = false;
session.RequestRecordPermission((granted) => {
  if (granted) {
    grantedPermission = true;
    string soundFile =
      Path.Combine(Environment.GetFolderPath(Environment.
      SpecialFolder.Personal), "sound.wav");
    soundFileUrl = new NSUrl(soundFile);
    NSDictionary recordingSettings =
      NSDictionary.FromObjectAndKey(AVAudioSettings.
      AVFormatIDKey,
      NSNumber.FromInt32((int)AudioFileType.Wave));
    this.audioRecorder = AVAudioRecorder.ToUrl(
      soundFileUrl, recordingSettings, out error);
  } else {
    this.lblStatus.Text = "Permission to microphone
      refused";
  }
});

this.btnStart.TouchUpInside += (s, e) => {
  if (grantedPermission) {
    this.audioRecorder.Record();
    this.lblStatus.Text = "Recording...";
  }
};
```

```
this.btnStop.TouchUpInside += (s, e) => {
  if (grantedPermission) {
    this.audioRecorder.Stop();
   this.lblStatus.Text = "Idle";
    AVAudioPlayer player =
      AVAudioPlayer.FromUrl(soundFileUrl);
    player.Play();
  }
};
```

4. Compile and run the app on the device. Tap the **Start** recording button to start recording the audio, for example, say something in order to record your voice. Tap the **Stop recording** button to stop recording and listen to the playback.

How it works...

The `AVAudioRecorder` class provides the recording functionality. It does this by streaming the captured audio directly to the filesystem. Prior to starting the actual recording, we need to prepare the shared audio session by using the following code:

```
NSError error = null;
AVAudioSession session = AVAudioSession.SharedInstance();
session.SetCategory(AVAudioSession.CategoryPlayAndRecord, out
  error);
session.SetActive(true, out error);
```

We need to adjust the audio session according to our app's needs so that the system *knows* how to handle the audio from other sources. By setting the category to `AVAudioSession.CategoryPlayAndRecord`, we state that our app will be able to play back the audio while it is getting recorded.

The first time we set the shared audio session's category to any value that requires the usage of the microphone, iOS automatically prompts the user to give permission to the app. By calling the `RequestRecordPermission` method, we can determine whether the user has granted microphone access to our app, as shown in the following code:

```
session.RequestRecordPermission((granted) => {
  if (granted) {
    grantedPermission = true;
    //..
```

Now that we have prepared the shared audio session, it's time to initialize an instance of `AVAudioRecorder` by using the following code:

```
this.audioRecorder = AVAudioRecorder.ToUrl(soundFileUrl,
  recordingSettings, out error);
```

If the file that corresponds to the NSUrl variable already exists, it will be overwritten.

The recordingSettings variable is of the NSDictionary type and contains the settings for the output sound file. We must provide at least some minimal settings to the AVAudioRecorder upon the initialization. Here, we set the sound format to plain WAV by using the following code:

```
NSDictionary recordingSettings =
    NSDictionary.FromObjectAndKey(AVAudioSettings.AVFormatIDKey,
    NSNumber.FromInt32((int)AudioFileType.WAVE));
```

To instruct the recorder to start recording, we just call its Record() method by using the following line of code:

```
this.audioRecorder.Record();
```

When the user taps on the **Stop recording** button, the recording stops and the saved sound starts playing with the AVAudioPlayer:

```
this.audioRecorder.Stop();
AVAudioPlayer player = AVAudioPlayer.FromUrl(soundFileUrl);
player.Play();
```

There's more...

The AVAudioRecorder class provides sound metering options as well. To enable the sound metering, set its MeteringEnabled property to true. We can then output the peak power in decibels on a specific channel. To do this for the first channel of our recording, add the following code right after the Record() method call:

```
ThreadPool.QueueUserWorkItem(delegate {
    while (this.audioRecorder.Recording)
    {
        this.audioRecorder.UpdateMeters();
        Console.WriteLine(this.audioRecorder.PeakPower(0));
    }
} );
```

The PeakPower method accepts the zero-based index of the channel and returns the peak of the channel in decibels. Call UpdateMeters() right before calling the PeakPower method to get the most recent reading.

Note that enabling the metering on the recorder requires using the CPU resources. Do not enable it if you do not intend on using the metering values.

Recording for a predefined amount of time

To record the audio for a predefined amount of time without the need for the user to stop the recording, call the `RecordFor(double)` method. Its parameter is the amount of time in seconds for which we want to record.

See also

▸ The *Playing music and sounds* recipe

Managing album items directly

In this recipe, we will discuss how to programmatically access the device's photo album.

Getting ready

Create a new **Single View Application** in Xamarin Studio and name it `ManageAlbumApp`.

 This example works on the simulator. At least one image must exist in the simulator's photo album.

How to do it...

Perform the following steps:

1. Add a button on the main view of the controller.

2. Enter the following `using` directive in the `MainController.cs` file:

   ```
   using MonoTouch.AssetsLibrary;
   ```

3. Add the following code in the `ViewDidLoad` method:

   ```
   this.btnEnumerate.TouchUpInside += (s, e) => {
     if (ALAssetsLibrary.AuthorizationStatus ==
     ALAuthorizationStatus.Authorized ||
       ALAssetsLibrary.AuthorizationStatus ==
         ALAuthorizationStatus.NotDetermined) {
       this.assetsLibrary = new ALAssetsLibrary();
       this.assetsLibrary.Enumerate(ALAssetsGroupType.All,
         this.GroupsEnumeration,
         this.GroupsEnumerationFailure);
     }
   } ;
   ```

4. Add the following methods in the class:

```
private void GroupsEnumeration(ALAssetsGroup assetGroup,
  ref bool stop)
{
  if (null != assetGroup)
  {
    stop = false;
    assetGroup.SetAssetsFilter(ALAssetsFilter.AllPhotos);
    assetGroup.Enumerate(this.AssetEnumeration);
  }
}
private void AssetEnumeration(ALAsset asset, int index, ref bool
stop)
{
  if (null != asset)
  {
    stop = false;
    Console.WriteLine("Asset url: {0}",
      asset.DefaultRepresentation.Url.AbsoluteString);
  }
}
private void GroupsEnumerationFailure(NSError error)
{
  if (null != error)
  {
    Console.WriteLine("Error enumerating asset groups!
      Message: {0}", error.LocalizedDescription);
  }
}
```

5. Compile and run the app. Tap the **Enumerate** button and watch the URLs of the saved photos get displayed in the **Application Output** pad.

How it works...

The ALAssetsLibrary class provides access to the album items of the device. These items are represented by the ALAsset class and are divided into groups, represented by the ALAssetGroup class.

The first thing we need to do is enumerate the asset groups. To do this, call the Enumerate method by using the following code:

```
this.assetsLibrary.Enumerate(ALAssetsGroupType.All,
    this.GroupsEnumeration, this.GroupsEnumerationFailure);
```

The first parameter is of the `ALAssetGroupTypes` type, and it instructs the assets library on the asset groups to be enumerated. Passing `ALAssetGroupTypes.All` means that we want to enumerate all the asset groups. The other two parameters are delegate types. The `GroupsEnumeration` method is where we read the group's data, while the `GroupsEnumerationFailure` method will be triggered if an error occurs. When the `Enumerate` method is called for the first time, the user is asked to grant access to the app to access the device's assets. If the user denies the access, the failure method will be triggered. The next time the `Enumerate` method gets called, the access message appears again.

The signature of the `GroupsEnumeration` method is as follows:

```
private void GroupsEnumeration(ALAssetsGroup assetGroup, ref
    bool stop)
```

The `assetGroup` parameter contains the group's information.

Note the `stop` parameter, which is declared as a `ref` parameter. When the enumeration occurs, the method is being triggered once to return the first group and does not get called for the second time, no matter how many more groups exist. To force it to keep getting called to enumerate all the groups, we have to set the `stop` variable to `false`. When all groups have been enumerated, the method gets called one last time, with the `assetGroup` variable set to `null`. So we need to check this. To put all this in code, take a look at the following example:

```
if (null != assetGroup)
{
  // Continue enumerating
  stop = false;
  // Determine what assets to enumerate
  assetGroup.SetAssetsFilter(ALAssetsFilter.AllPhotos);
  // Enumerate assets
  assetGroup.Enumerate(this.AssetEnumeration);
}
```

After calling the `SetAssetsFilter` method on the instance of the `ALAssetGroup` class, we instruct it to filter what types of assets we want it to look for. After this, the process becomes similar to the group's enumeration. The `ALAssetGroup` class also contains an `Enumerate` method. It accepts a parameter of a delegate type, represented here by the `AssetsEnumeration` method. Its implementation is similar to the `GroupsEnumeration` method, as shown in the following code:

```
if (null != asset)
{
  // Continue enumerating assets
  stop = false;
  // Output the asset url
  Console.WriteLine("Asset url: {0}",
    asset.DefaultRepresentation.Url.AbsoluteString);
}
```

The `ALAsset` class contains various kinds of information and properties. Most of the information is stored in its `DefaultRepresentation` property, which is of the `ALAssetRepresentation` type.

There's more...

If the asset we are interested in is an image, we can get the actual image through the `DefaultRepresentation` property by using the following code:

```
CGImage image = asset.DefaultRepresentation.GetImage();
```

Reading EXIF data

We can read a photo's **EXchangeable Image File** (**EXIF**) format metadata through the `Metadata` property of `ALAssetRepresentation`, which is of the `NSDictionary` type, as shown in the following code:

```
NSDictionary metaData = asset.DefaultRepresentation.Metadata;
if (null != metaData)
{
  NSDictionary exifData = (NSDictionary)metaData[new
  NSString("{Exif}")];
}
```

Retrieving individual assets

We can also retrieve an individual asset, if we know the asset's URL, through the `AssetForUrl` method of `ALAssetLibrary`.

Checking for permission

We can check whether the user has granted access to the asset library through the `ALAssetsLibrary.AuthorizationStatus` static property. The possible values of the `ALAuthorizationStatus` enumeration are the following:

- ▸ `Authorized`: This means that the user has authorized our app.
- ▸ `Denied`: This means that the user has denied access to the albums.
- ▸ `NotDetermined`: This means that our app never requested access to the albums.
- ▸ `Restricted`: This means that the app is not authorized to access the albums and the user cannot grant access, possibly due to parental restrictions.

Note that accessing the `AuthorizationStatus` property does not prompt the user for permission. When we actually try to access the library in this example, by calling the `Enumerate` method, is when iOS prompts the user for permission.

See also

- ▸ The *Selecting images and videos* recipe

8

Integrating iOS Features

In this chapter, we will cover the following:

- ▶ Starting phone calls
- ▶ Sending text messages and e-mails
- ▶ Using text messaging in our application
- ▶ Using e-mail messaging in our application
- ▶ Managing the address book
- ▶ Displaying contacts
- ▶ Managing the calendar

Introduction

Mobile devices offer a handful of features to the user. Creating an app that interacts with these features to provide a complete experience to users can surely be considered as an advantage.

In this chapter, we will discuss some of the most common features of iOS and how to integrate some or all of their functionality into our apps. We will see how to offer the user the ability to make telephone calls and send SMS and e-mails, either using the native platform apps or by integrating the native user interface in our projects. Also, we will discuss the following components:

- ▶ **MFMessageComposeViewController**: This controller is suitable for sending text (SMS) messages

- ▶ **MFMailComposeViewController**: This controller is used for sending e-mails with or without attachments

- ▶ **ABAddressBook**: This class provides us access to the address book database

- ▶ **ABPersonViewController**: This controller displays and/or edits contact information from the address book

- ▶ **EKEventStore**: This class is responsible for managing calendar events

Furthermore, we will learn how to read and save contact information, how to display contact details, and interact with the device's calendar.

Note that some of the examples in this chapter will require a device. For example, the simulator does not contain the *Messaging* app. To deploy a simulator to a device, you will need to enroll as an iOS Developer through Apple's Developer Portal.

Starting phone calls

In this recipe, we will learn how to invoke the native *Phone* app to allow the user to place a phone call.

Getting ready

Create a new **Single View Application** in Xamarin Studio and name it `PhoneCallApp`.

 The native *Phone* app is not available on the simulator. It is only available on an iPhone device.

How to do it...

Perform the following steps to allow the user to place phone calls:

1. Add a button on the view of `PhoneCallAppViewController`.

2. Add the following code in the `ViewDidLoad` method:

```
this.btnCall.TouchUpInside += (s, e) => {
  NSUrlurl = new NSUrl("tel:+123456789012");
  if (UIApplication.SharedApplication.CanOpenUrl(url))
  {
    UIApplication.SharedApplication.OpenUrl(url);
  } else
```

```
    {
        Console.WriteLine("Cannot open url: {0}",
          url.AbsoluteString);
    }
  } ;
```

3. Compile and run the app on the device. Tap the **Call phone number** button to start the call. The following screenshot shows the *Phone* app placing a call:

How it works...

Through the `UIApplication.SharedApplication` static property, we have access to the app's `UIApplication` object. We can use its `OpenUrl` method that accepts an `NSUrl` variable to initiate a call using the following line of code:

```
UIApplication.SharedApplication.OpenUrl(url);
```

Because not all iOS devices support the native *Phone* app, it would be useful to check for availability first. You can do this using the following code:

```
if (UIApplication.SharedApplication.CanOpenUrl(url))
```

When the `OpenUrl` method is called, the native *Phone* app will be executed and start calling the number immediately. Note that the `tel:` prefix is needed to initiate the call.

There's more...

Xamarin.iOS also supports the CoreTelephony Framework through the `MonoTouch.CoreTelephony` namespace. This is a simple framework that provides information on call state, connection, carrier information, and so on. Note that when a call starts, the native *Phone* app enters into the foreground, causing the app to be suspended. A simple usage of the CoreTelephony Framework is as follows:

```
CTCallCenter callCenter = new CTCallCenter();
callCenter.CallEventHandler = delegate(CTCall call) {
    Console.WriteLine(call.CallState);
} ;
```

Note that the handler is assigned with an equals sign (=) instead of the common plus-equals (+=) combination. This is because `CallEventHandler` is a property and not an event. When the app enters into the background, events are not distributed to it. The event that occurred last, however, will be distributed when the app returns to the foreground.

More information on OpenUrl

The `OpenUrl` method can be used to open various native and non-native applications. For example, to open a web page in Safari, just create an `NSUrl` object with the link, as follows:

```
NSUrl url = new NSUrl("http://www.packtpub.com");
```

See also

> ▸ The *Sending text messages and e-mails* recipe

Sending text messages and e-mails

In this recipe, we will learn how to invoke the native *Mail* and *Messaging* apps within our own app.

Getting ready

Create a new **Single View Application** in Xamarin Studio and name it `SendTextApp`.

Perform the following steps to invoke the apps:

1. Add two buttons on the view of `SendTextAppViewController`.

2. Add the following code in the `ViewDidLoad` method:

```
this.btnSendText.TouchUpInside += (s, e) => {
  NSUrl textUrl = new NSUrl("sms:+123456789");
  if (UIApplication.SharedApplication.CanOpenUrl(textUrl))
  {
    UIApplication.SharedApplication.OpenUrl(textUrl);
  } else
  {
    Console.WriteLine("Cannot send text message!");
  }
} ;
this.btnSendEmail.TouchUpInside += (s, e) => {
  NSUrl emailUrl = new NSUrl("mailto:mail@example.com");
  if (UIApplication.SharedApplication.CanOpenUrl(emailUrl))
  {
    UIApplication.SharedApplication.OpenUrl(emailUrl);
  } else
  {
    Console.WriteLine("Cannot send email message!");
  }
} ;
```

3. Compile and run the app on the device. Click on one of the buttons to open the corresponding app.

Once again, using the `OpenUrl` method, we can send text or e-mail messages. Just using the `sms:` prefix from the preceding example code will open the native text messaging app, as follows:

```
UIApplication.SharedApplication.OpenUrl(new
  NSUrl("sms:+123456789012"));
```

Adding a cell phone number after the `sms:` prefix will open the native *Messaging* app, as shown in the following screenshot:

For opening the native e-mail app, the process is similar. Pass the `mailto:` prefix, as follows:

```
UIApplication.SharedApplication.OpenUrl(new
    NSUrl("mailto:mail@example.com"));
```

This opens the edit mail controller, as shown in the following screenshot:

The `mailto:` URL scheme supports various parameters for customizing an e-mail message. These parameters allow us to enter the sender address, subject, and message, as follows:

```
UIApplication.SharedApplication.OpenUrl("mailto:recipient@example.
    com?subject=Email%20with%20Xamarin.iOS!&body=
    This%20is%20the%20message%20body!");
```

There's more...

Although iOS provides access to opening the native *Messaging* apps, predefining message content in the case of e-mails is where the control from inside the app stops. There is no way of actually sending the message through code. It is the user that will decide whether to send the message or not.

More information on opening external apps

The `OpenUrl` method provides an interface for opening external apps. Opening external apps has one drawback, that is, the app that calls the `OpenUrl` method transitions to the background. Up to iOS Version 3.*, this was the only way of messaging through an application. Since iOS Version 4.0, Apple has provided the messaging controllers to the SDK. The following recipes discuss their usage.

See also

> ▶ The *Starting phone calls* and *Using text messaging in our application* recipes

Using text messaging in our application

In this recipe, we will learn how to display the text messaging controller inside our app.

Getting ready

Create a new **Single View Application** in Xamarin Studio and name it `TextMessageApp`.

How to do it...

Perform the following steps to display the text messaging controller in our app:

1. Add a button on the view of the controller.
2. Enter the following `using` directive in the `TextMessageAppViewController` file:

   ```
   using MonoTouch.MessageUI;
   ```

3. Implement the `ViewDidLoad` method with the following code, changing the recipient number and/or the message body at your discretion:

```
private MFMessageComposeViewController messageController;
public override void ViewDidLoad ()
{
  base.ViewDidLoad ();
  this.btnSendMessage.TouchUpInside += async (s, e) => {
  if (MFMessageComposeViewController.CanSendText)
    {
      this.messageController =
        new MFMessageComposeViewController ();
      this.messageController.Recipients =
        new string[] { "+123456789012" };
      this.messageController.Body =
        "Text from Xamarin.iOS";
      this.messageController.Finished +=
        MessageController_Finished;
      await this.PresentViewControllerAsync (this.
        messageController, true);
    } else
    {
      Console.WriteLine ("Cannot send text message!");
    }
  } ;
}
```

4. Add the following method:

```
private async void MessageController_Finished(object
  sender, MFMessageComposeResultEventArgs e) {
  switch (e.Result) {
  case MessageComposeResult.Sent:
    Console.WriteLine ("Message sent!");
    break;
  case MessageComposeResult.Cancelled:
    Console.WriteLine ("Message cancelled!");
    break;
  default:
    Console.WriteLine ("Message failed!");
    break;
  }
  e.Controller.Finished -= MessageController_Finished;
  await e.Controller.DismissViewControllerAsync (true);
}
```

5. Compile and run the app on the device. Tap the **Send message** button to open the message controller. Tap the **Send** button to send the message, or on the **Cancel** button to return to the app.

How it works...

The `MonoTouch.MessageUI` namespace contains the necessary UI elements that allow us to implement messaging in an iOS app. For text messaging (SMS), we need the `MFMessageComposeViewController` class.

We need to check for texting availability, because not all devices can send text messages. The `MFMessageComposeViewController` class contains a static method named `CanSendText`, which returns a boolean value indicating whether we can use this functionality. The important thing in this case is that we check if the functionality of sending text messages is available prior to initializing the controller. This is because when you try to initialize the controller on a device that does not support text messaging or on the simulator, you will get an exception.

To determine when the user has taken action in the message UI, we subscribe to the `Finished` event, as follows:

```
this.messageController.Finished += MessageController_Finished;
```

Inside the `Finished` method, we can provide functionality according to the `MessageComposeResult` parameter. It can have one of the following three values:

- Sent: This means the message was sent successfully.
- Cancelled: This means the user has tapped the **Cancel** button. The message will not be sent.
- Failed: This means the message sending failed.

The last thing to do is unsubscribe the event and dismiss the message controller, as follows:

```
e.Controller.Finished -= MessageController_Finished;
await e.controller.DismissViewControllerAsync(true);
```

After initializing the controller, we can set the recipients and body message to the appropriate properties, as follows:

```
this.messageController.Recipients =
  new string[] { "+123456789012" };
this.messageController.Body = "Text from Xamarin.iOS";
```

The `Recipients` property accepts a `string` array that allows multiple recipient numbers.

There's more...

The fact that SDK allows the user interface to send text messages does not mean that it is customizable. Just like invoking the native *Messaging* app, it is the user who will decide whether to send the message or discard it. In fact, after the controller is presented on the screen, any attempts to change the actual object or any of its properties will simply fail. Furthermore, the user can change or delete both the recipients and the message body. The real benefit, though, is that the messaging user interface is displayed within our app instead of running separately.

Attachments

Starting with iOS 7, the `MFMessageComposeViewController` class supports attachments. We can attach a file to a message through the `AddAttachment` method, as follows:

```
this.messageController.AddAttachment(new NSUrl("path/to/file"),
    "A wonderful image");
```

The second parameter is the string that will appear as a filename on the UI. If null is passed, the actual filename will appear.

Using e-mail messaging in our application

In this recipe, we will learn how to use the e-mail messaging interface within an application.

Getting ready

Create a new **Single View Application** in Xamarin Studio and name it `EmailMessageApp`.

How to do it...

Perform the following steps:

1. Add a button on the view of `EmailMessageAppViewController` and the `MonoTouch.MessageUI` namespace in the `EmailMessageAppViewController.cs` file.

2. Enter the following code in the `ViewDidLoad` method:

```
this.btnSendEmail.TouchUpInside += async (s, e) => {
  if (MFMailComposeViewController.CanSendMail)
  {
  this.mailController = new MFMailComposeViewController();
  this.mailController.SetToRecipients(new string[]
    { "recipient@example.com" });
```

```
      this.mailController.SetSubject("Email from
        Xamarin.iOS!");
      this.mailController.SetMessageBody("This is the message
        body!", false);
      this.mailController.Finished +=
        this.MailController_Finished;
        await this.PresentViewControllerAsync(
          this.mailController, true);
    }   else
    {
      Console.WriteLine("Cannot send email!");
    }
  } ;
```

3. Add the following method:

```
private async void MailController_Finished (object sender,
  MFComposeResultEventArgs e)
{
  switch (e.Result)
  {
  case MFMailComposeResult.Sent:
    Console.WriteLine("Email sent!");
  break;
  case MFMailComposeResult.Saved:
    Console.WriteLine("Email saved!");
  break;
  case MFMailComposeResult.Cancelled:
    Console.WriteLine("Email sending cancelled!");
  break;
  case MFMailComposeResult.Failed:
    Console.WriteLine("Email sending failed!");
    if (null != e.Error)
    {
      Console.WriteLine("Error message: {0}",
        e.Error.LocalizedDescription);
    }
  break;
  }
  e.Controller.Finished -= MailController_Finished;
  await e.Controller.DismissViewControllerAsync(true);
}
```

4. Compile and run the app either on the simulator or on the device. Click on the **Send
   email** button to display the mail user interface.

Send or cancel the message. The app will work on the simulator and behave just like the native *Mail* app on devices, except for the fact that messages will not actually be sent or saved.

How it works...

The `MFMailComposeViewController` class provides the native mail composing interface. To determine whether the device is capable of sending e-mails, we first check its `CanSendMail` property, as follows:

```
if (MFMailComposeViewController.CanSendMail)
```

Just like we did with the `MFMessageComposeViewController` class, we subscribe to the `Finished` event of the `MFMailComposeViewController` class. We use this event to respond to user actions, without having to implement a `Delegate` object. We do this inside the `MailController_Finished` method based on the `MFComposeResultEventArgs.Result` property, which is of the `MFMailComposeResult` type. The possible values of the `MFMailComposeResult` enumeration will be one of the following:

▶ Sent: This means the e-mail message is queued for sending.

▶ Saved: This means the user clicked on the **Cancel** button, and the **Save Draft** option of the action sheet automatically appears. The following screenshot shows the action sheet that appears when the user clicks on the **Cancel** button:

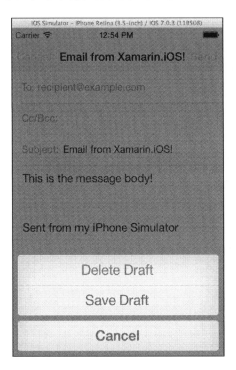

- ▶ Cancelled: This means the user clicked on the **Cancel** button on the controller and selected the **Delete Draft** option on the action sheet.

- ▶ Failed: This means the e-mail message sending failed.

After initializing the object, we can assign a recipient list, subject, and message body through the corresponding set of the `Set` prefixed methods, as follows:

```
this.mailController.SetToRecipients(new string[] {
    "recipient@example.com" });
this.mailController.SetSubject("Email from MonoTouch!");
this.mailController.SetMessageBody("This is the message body!",
    false);
```

If the second parameter of the `SetMessageBody` message is set to `true`, it informs the controller that the message should be treated as HTML.

There's more...

Apart from simple or HTML formatted text, we can also send attachments. We can do this with the `AddAttachmentData` method using the following line of code:

```
this.mailController.AddAttachmentData(UIImage.FromFile(
    "image.jpg").AsJPEG(), "image/jpg", "image.jpg");
```

The first parameter is of the `NSData` type and is the actual content of the attachment. In this case, we attach an image through the `UIImage.AsJPEG()` method, which returns the image contents inside an `NSData` object. The second parameter represents the **Multipurpose Internet Mail Extensions** (**MIME**) type of the attachment, and the third parameter represents its filename that will be shown to the user.

See also

- ▶ The *Using text messaging in our application* recipe

Managing the address book

In this recipe, we will discuss how to access and manage the user's stored contacts in the device's address book.

Getting ready

Create a new **Single View Application** in Xamarin Studio and name it `AddressBookApp`.

How to do it...

Perform the following steps:

1. Add a button on the view of the controller.

2. Enter the following using directive in the `AddressBookAppViewController.cs` file:

   ```
   using MonoTouch.AddressBook;
   ```

3. Override the `ViewDidLoad` method:

   ```
   public override void ViewDidLoad ()
   {
     base.ViewDidLoad ();
     this.btnReadContacts.TouchUpInside += (s, e) => {
     ABAuthorizationStatus abStatus =
       ABAddressBook.GetAuthorizationStatus();
     NSError error;
     ABAddressBook addressBook =
       ABAddressBook.Create(out error);
     if (abStatus == ABAuthorizationStatus.NotDetermined)
     {
       addressBook.RequestAccess((g, err) => {
         if (!g)
         {
           Console.WriteLine("User denied address
             book access!");
         } else
         {
           this.InvokeOnMainThread(() =>
             this.ReadContacts(addressBook));
         }
       });
     } else if (abStatus == ABAuthorizationStatus.Authorized)
     {
       this.ReadContacts(addressBook);
     } else
     {
       Console.WriteLine("App does not have access
         to the address book!");
     }
     };
   }
   ```

4. Add the following method:

```
private void ReadContacts(ABAddressBook addressBook)
{
  ABPerson[] contacts = addressBook.GetPeople();
  foreach (ABPerson eachPerson in contacts)
  {
    Console.WriteLine("{0} {1}", eachPerson.LastName,
      eachPerson.FirstName);
  }
}
```

5. Compile and run the app on the simulator. Click on the **Get contacts** button and either accept or deny access to the address book. The following screenshot displays the alert that appears when we request access to the address book:

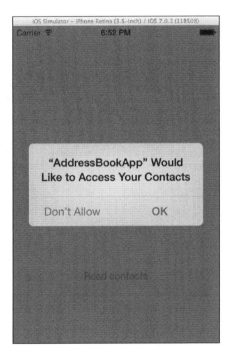

 The simulator's address book contains some fake contacts that we can work with.

How it works...

The `MonoTouch.AddressBook` namespace contains all the classes that allow us to manage the device's address book. To access the address book, we first need to check if the user has previously granted address book access to our app and instantiate an `ABAddressBook` instance, as follows:

```
ABAuthorizationStatus abStatus =
  ABAddressBook.GetAuthorizationStatus();
NSError error;
ABAddressBook addressBook = ABAddressBook.Create(out error);
```

If the status is `NotDermined`, we call the `RequestAccess` method, which accepts an `Action<bool, NSError>` delegate, as follows:

```
addressBook.RequestAccess((g, err) => {
      if (!g)
      {
        Console.WriteLine("User denied address book access!");
      } else
      {
        this.InvokeOnMainThread(() =>
          this.ReadContacts(addressBook));
      }
    });
```

The `bool` parameter informs us if the user has granted access. If it is `true`, we call the `ReadContacts` method so that we proceed with reading the address book information we want. Note that we wrap the call of the `ReadContacts` method with an `InvokeOnMainThread` call, although it is not accessing the UI. This is because the `RequestAccess` method is called on a separate thread.

 We can access the address book from other threads other than the main one; however, every instance of `ABAddressBook` needs to be used on the same thread.

Inside the `ReadContacts` method, we enumerate the individual contact through the `GetPeople` method, as follows:

```
ABPerson[] contacts = addressBook.GetPeople();
foreach (ABPerson eachPerson in contacts)
{
  Console.WriteLine("{0} {1}", eachPerson.LastName,
    eachPerson.FirstName);
}
```

The `ABPerson` class contains the contact information we want.

There's more...

To get a contact's stored phone number(s), call the `GetPhones()` method, as follows:

```
ABMultiValue<string> phones = eachPerson.GetPhones();
Console.WriteLine(phones[0].Value);
```

It returns an object of the `ABMultiValue<string>` type. `ABMultiValue<T>` is a generic collection, especially designed for multiple address book values.

Adding a phone number to a contact

To add a phone number to a contact, we can use the `ABPerson` class' `SetPhones` method. It accepts an `ABMultiValue<string>` object as its parameter, but we cannot add new values to the `ABMultiValue` objects. We can, however, write values to an `ABMutableMultiValue<T>` object, as follows:

```
ABMutableMultiValue<string> newPhones =
    phones.ToMutableMultiValue();
```

This line of code creates a new instance of the `ABMutableMultiValue<string>` object, which we then use to add the phone number(s) we want, as follows:

```
newPhones.Add("+120987654321", ABPersonPhoneLabel.iPhone);
eachPerson.SetPhones(newPhones);
addressBook.Save();
```

The second parameter of the `Add` method is the label that the phone number will have when it is saved to the contact. It is important to call the `ABAddressBook.Save()` method, or else, the changes will not be saved.

Displaying contacts

In this recipe, we will learn how to use the native address book user interface to display contact information.

Getting ready

Create a new **Single View Application** in Xamarin Studio and name it `DisplayContactApp`.

How to do it...

Perform the following steps:

1. Add a button on the controller.

2. In the `AppDelegate.cs` file, add the `DisplayContactAppViewController` to a navigation controller, as follows:

```
window.RootViewController =
    new UINavigationController(viewController);
```

3. Add the following namespaces in the `DisplayContactAppViewController.cs` file:

```
using MonoTouch.AddressBook;
using MonoTouch.AddressBookUI;
```

4. Add the following code in the `ViewDidLoad` method:

```
this.btnDisplayContact.TouchUpInside += (sender, e) => {
    ABAuthorizationStatus status =
        ABAddressBook.GetAuthorizationStatus();
    NSError error;
    ABAddressBook addressBook =
        ABAddressBook.Create(out error);
    if (status == ABAuthorizationStatus.NotDetermined)
    {
        addressBook.RequestAccess((g, err) => {
            if (g)
            {
                this.InvokeOnMainThread(() =>
                    this.DisplayContactCard(addressBook));
            } else
            {
                Console.WriteLine("User denied access to the
                    address book!");
            }
        });
    } else if (status == ABAuthorizationStatus.Authorized)
    {
        this.DisplayContactCard(addressBook);
    } else
    {
        Console.WriteLine("App does not have access to the
            address book!");
    }
};
```

5. Add the following method:

```
private void DisplayContactCard(ABAddressBookaddressBook)
{
  ABPerson[] contacts = addressBook.GetPeople();
  ABPersonViewController personController =
    new ABPersonViewController();
  personController.DisplayedPerson = contacts[0];
  this.NavigationController.PushViewController(
    personController, true);
}
```

6. Compile and run the application on the simulator. Tap the button to show the contact card screen. The result should be similar to the following screenshot:

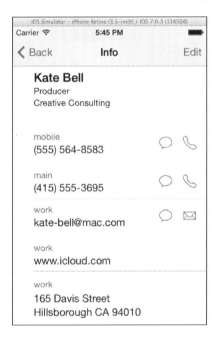

How it works...

The `MonoTouch.AddressBookUI` namespace contains the controllers that the native *Contacts* app uses to allow the user to display and manage contacts. Each contact's details can be viewed with `ABPersonViewController`. This controller must be pushed to `UINavigationController`, or else it will not display correctly.

After initializing it, we set the `ABPerson` object, which we want to be displayed, to its `DisplayedPerson` property, as follows:

```
ABPersonViewController personController =
  new ABPersonViewController();
personController.DisplayedPerson = contacts[0];
```

Then, we push it to the navigation controller's stack using the following line of code:

```
this.NavigationController.PushViewController(personController,
  true);
```

There's more...

The `ABPersonViewController` class can also be used for editing. To do this, set the `AllowsEditing` property to `true`, as follows:

```
personController.AllowsEditing = true;
```

Note that the changes are saved normally through the `ABPersonViewController` class.

Other address book controllers

The `MonoTouch.AddressBookUI` namespace contains all the controllers we need to create our own custom contacts application, as follows:

- ▶ `ABPeoplePickerNavigationController`: This is a navigation controller that displays the saved contacts. The user can select a contact from the list.
- ▶ `ABPersonViewController`: This is described in the example given in this recipe.
- ▶ `ABNewPersonViewController`: This is the controller that creates a new contact.
- ▶ `ABUnknownPersonViewController`: This is the controller that is displayed with partial data for creating a new contact. This is similar to the controller that is displayed when we tap on an unknown number in the list of recent calls on the device.

See also

- ▶ The *Managing the address book* recipe

Managing the calendar

In this recipe, we will learn how create an event and save it to the device's calendar database.

Getting ready

Create a new **Single View Application** in Xamarin Studio and name it `CalendarEventsApp`.

The app we will be creating will output the calendar events of the next 30 days. Make sure you have some calendar events in that period.

How to do it...

Let's create an event and save it to the device's calendar database by performing the following steps:

1. Add a button on the main view of the controller.

2. Add the `MonoTouch.EventKit` namespace in the `CalendarEventAppViewController.cs` file.

3. Enter the following code in the `ViewDidLoad` method:

```
this.btnDisplayEvents.TouchUpInside += async (sender, e) => {
  EKAuthorizationStatus status = EKEventStore.
    GetAuthorizationStatus(EKEntityType.Event);
  EKEventStore evStore = new EKEventStore();
  if (status == EKAuthorizationStatus.NotDetermined)
  {
    if (await
      evStore.RequestAccessAsync(EKEntityType.Event))
    {
      this.DisplayEvents(evStore);
    } else
    {
      Console.WriteLine("User denied access to the
        calendar!");
    }
  } else if (status == EKAuthorizationStatus.Authorized)
  {
    this.DisplayEvents(evStore);
  } else
  {
    Console.WriteLine("App does not have access to the
      calendar!");
  }
};
```

4. Add the following method:

```
private void DisplayEvents (EKEventStoreevStore)
{
  NSPredicate evPredicate =
    evStore.PredicateForEvents(DateTime.Now,
      DateTime.Now.AddDays(30),
      evStore.GetCalendars(EKEntityType.Event));
  evStore.EnumerateEvents(evPredicate,
    delegate(EKEventcalEvent, ref bool stop) {
    if (null != calEvent) {
      stop = false;
      Console.WriteLine("Event title: {0}\nEvent start
        date: {1}", calEvent.Title, calEvent.StartDate);
    }
  });
}
```

5. Compile and run the app on the device. Click on the **Display events** button to output the calendar events of the next 30 days in the **Application Output** pad.

How it works...

The `MonoTouch.EventKit` namespace is responsible for managing the calendar events. To read the stored events, we first check if we have access to the calendar and initialize an `EKEventStore` object, as follows:

```
EKAuthorizationStatus status =
  EKEventStore.GetAuthorizationStatus(EKEntityType.Event);
  EKEventStore evStore = new EKEventStore();
```

If the authorization status is `NotDetermined`, we call the `RequestAccessAsync` method so that the user is prompted for access, as follows:

```
if (await evStore.RequestAccessAsync(EKEntityType.Event))
```

If the result is `true`, it means that the user has granted calendar access to our app. Now, we call the `DisplayEvents` method to read and output the events.

The `EKEventStore` class provides us access to the stored events. To retrieve the calendar events, we need a predicate of the `NSPredicate` type. We can create an instance through the `PredicateForEvents` method of the `EKEventStore` class using the following code snippet:

```
NSPredicate evPredicate =
    evStore.PredicateForEvents(DateTime.Now,
      DateTime.Now.AddDays(30),
      evStore.GetCalendars(EKEntityType.Event));
```

The first two parameters are of the `NSDate` type (which can be implicitly converted to `DateTime`) and represent the start and end dates for which to search events. The third parameter is of the `EKCalendar[]` type, and is an array of the calendars to search. To search all the available calendars, we pass the return value of the `GetCalendars` method.

Finally, we call the `EnumerateEvents` method using the following line of code:

```
evStore.EnumerateEvents(evPredicate, delegate(EKEventcalEvent, ref
bool stop) {
//...
```

We pass the predicate we created earlier to the first parameter. The second parameter is a delegate of the `EKEventSearchCallback` type. To read each event's data, we use its `EKEvent` object. Note that the process of enumerating calendar events is similar to the one that is used for enumerating assets from the assets library, discussed in the previous chapter. This means that if the `EKEvent` object is not null, we must explicitly set the `stop` parameter to `false` so that the `EKEventStore` class continues enumerating the calendar events.

There's more...

Except from enumerating events, the `EKEventStore` class also allows us to create new events. The following example creates and saves a new calendar event:

```
EKEvent newEvent = EKEvent.FromStore(evStore);
newEvent.StartDate = DateTime.Now.AddDays(1);
newEvent.EndDate = DateTime.Now.AddDays(1.1);
newEvent.Title = "Xamarin event!";
newEvent.Calendar = evStore.DefaultCalendarForNewEvents;
NSError error = null;
evStore.SaveEvent(newEvent, EKSpan.ThisEvent, out error);
```

For creating a new EKEvent instance, we use the EKEvent.FromStore static method. We then set the start and end dates, a title, and the calendar to which the event will be stored. Here, we use the default calendar that we can get with the DefaultCalendarForNewEvents property of EKEventStore. When we have everything set up, we call the SaveEvent method to save it.

Reminders

You may have noticed the usage of the EKEntityType enumeration. This defines the entity type we want to have access to. Other than Event, which refers to the calendar events, we can also use the Reminder value so that we can work with the tasks the user has in the *Reminders* app.

We need to explicitly ask for the **Reminders** permission, even if the user has already granted access to the calendar.

See also

▸ The *Managing album items directly* recipe in *Chapter 7, Multimedia Resources*

9

Interacting with Device Hardware

In this chapter, we will cover the following topics:

- ▶ Detecting the device orientation
- ▶ Adjusting the UI orientation
- ▶ The proximity sensor
- ▶ Retrieving the battery information
- ▶ Handling motion events
- ▶ Handling touch events
- ▶ Recognizing gestures
- ▶ Custom gestures
- ▶ Using the accelerometer
- ▶ Using the gyroscope

Introduction

Today's mobile devices are equipped with very advanced hardware, be it accelerometers to detect motion and orientation, proximity sensors, GPS modules and, among many other components, sophisticated multitouch screens.

In this chapter, we will focus on how to use this hardware within our apps to provide the user with an experience that extends into the 3D world. Specifically, we will discuss how to adjust the user interface orientation according to the position of the device, how to use the proximity sensor, and how to read the battery information. In a series of four tasks, we will learn how to capture user touches on the screen and recognize gestures.

Last but not least, we will create advanced apps that read the raw data from the accelerometer and gyroscope sensors to detect the device motion and rotation with detailed and simple guides.

Detecting the device orientation

In this recipe, we will learn how to make an app that is aware of changes in the device orientation.

Getting ready

Create a new **Single View Application** in Xamarin Studio and name it DeviceOrientationApp.

How to do it...

Perform the following steps:

1. Add a label to the controller.

2. In the DeviceOrientationAppViewController class, override the ViewWillAppear method and implement it with the following code:

```
private NSObject orientationObserver;
public override void ViewWillAppear (bool animated)
{
  base.ViewWillAppear (animated);
  UIDevice.CurrentDevice.
    BeginGeneratingDeviceOrientationNotifications();
  this.orientationObserver =
    UIDevice.Notifications.ObserveOrientationDidChange((s,
    e) => {
    this.lblOrientation.Text =
      UIDevice.CurrentDevice.Orientation.ToString();
  });
}
```

3. Override the ViewWillDisappear method by using the following code:

```
public override void ViewWillDisappear (bool animated)
{
  base.ViewWillDisappear (animated);
  NSNotificationCenter.DefaultCenter.RemoveObserver(
    this.orientationObserver);
    UIDevice.CurrentDevice.
      EndGeneratingDeviceOrientationNotifications();
}
```

4. Compile and run the app on the simulator. Rotate the simulator by holding the *Command* key on your Mac and by pressing the left or right arrow keys.

How it works...

Although the simulator lacks the accelerometer hardware, it supports notifications for orientation changes.

The device orientation notification mechanism can be accessed through the `UIDevice.CurrentDevice` static property. To receive notifications, we first need to instruct the runtime to issue them. We do this with the following method:

```
UIDevice.CurrentDevice.
BeginGeneratingDeviceOrientationNotifications();
```

This method turns the accelerometer on and starts generating orientation notifications. We then need to start observing the notifications in order to respond to changes, as shown in the following code:

```
this.orientationObserver =
    UIDevice.Notifications.ObserveOrientationDidChange((s, e) => {
    this.lblOrientation.Text =
    UIDevice.CurrentDevice.Orientation.ToString();
});
```

Each time the device orientation changes, the observer triggers the anonymous method. In the anonymous method, we output the orientation, which we get from the `Orientation` property, to the label.

The `ViewWillDisappear` method is the method that is being called when the view controller is about to hide (for example, when we push another view controller on a navigation controller). Inside it, we make sure that we remove the orientation observer, and we instruct the runtime to stop generating orientation notifications by using the following code:

```
NSNotificationCenter.DefaultCenter.RemoveObserver(this.orientation
    Observer);
UIDevice.CurrentDevice.
    EndGeneratingDeviceOrientationNotifications();
```

There's more...

The `Orientation` property of the `UIDevice` class returns an enumeration of the `UIDeviceOrientation` type. Its possible values are the following:

▸ `Unknown`: This means that the device orientation is unknown

▸ `Portrait`: This means that the device is in its normal portrait orientation, with the home button on the bottom side

- ▶ PortraitUpsideDown: This means that the device is in an upside-down portrait orientation, with the home button on the top side
- ▶ LandscapeLeft: This means that the device is in the landscape orientation, with the home button on the left side
- ▶ LandscapeRight: This means that the device is in the landscape orientation, with the home button on the right side
- ▶ FaceUp: This means that the device is parallel to the ground, with the screen facing up
- ▶ FaceDown: This means that the device is parallel to the ground, with the screen facing down

FaceUp and FaceDown are two values that cannot be reproduced on the simulator.

The device orientation and user interface orientation

The user interface—in this case, the view controller—will also rotate and adjust to the new screen orientation by default. It is, however, important to note that the device orientation and the user interface orientation can be different. For example, the device can be in landscape, with UIDevice.CurrentDevice.Orientation returning LandscapeLeft without any change to the appearance of the view controller.

See also

- ▶ The *Adjusting the UI orientation* recipe
- ▶ The *Using the accelerometer* recipe

Adjusting the UI orientation

In this chapter, we will learn how to rotate the user interface according to the screen orientation.

Getting ready

Create a new **Single View Application** in Xamarin Studio and name it UIOrientationApp.

How to do it...

Perform the following steps:

1. Add a label to the view the controller.
2. Override the ShouldAutoRotate method:

```
public override bool ShouldAutorotate ()
{
    return true;
}
```

3. Override the `GetSupportedInterfaceOrientations` method:

```
public override UIInterfaceOrientationMask
  GetSupportedInterfaceOrientations ()
{
  return UIInterfaceOrientationMask.All;
}
```

4. Override the `DidRotate` method:

```
public override void DidRotate (UIInterfaceOrientation
  fromInterfaceOrientation)
{
  base.DidRotate (fromInterfaceOrientation);
  this.lblOrientation.Text =
    this.InterfaceOrientation.ToString();
}
```

5. Compile and run the app on the simulator. Rotate the simulator by pressing the *Command* key and either the left or right arrow keys. The current user interface orientation will be shown on the simulator's screen.

   Try rotating the simulator twice to turn the portrait orientation upside down. You will notice that the user interface will not rotate to this orientation and will remain on the landscape, as shown in the following screenshot:

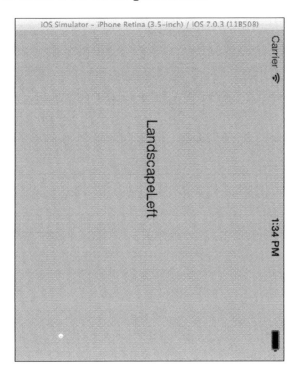

How it works...

On every view controller that is loaded, the system calls the `ShouldAutoRotate` method to determine whether it should rotate the specific controller. If the method returns `true`, then the system calls the `GetSupportedInterfaceOrientations` method to determine which orientations the controller is allowed to be rotated to. The `GetSupportedInterfaceOrientations` method implementation is shown in the following code:

```
public override UIInterfaceOrientationMask
   GetSupportedInterfaceOrientations ()
{
   return UIInterfaceOrientationMask.All;
}
```

However, there is an app-wide setting in the `Info.plist` file that takes priority over orientations for all view controllers. This can be accessed through the project options under the **iOS Application** node. The default setting is shown in the following screenshot:

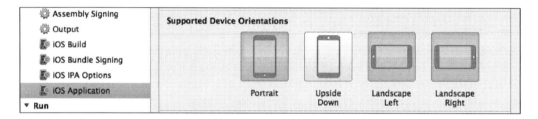

This also explains why our user interface will not rotate when the device is turned upside down, despite the fact that we return `UIInterfaceOrientationMask.All` from the `GetSupportedInterfaceOrientations` method. To make the view controller support the `PortraitUpsideDown` orientation, we have to enable the **Upside Down** option through the orientation settings.

Similarly, if we wanted our user interface to only remain in a specific orientation, say, a portrait, we would just return `UIInterfaceOrientationMask.Portrait` from the `GetSupportedInterfaceOrientations` method, making sure that at least the **Portrait** orientation is enabled in the project settings.

There's more...

As long as the app supports an orientation, the view controller will adjust to it at the runtime, if we want it to. For example, if we would present a second view controller modally and we only want that view controller to be shown in the landscape orientations, we would implement its `GetSupportedInterfaceOrientations` method as shown in the following code:

```
public override UIInterfaceOrientationMask
  GetSupportedInterfaceOrientations() {
  return UIInterfaceOrientationMask.LandscapeLeft |
    UIInterfaceOrientationMask.LandscapeRight;
}
```

User interface orientation on child controllers

In the project that we created here, if the `UIOrientationAppViewController` was presented as a child view controller (for example, through `UINavigationController`), its `ShouldAutoRotate` and `GetSupportedInterfaceOrientations` methods would not have been called but the ones from `UINavigationController` would have been called instead, returning the corresponding default values.

In this situation, to make sure the user interface would rotate according to the current controller, we would have to subclass `UINavigationController` and override these two methods, returning the corresponding values from the currently active view controller in the navigation stack, as shown in the following code:

```
// Inside our UINavigationController subclass:
public override ShouldAutoRotate() {
  return this.TopViewController.ShouldAutoRotate();
}
public override UIInterfaceOrientationMask
  GetSupportedInterfaceOrientations() {
  return this.TopViewController.
    GetSupportedInterfaceOrientations();
}
```

This applies to any parent-child controller relationship, for example, if our parent controller was `UITabBarController` and so on.

See also

▸ The *Detecting the device orientation* recipe

▸ The *Using the accelerometer* recipe

▸ The *Navigating through different view controllers* recipe in Chapter 3, *User Interface – View Controllers*

Proximity sensor

In this recipe, we will discuss how to use the proximity sensor to disable the device screen.

Getting ready

Create a new **Single View Application** in Xamarin Studio and name it `ProximitySensorApp`.

 The simulator does not support the proximity sensor.

How to do it...

Perform the following steps:

1. For this project, no controls are needed on the view controller. Declare an `NSObject` field that will hold the notification observer by using the following command:

```
private NSObject proximityObserver;
```

2. Override the `ViewWillAppear` method of the controller and implement it according to the following code:

```
public override void ViewWillAppear (bool animated)
{
  base.ViewWillAppear (animated);
  UIDevice.CurrentDevice.ProximityMonitoringEnabled = true;
  if (UIDevice.CurrentDevice.ProximityMonitoringEnabled)
  {
    this.proximityObserver = UIDevice.Notifications.
      ObserveProximityStateDidChange ((s, e) => {
      Console.WriteLine ("Proximity state: {0}",
        UIDevice.CurrentDevice.ProximityState);
    });
  }
}
```

3. Compile and run the app on the device. Put your finger over the proximity sensor (it is next to the speaker on an iPhone), and watch the **Application Output** pad in Xamarin Studio display the sensor state.

How it works...

Although the functionality of the proximity sensor is quite simple, it provides a very important feature. iOS devices have only one button on the front, which is the home button. Almost every user-device interaction is based on the touch-sensitive screen. This poses a problem on the iPhone; apart from its multiple features, it is also a phone. This means that it will most likely spend some time on the side of the user's face to make calls.

To avoid accidental virtual buttons being tapped, the proximity sensor gets activated when the phone app is running in order to disable the screen when the device is near the user's ear or whatever is over the sensor.

To enable the proximity sensor, set the property of the `UIDevice.CurrentDevice.ProximityMonitoringEnabled` property to `true`:

```
UIDevice.CurrentDevice.ProximityMonitoringEnabled = true;
```

If the device does not support the proximity sensor, this property will return `false` even after it has been set to `true`. So after setting it to `true`, we can check it to see whether the device supports the sensor by using the following code:

```
if (UIDevice.CurrentDevice.ProximityMonitoringEnabled)
```

After checking the support for a proximity sensor, we can add an observer to get notified of the sensor's state by using the following code:

```
this.proximityObserver =
  UIDevice.Notifications.ObserveProximityStateDidChange((
  s, e) => {
  Console.WriteLine("Proximity state: {0}",
    UIDevice.CurrentDevice.ProximityState);
});
```

The `ProximityState` property returns `true` if the sensor has turned the screen off and `false` if it has turned it back on.

There's more...

The proximity sensor usage is not limited to the phone call functionality. For example, if you are developing an app that could do some work while the device is in the user's pocket or purse, enabling the proximity sensor would help you make sure that no accidental controls are tapped. You can even save the battery power by just turning the screen off.

See also

▶ The *Retrieving the battery information* recipe

Retrieving the battery information

In this recipe, we will learn how to read the charging states of the device and its battery usage.

Getting ready

Create a new **Single View Application** in Xamarin Studio and name it `BatteryInfoApp`.

How to do it...

Perform the following steps:

1. Add a label to the view of the controller.

2. Override the `ViewWillAppear` method in the controller class as follows:

```
private NSObject batteryStateChangeObserver;
public override void ViewWillAppear (bool animated)
{
  base.ViewWillAppear (animated);
  UIDevice.CurrentDevice.BatteryMonitoringEnabled = true;
  this.batteryStateChangeObserver =
    UIDevice.Notifications.ObserveBatteryStateDidChange((s,
    e) => {
    this.lblOutput.Text = string.Format("Battery level:
      {0}", UIDevice.CurrentDevice.BatteryLevel);
    Console.WriteLine("Battery state: {0}",
      UIDevice.CurrentDevice.BatteryState);
  });
}
```

3. Compile and run the app on the device. After the app loads, disconnect and/or connect the USB cable of the device. The battery level will be displayed on the label and the current state will be displayed in the **Application Output** pad.

How it works...

We can retrieve the battery information through the `UIDevice` class. The first thing we have to do is to enable the battery monitoring:

```
UIDevice.CurrentDevice.BatteryMonitoringEnabled = true;
```

On the simulator, which does not support battery monitoring, this property will return `false` even after we have set it to `true`.

We can then add an observer for the battery state change notifications, through the `UIDevice.BatteryStateDidChangeNotification` key, as indicated in the highlighted code in the preceding section. The battery level can be retrieved through the `BatteryLevel` property, which returns the charge percentage of the battery in the range of `0` through `1` (`0` meaning fully discharged and `1` meaning 100 percent charged) by using the following code:

```
this.lblOutput.Text = string.Format("Battery level: {0}",
    UIDevice.CurrentDevice.BatteryLevel);
```

Similarly, we can retrieve the state of the battery through the `BatteryState` property by using the following code:

```
Console.WriteLine("Battery state: {0}",
    UIDevice.CurrentDevice.BatteryState);
```

The possible values of the `BatteryState` property are as follows:

- ▶ `Unknown`: This means that the battery state cannot be determined or the battery monitoring is disabled
- ▶ `Unplugged`: This means that the device is running on the battery power
- ▶ `Charging`: This means that the device battery is getting charged, and the USB cable is connected
- ▶ `Full`: This means that the device battery is full and the USB cable is connected

There's more...

Apart from the battery state, we can get information on its power level. To do this, we need to add an observer for the `UIDevice.BatteryLevelDidChangeNotification` key, as shown in the following code:

```
private NSObject batteryLevelChangedObserver;
//...
this.batteryLevelChangedObserver =
    UIDevice.Notifications.ObserveBatteryLevelDidChange((s, e) =>
    {..//
```

Disabling battery monitoring

Always disable battery monitoring when not needed. The actual monitoring mechanism itself consumes a significant amount of battery power.

See also

▸ The *Proximity sensor* recipe

Handling motion events

In this recipe, we will learn how to intercept and respond to shake gestures.

Getting ready

Create a new **Single View Application** in Xamarin Studio and name it `MotionEventsApp`.

How to do it...

Perform the following steps:

1. Add a label to the view of the controller.
2. Enter the following code in the `MotionEventsAppViewController` class:

```
public override bool CanBecomeFirstResponder
{
  get {  return true; }
}
public override void ViewDidAppear (bool animated)
{
  base.ViewDidAppear (animated);
  this.BecomeFirstResponder ();
}
public override void MotionBegan (UIEventSubtype motion, UIEvent
evt)
{
  base.MotionBegan (motion, evt);
  this.lblOutput.Text = "Motion started!";
}
public override void MotionEnded (UIEventSubtype motion, UIEvent
evt)
{
  base.MotionEnded (motion, evt);
  this.lblOutput.Text = "Motion ended!";
}
public override void MotionCancelled (UIEventSubtype motion,
UIEvent evt)
{
```

```
      base.MotionCancelled (motion, evt);
      this.lblOutput.Text = "Motion cancelled!";
   }
```

3. Compile and run the app on the device. Shake the device and watch the output on the label.

 You can also test this app on the simulator. After it loads, navigate to **Hardware | Shake Gesture** on the menu bar.

How it works...

By overriding the motion methods of the `UIViewController` class, we can intercept and respond to the motion events sent by the system. Just overriding these methods is not enough, though. For a controller to receive the motion events, it needs to be the first responder. To make sure that this happens, we first override the `CanBecomeFirstResponder` property and return `true` from it, as shown in the following code:

```
public override bool CanBecomeFirstResponder
{
   get {   return true; }
}
```

Then, we make sure that our controller becomes the first responder when its view appears, by calling the `BecomeFirstResponder` method in the `ViewDidAppear` override, as shown in the following code:

```
public override void ViewDidAppear (bool animated)
{
   base.ViewDidAppear (animated);
   this.BecomeFirstResponder ();
}
```

The `ViewDidAppear` method gets called after the view has appeared on the screen.

The system determines whether a motion is a shake gesture and calls the appropriate methods. The methods with which we can override and capture shake gestures are the following:

▶ `MotionBegan`: This means that the shaking motion has started

▶ `MotionEnded`: This means that the shaking motion has ended

▶ `MotionCancelled`: This means that the shaking motion has been cancelled

When the device starts moving, the `MotionBegan` method is called. If the motion lasts for about a second or less, the `MotionEnded` method is called. If it lasts longer, the system classifies it as not being a shake gesture and calls the `MotionCancelled` method. It is advisable to override all the three methods and react accordingly when we want to implement the shake gestures in an app.

There's more...

Motion events are only sent to objects that inherit the `UIResponder` class. This includes the `UIView` and `UIViewController` classes.

More information on motion events

The motion event mechanism is fairly simple. It merely detects near-instant device shakes, without providing any information on their direction or rate. To handle the motion events based on different characteristics, the accelerometer can be used in combination.

See also

▶ The *Using the accelerometer* recipe

Handling touch events

In this recipe, we will learn how to intercept and respond to user touches.

Getting ready

Create a new **Single View Application** in Xamarin Studio and name it `TouchEventsApp`.

How to do it...

Perform the following steps:

1. Add a label to the view the controller.
2. Enter the following code in the `TouchEventsAppViewController` class:

```
public override void TouchesMoved (NSSet touches,
  UIEvent evt)
{
  base.TouchesMoved (touches, evt);
  UITouch touch = touches.AnyObject as UITouch;
  UIColor currentColor = this.View.BackgroundColor;
  float red, green, blue, alpha;
```

```
currentColor.GetRGBA(out red, out green, out blue, out
    alpha);
PointF previousLocation =
touch.PreviousLocationInView(this.View);
PointF touchLocation = touch.LocationInView(this.View);
if (previousLocation.X != touchLocation.X)
{
    this.lblOutput.Text = "Changing background color...";
    float colorValue = touchLocation.X /
        this.View.Bounds.Width;
    this.View.BackgroundColor = UIColor.FromRGB(colorValue,
        colorValue, colorValue);
}
}
```

3. Compile and run the app on the simulator. Click-and-drag the cursor sideways on the simulator's screen and watch the view's background color gradually change from white to black. Note that clicking with the cursor on the simulator screen is the equivalent of touching the device's screen with a finger.

How it works...

To respond to user touches, the object that acts as a touch receiver must have its `UserInteractionEnabled` property set to `true`. Almost all objects are enabled for user interaction by default, except for those whose primary usage is not intended for direct user interaction, for example the `UILabel` and the `UIImageView` object. We need to set `UserInteractionEnabled` to these objects explicitly if we want them to be sensitive to user touches. Apart from this, the objects that can handle touch events must inherit from the `UIResponder` class. Note that although the `UIViewController` class inherits from `UIResponder` and can therefore capture touch events, it does not have a `UserInteractionEnabled` property, and it is its main property of `UIView`, which controls the delivery of touch events. What this means is that if you override the touch methods of `UIViewController` but its view's `UserInteractionEnabled` property is set to `false`, these methods will not respond to user touches.

The methods responsible of handling the touch events are the following:

▶ `TouchesBegan`: It is called when the user has touched the screen

▶ `TouchesMoved`: It is called when the user is dragging his/her finger on the screen

▶ `TouchesEnded`: It is called when the user has lifted his/her finger from the screen

▶ `TouchesCancelled`: It is called when the touch event has been cancelled by a system event, for example, when a notification alert is displayed

The full project can be found in the downloadable source code. The `TouchesMoved` method implementation has been explained here.

Every touch method has two parameters. The first parameter is of the `NSSet` type and contains the `UITouch` objects. The `NSSet` class represents a collection of objects, while the `UITouch` class holds the information for each user touch. The second parameter is of the `UIEvent` type and holds the information of the actual event.

We can retrieve the `UITouch` object related to the actual touch through the `NSSet`. `AnyObject` return value by using the following code:

```
UITouch touch = touches.AnyObject as UITouch;
```

It returns an object of the `NSObject` type, which we convert to `UITouch`. We can get the previous and current locations of the touch through the following methods:

```
PointF previousLocation =
    touch.PreviousLocationInView(this.View);
PointF touchLocation = touch.LocationInView(this.View);
```

Both of the preceding methods return a `PointF` struct, which contains the location of the touch in the receiver's coordinate system. After receiving the location of the touch, we adjust the background color accordingly.

There's more...

This example is based on single user touches. To enable a view to respond to multiple touches, we have to set its `MultipleTouchEnabled` property to `true`. We can then get all the `UITouch` objects in an array:

```
UITouch[] allTouches = touches.ToArray<UITouch>();
```

Getting the tap count

We can determine the number of consecutive user taps through the `UITouch.TapCount` property inside the `ToucheEnded` method.

See also

- ▶ The *Handling motion events* recipe
- ▶ The *Recognizing gestures* recipe
- ▶ The *Custom gestures* recipe

Recognizing gestures

In this recipe, we will discuss how to recognize touch gestures and respond accordingly.

Getting ready

Create a new **Single View Application** in Xamarin Studio and name it `GestureApp`.

How to do it...

Perform the following steps:

1. Add a label to the view of the controller.

2. Add the following method in the `GestureAppViewController` class:

   ```
   private void OnPinchGesture(UIPinchGestureRecognizer pinch)
   {
     switch (pinch.State)
     {
     case UIGestureRecognizerState.Began:
       this.lblOutput.Text = "Pinch began!";
       break;
     case UIGestureRecognizerState.Changed:
       this.lblOutput.Text = "Pinch changed!";
       break;
     case UIGestureRecognizerState.Ended:
       this.lblOutput.Text = "Pinch ended!";
       break;
     }
   }
   ```

3. Add the following code in the `ViewDidLoad` method:

   ```
   UIPinchGestureRecognizer pinchGesture = new
     UIPinchGestureRecognizer(this.OnPinchGesture);
   this.View.AddGestureRecognizer(pinchGesture);
   ```

4. Compile and run the app on the simulator. Hold down the *option* key and click-and-drag the mouse to perform the equivalent of a pinch on the simulator screen.

   Holding down the Option key and dragging with the mouse cursor on the simulator is the equivalent of touching a device's screen with two fingers, as shown in the following screenshot:

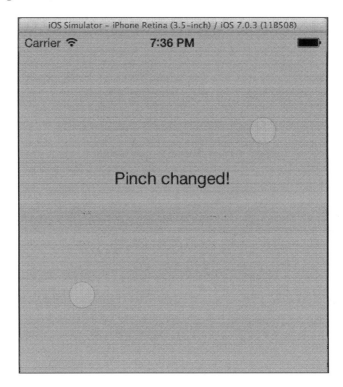

How it works...

As the iOS Version 3.2 was released along with the iPad, Apple introduced the UIGestureRecognizer class and its derivatives. The gesture recognizers make use of the multitouch screens on iOS devices. Gestures are basically touch combinations that can be performed for specific actions.

For example, pinching on a fullscreen image in the native *Photos* app will zoom out. The action of pinching is the gesture that the user performs, while the gesture recognizer is responsible for recognizing and delivering the gesture event to its receiver.

In this example, we create a `UIPinchGestureRecognizer` instance, which will recognize the pinches performed on the screen. Its instance is created with the following code:

```
UIPinchGestureRecognizer pinchGesture = new
    UIPinchGestureRecognizer(this.OnPinchGesture);
```

The constructor that initializes the instance takes one parameter, which is of the `Action<UI PinchGestureRecognizer>` type and represents the method that will be called when the recognizer receives a gesture.

Inside the method, we read the `State` property of the gesture recognizer object and respond accordingly, as shown in the following code:

```
switch (pinch.State) {
//…
```

There's more...

The state of each gesture recognizer is represented by an enumeration of the `UIGestureRecognizerState` type. Its possible values are shown as follows:

- `Possible`: This indicates that the gesture has not been recognized yet. This is the default value.
- `Began`: This indicates that the gesture has started.
- `Changed`: This indicates that the gesture has changed.
- `Ended`: This indicates that the gesture has ended.
- `Cancelled`: This indicates that the gesture has been canceled.
- `Failed`: This indicates that the gesture cannot be recognized.
- `Recognized`: This indicates that the gesture has been recognized.

The advantage of gesture recognizers

The advantage of gesture recognizers is that they save developers the time to create their own gesture recognition mechanisms through the touch events. Furthermore, they are based on the gestures that users are accustomed to using on iOS devices.

See also

- The *Handling touch events* recipe
- The *Custom gestures* recipe

Custom gestures

In this recipe, we will learn how to create a custom gesture recognizer to create our own gesture response mechanism.

Getting ready

Create a new **Single View Application** in Xamarin Studio and name it `CustomGestureApp`.

How to do it...

Perform the following steps:

1. Add a label to the view of the controller.

2. Create the following nested class in the `CustomGestureAppViewController` class:

```
private class DragLowerLeftGesture : UIGestureRecognizer
{
  private PointF startLocation;
  private RectangleF lowerLeftCornerRect;
  public override UIGestureRecognizerState State
  {
    get
    {
      return base.State;
    }   set
    {
      base.State = value;
    }
  }
  public override void TouchesBegan (NSSet touches, UIEvent
    evt)
  {
    base.TouchesBegan (touches, evt);
    UITouch touch = touches.AnyObject as UITouch;
    this.startLocation = touch.LocationInView(this.View);
    RectangleF viewBounds = this.View.Bounds;
    this.lowerLeftCornerRect = new RectangleF(0f,
      viewBounds.Height - 50f, 50f, 50f);
    if (this.lowerLeftCornerRect.
      Contains(this.startLocation))
    {
```

```
      this.State = UIGestureRecognizerState.Failed;
    } else
    {
      this.State = UIGestureRecognizerState.Began;
    }
  }
public override void TouchesMoved (NSSet touches,
  UIEvent evt)
{
  base.TouchesMoved (touches, evt);
  this.State = UIGestureRecognizerState.Changed;
}
public override void TouchesEnded (NSSet touches,
  UIEvent evt)
{
  base.TouchesEnded (touches, evt);
  UITouch touch = touches.AnyObject as UITouch;
  PointF touchLocation = touch.LocationInView(this.View);
  if (this.lowerLeftCornerRect.Contains(touchLocation))
  {
    this.State = UIGestureRecognizerState.Ended;
  } else
  {
    this.State = UIGestureRecognizerState.Failed;
  }
  }
}
```

3. Add the following method to the class:

```
private void OnDragLowerLeft(NSObject gesture)
{
  DragLowerLeftGesture drag =
    (DragLowerLeftGesture)gesture;
  switch (drag.State)
  {
  case UIGestureRecognizerState.Began:
    this.lblOutput.Text = "Drag began!";
    break;
  case UIGestureRecognizerState.Changed:
    this.lblOutput.Text = "Drag changed!";
    break;
  case UIGestureRecognizerState.Ended:
    this.lblOutput.Text = "Drag ended!";
    break;
```

```
    case UIGestureRecognizerState.Failed:
      this.lblOutput.Text = "Drag failed!";
      break;
  }
}
```

4. Initialize and add the gesture recognizer in the `ViewDidLoad` method as shown in the following code:

```
DragLowerLeftGesture dragGesture = new
  DragLowerLeftGesture();
dragGesture.AddTarget(this.OnDragLowerLeft);
this.View.AddGestureRecognizer(dragGesture);
```

5. Compile and run the app on the simulator. Click-and-drag on the simulator's screen towards the lower-left corner.

How it works...

To create a gesture recognizer, we need to declare a class that inherits from the `UIGestureRecognizer` class. In this example, we are creating a gesture that will be recognized by dragging the finger on the screen towards a 50 x 50 point area in the lower-left corner of the screen. The following line of code shows the class declaration:

```
private class DragLowerLeftGesture : UIGestureRecognizer
```

The `UIGestureRecognizer` class contains the same touch methods that we use to intercept touches in views. We also have access to the view it was added to through its `View` property. Inside the `TouchesBegan` method, we determine the initial touch location. If it is outside the lower-left portion of the view, we set the `State` property to `Began`. If it is inside the lower-left portion, we set the `State` property to `Failed` so that the callback will not be called.

Inside the `TouchesEnded` method, we consider the gesture as `Ended` if the touch's location was inside the lower-left portion of the view. If it was not, the gesture recognition is considered as `Failed`.

The `TouchesMoved` method is where the `Changed` state will be set. For this simple gesture recognizer that we are creating, no other logic is needed.

As the `UIGestureRecognizer` class does not have a constructor that accepts an `Action<T>` object for the gesture handler, we initialize it with the default constructor and use the `AddTarget` method for this purpose by using the following code:

```
dragGesture.AddTarget(this.OnDragLowerLeft);
```

The only difference in this case is that the parameter is of the `Action<NSObject>` type, which we can cast to our own custom type, as shown in the following line of code:

```
DragLowerLeftGesture drag = (DragLowerLeftGesture)gesture;
```

There's more...

This is a simple gesture recognizer that depends on a single touch. With the information provided in the touch methods, we can create more complex gestures that will support multiple touches.

Another use of custom gesture recognizers

There are some views that inherit from the `UIView` class, which, according to the Apple developer documentation, should not be subclassed. The `MKMapView` class represents one of these views that is used to display the maps. This poses a problem if we want to intercept the touch events from these views. Although we could use another view over it and intercept that view's touch events, it is quite complex (and error prone) to do so. A more simple approach is to create a simple custom gesture recognizer and add it to the view that we cannot subclass. This way, we can intercept its touches without having to subclass it.

See also

- ▸ The *Recognizing gestures* recipe
- ▸ The *Handling touch events* recipe

Using the accelerometer

In this recipe, we will learn how to receive the accelerometer events to create an app that is aware of the device movement.

Getting ready

Create a new **Single View Application** in Xamarin Studio and name it `AccelerometerApp`.

 The simulator does not support the accelerometer hardware. The project in this example will work correctly on a device.

How to do it...

Perform the following steps:

1. Add two buttons and a label on the view of the controller.

2. In the `ViewDidLoad` method, add the following code:

```
this.btnStop.Enabled = false;
UIAccelerometer.SharedAccelerometer.UpdateInterval = 1 /
```

```
      10;
    this.btnStart.TouchUpInside += delegate {
      this.btnStart.Enabled = false;
      UIAccelerometer.SharedAccelerometer.Acceleration +=
        this.Acceleration_Received;
      this.btnStop.Enabled = true;
    } ;
    this.btnStop.TouchUpInside += delegate {
      this.btnStop.Enabled = false;
      UIAccelerometer.SharedAccelerometer.Acceleration -=
        this.Acceleration_Received;
      this.btnStart.Enabled = true;
    } ;
```

3. Add the following method in the class:

```
    private void Acceleration_Received (object sender,
      UIAccelerometerEventArgs e)
    {
      this.lblOutput.Text = string.Format("X: {0}\nY: {1}\nZ:
        {2}", e.Acceleration.X, e.Acceleration.Y,
        e.Acceleration.Z);
    }
```

4. Compile and run the app on the device. Tap the **Start accelerometer** button and watch the values get displayed on the label while moving or shaking the device.

How it works...

The UIAccelerometer class provides access to the accelerometer hardware through its SharedAccelerometer static property. To activate it, all we need to do is to assign a handler to its Acceleration event by using the following code:

```
    UIAccelerometer.SharedAccelerometer.Acceleration +=
    this.Acceleration_Received;
```

Inside the handler, we receive the accelerometer values through the UIAccelerometerEventArgs.Acceleration property. The property returns an object of the UIAcceleration type, which contains the accelerometer amount in three properties: X, Y, and Z. These properties represent the motion in the x-, y-, and z-axis. Consider the following screenshot:

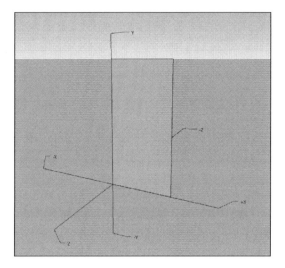

Each of these values measure the amount of G-force by which the device moved on each axis. For example, if X has a value of 1, the device is moving on the x axis to the right with an acceleration of 1G. If X has a value of -1, the device is moving on the x axis to the left with an acceleration of 1G. When the device is placed on a table with its back facing the floor and is not moving, the normal values of the acceleration should be close or equal to the following:

- X: 0

- Y: 0

- Z: -1

Although the device is not moving, Z will be -1 because the device measures the earth's gravity.

We can set the interval by which the accelerometer will issue the acceleration events, by setting its `UpdateInterval` property by using the following code:

```
UIAccelerometer.SharedAccelerometer.UpdateInterval = 1 / 10;
```

The property accepts a number of type `double`, which represents the interval by which the accelerometer will issue its acceleration events in seconds. Care must be taken when setting the update interval because the more events the accelerometer has to issue for a specific period of time, the more battery power it consumes.

To stop using the accelerometer, all we need to do is unhook the handler from the `Acceleration` event by using the following code:

```
UIAccelerometer.SharedAccelerometer.Acceleration -=
this.Acceleration_Received;
```

There's more...

The `UIAcceleration` class contains another useful property, named `Time`. It is a `double` that represents the relative time on which the acceleration event occurred. It is relative to the CPU time, and it is not suggested that you use this value to calculate the exact timestamp of the event.

Consideration when using the accelerometer

Although the iPhone's accelerometer is a very accurate and sensitive sensor, it should not be used for precise measurements. Also, the results it produces may vary among different iOS devices, even if they're of the same model.

See also

 ▸ The *Using the gyroscope* recipe

Using the gyroscope

In this recipe, we will learn how to use the device's built-in gyroscope.

Getting ready

Create a new project in Xamarin Studio and name it `GyroscopeApp`.

 The simulator does not support the gyroscope hardware. Also, only newer devices contain a gyroscope. If this app is executed on a device without a gyroscope or on the simulator, no error will occur but no data will be displayed.

How to do it...

Perform the following steps:

1. Add two buttons and a label to the view the controller.

2. Add the `MonoTouch.CoreMotion` namespace in the `GyroscopeAppViewController.cs` file.

3. Enter the following private field in the class:

   ```
   private CMMotionManager motionManager;
   ```

4. Implement the `ViewDidLoad` method with the following code:

```
this.motionManager = new CMMotionManager();
this.motionManager.GyroUpdateInterval = 1 / 10;
this.btnStart.TouchUpInside += delegate {
  this.motionManager.StartGyroUpdates(
    NSOperationQueue.MainQueue, this.GyroData_Received);
} ;
this.btnStop.TouchUpInside += delegate {
  this.motionManager.StopGyroUpdates();
} ;
```

Add the following method:

```
private void GyroData_Received(CMGyroData gyroData,
  NSError error)
{
  Console.WriteLine("rotation rate x: {0}, y: {1}, z: {2}",
    gyroData.RotationRate.x, gyroData.RotationRate.y,
    gyroData.RotationRate.z);
}
```

5. Compile and run the app on the device. Tap the **Start gyroscope** button and rotate the device in all axes. Watch the values get displayed in the **Application Output** pad.

How it works...

The gyroscope is a mechanism that measures orientation. Newer iOS devices support the gyroscope hardware, along with the accelerometer, to give even more accurate measurements of the device motion.

The `MonoTouch.CoreMotion` namespace wraps the objects contained in the native CoreMotion framework. The process of using the gyroscope hardware in code is similar to the one used for the accelerometer. The first difference is that there is no single object for the gyroscope in the `UIApplication` class. So, we need to create an instance of the `CMMotionManager` class as shown in the following code:

```
private CMMotionManager motionManager;
//...
    this.motionManager = new CMMotionManager();
```

Just like how we use the accelerometer, we can set the interval by which we will receive the gyroscope events in seconds by using the following code:

```
this.motionManager.GyroUpdateInterval = 1 / 10;
```

To start receiving the gyroscope events, we call the object's `StartGyroUpdates` method as shown in the following code:

```
this.motionManager.StartGyroUpdates(NSOperationQueue.MainQueue,
    this.GyroData_Received);
```

This method is overloaded; the first overload is parameterless and when called, the values of the gyroscopic measurements are set to the `GyroData` property. Using this overload is quite simple and easy, but no events are triggered here, and we have to provide a mechanism to read the measurements from the property.

The second overload, which is used in this example, accepts two parameters. The first parameter is the `NSOperationQueue` parameter on which the updates will occur, and the second parameter is the handler that will be executed when an update occurs.

The `NSOperationQueue` class represents an iOS mechanism to manage the `NSOperation` objects' execution. We access the runtime's main operation queue through the static `NSOperationQueue.MainQueue` property. Basically, this way, we instruct the runtime to manage the delivery of the handler in a more effective manner.

The second parameter is a delegate of the `CMGyroHandler` type. Its signature, represented by the method we created, is similar to the following code:

```
private void GyroData_Received(CMGyroData gyroData, NSError error)
```

The `CMGyroData` object contains the actual measurement values received from the gyroscope through its `RotationRate` property. The following code outputs the data from the property:

```
Console.WriteLine("rotation rate x: {0}, y: {1}, z: {2}",
    gyroData.RotationRate.x, gyroData.RotationRate.y,
    gyroData.RotationRate.z);
```

The rotation rate is reflected on the x, y, and z axis, represented by the corresponding `X`, `Y`, and `Z` properties. Each value is the amount of the rotation angle per second, which occurred on that axis, in radians.

Although it might seem a bit complicated at first, it is actually quite simple. For example, a value of 0.5 in the z axis means that the device rotated with a rate of 0.5 radians/sec to the left. A value of -0.5 in the z-axis means that the device rotated with a rate of 0.5 radians/sec to the right. The pattern to determine the rotation direction is based on the right-hand rule.

There's more...

If you want your app to be available only for devices that support the gyroscope, add the `UIRequiredDeviceCapabilities` key in your project's `Info.plist` file with the `gyroscope` value. If your app's functionality is based fully on the gyroscope, adding this key must be considered essential to avoid the app being downloaded by users with older devices, ending up with an app that does not work.

Determining the availability of the gyroscope hardware

To determine whether the device the app is running on supports the gyroscope hardware, check the value of the `GyroAvailable` property of the `CMMotionManager` instance.

Converting radians to degrees

A radian is an angle measurement unit. To convert an angle measurement from radians to degrees, consider the following helper method:

```
public static double RadiansToDegrees (double radians)
{
    return (radians * 180 / Math.PI);
}
```

See also

▸   The *Using the accelerometer* recipe

10
Location Services and Maps

In this chapter, we will cover the following:

- ▸ Determining location
- ▸ Determining heading
- ▸ Using region monitoring
- ▸ Using a significant-change location service
- ▸ Location services in the background
- ▸ Displaying maps
- ▸ Geocoding
- ▸ Adding map annotations
- ▸ Adding map overlays

Introduction

Today's smartphones and hand-held devices are equipped with high-accuracy Global Positioning System (GPS) hardware. The GPS hardware receives location information from a constellation of satellites. Apart from the satellites, iOS devices take advantage of the cellular and Wi-Fi networks to provide location information to the user.

In this chapter, we will discuss how to use the appropriate frameworks to take advantage of the location services of the device. Furthermore, we will learn how to display maps and annotate them. Specifically, we will focus on the following subjects:

- **Location services**: Here, the services available on a device for providing location information will be discussed. These services are as follows:

  - **Standard location service**: This location service depends fully on the device's GPS module and provides location data of the highest accuracy

  - **Region monitoring service**: This location service monitors boundary crossings

  - **Significant-change location service**: This service monitors significant changes in the location of the device

- `CLLocationManager`: This class allows us to use the location services

- `Compass`: This class shows how to use the built-in compass

- `MKMapView`: This view is used to display maps

- `CLGeocoder`: This class provides geocoding features

- `MKAnnotation`: This class allows us to add annotations on maps

- `MKOverlay`: This class allows us to add overlays on maps

Determining location

We will now learn how to receive the location information from the built-in GPS hardware.

Getting ready

Create a new **Single View Application** in Xamarin Studio and name it `LocationApp`. Add two buttons and a label on the view of the controller.

How to do it...

Perform the following steps to receive the location of the device:

1. To retrieve location information from the built-in GPS hardware, we need to use the Core Location framework. It is exposed through the `MonoTouch.CoreLocation` namespace as follows:

   ```
   using MonoTouch.CoreLocation;
   ```

2. Add the following code in the `LocationAppViewController` class:

   ```
   private CLLocationManager locationManager;
   public override void ViewDidLoad ()
   ```

```
{
  base.ViewDidLoad ();
  this.locationManager = new CLLocationManager();
  this.locationManager.LocationsUpdated +=
    LocationManager_LocationsUpdated;
  this.locationManager.Failed +=
    this.LocationManager_Failed;

  this.btnStart.TouchUpInside += delegate {
    this.lblOutput.Text = "Determining location...";
    this.locationManager.StartUpdatingLocation();
  } ;
  this.btnStop.TouchUpInside += delegate {
    this.locationManager.StopUpdatingLocation();
    this.lblOutput.Text = "Location update stopped.";
  } ;
}
private void LocationManager_LocationsUpdated (object
  sender, CLLocationsUpdatedEventArgs e)
{
  CLLocation location = e.Locations[0];
  double latitude =
    Math.Round(location.Coordinate.Latitude, 4);
  double longitude =
    Math.Round(location.Coordinate.Longitude, 4);
  double accuracy = Math.Round(location.HorizontalAccuracy,
    0);
  this.lblOutput.Text = string.Format("Latitude:
    {0}\nLongitude: {1},\nAccuracy: {2}m", latitude,
    longitude, accuracy);
}
private void LocationManager_Failed (object sender,
  NSErrorEventArgs e)
{
  this.lblOutput.Text = string.Format("Location update
    failed! Error message: {0}",
    e.Error.LocalizedDescription);
}
```

3. Compile and run the app on the device. Tap the start button to view your location coordinates on the screen.

Projects using the Core Location framework to determine the current position of a device can work on the simulator. By navigating to the **Debug | Location** menu of the simulator, we can customize the location that the device will be using.

How it works...

The location data that the GPS module provides can be accessed through the `CLLocationManager` class. After initializing an instance of the class, we need to subscribe to its `LocationsUpdated` event as follows:

```
this.locationManager = new CLLocationManager();
this.locationManager.LocationsUpdated +=
  LocationManager_LocationsUpdated;
```

Location data will become available, as they are issued through this event. It is also a good practice to subscribe to the `Failed` event as follows:

```
this.locationManager.Failed += this.LocationManager_Failed;
```

When the location manager first requests for location updates, the user is informed through a system-specific alert, which is similar to the one shown in the following screenshot:

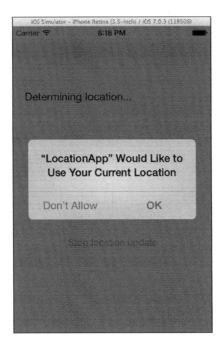

This alert basically asks for user permission to allow the app to retrieve location data. If the user denies this request, the `Failed` event will be triggered with the appropriate message. Future location requests will not trigger the permission alert, and the user will have to enable location services for the app through the device's settings, so we need to handle this scenario accordingly.

After subscribing to the appropriate events, we request the delivery of location updates through the `StartUpdatingLocation` method as follows:

```
this.locationManager.StartUpdatingLocation();
```

To stop receiving location updates, we call the `StopUpdatingLocation` method as follows:

```
this.locationManager.StopUpdatingLocation();
```

There's more...

The `LocationsUpdated` event accepts the delegates of the `EventHandler<CLLocationsUpdatedEventArgs>` type. The `CLLocationsUpdatedEventArgs` parameter contains one property that returns an array of `CLLocation` objects. The last item in the array contains the most recent location data that were retrieved from location services. The array will always contain at least one `CLLocation` item.

The coordinates are returned as values of the `double` type and represent the coordinates of the position in degrees as follows:

```
CLLocation location = e.Locations[0];
double latitude = Math.Round(location.Coordinate.Latitude, 4);
double longitude = Math.Round(location.Coordinate.Longitude, 4);
double accuracy = Math.Round(location.HorizontalAccuracy, 0);
```

Negative latitude values indicate south coordinates and positive values indicate north coordinates. Negative longitude values indicate west coordinates, while positive longitude values indicate east coordinates.

The `HorizontalAccuracy` property returns the accuracy of the GPS fix in meters. For example, a value of 17 m indicates that the location is determined within a circle of a diameter 17 m. Lower values indicate better accuracy.

GPS accuracy

There is always a margin of error in location data, which is independent of GPS hardware, and there are variable factors that define it, such as the surrounding buildings and various obstacles. You will notice that the `HorizontalAccuracy` property will return lower values when the device is outdoors, while higher values will be returned when we use the GPS indoors or on a city street with tall buildings.

Location services availability

Not all devices are equipped with location services hardware. Furthermore, even if a device is equipped with the appropriate hardware, location services could be disabled by the user.

To determine if the location services are available or enabled on the device, we read the return value of the `CLLocationManager.LocationServicesEnabled` static property before initializing the location manager object as follows:

```
if (CLLocationManager.LocationServicesEnabled) {
  // Initialize the location manager
  //...
}
```

Furthermore, we can check for the authorization status of location services through the `CLLocationManager.Status` property as follows:

```
if (CLLocationManager.Status == CLAuthorizationStatus.Authorized) {
  //..
}
```

Location services usage indicator

When any type of location service is used, the location services icon appears on the right-hand side of the status bar next to the battery indicator, as shown in the following screenshot:

See also

▶ The *Determining heading* and *Location services in the background* recipes

Determining heading

In this recipe, we will learn how to use the built-in compass to determine the heading of the device.

Getting ready

Create a new **Single View Application** in Xamarin Studio and name it `HeadingApp`. Just as you did in the previous recipe, add two buttons and a label on the view of the controller.

 The project in this recipe cannot be tested on the simulator. A device with compass hardware (magnetometer) is required.

How to do it...

Perform the following steps to determine the heading of the device:

1. Add the following code in the `HeadingAppViewController` class:

```
private CLLocationManager locationManager;
public override void ViewDidLoad ()
{
  base.ViewDidLoad ();
  // Perform any additional setup after loading the view,
    typically from a nib.
  this.locationManager = new CLLocationManager();
  this.locationManager.UpdatedHeading +=
    LocationManager_UpdatedHeading;
  this.locationManager.Failed += (sender, e) =>
    Console.WriteLine("Failed! {0}",
    e.Error.LocalizedDescription);

  this.btnStart.TouchUpInside += delegate {
    this.lblOutput.Text = "Starting updating heading...";
    this.locationManager.StartUpdatingHeading();
  } ;
  this.btnStop.TouchUpInside += delegate {
    this.locationManager.StopUpdatingHeading();
    this.lblOutput.Text = "Stopped updating heading.";
  };
}
private void LocationManager_UpdatedHeading (object sender,
  CLHeadingUpdatedEventArgs e)
{
  this.lblOutput.Text = string.Format("Magnetic heading:
    {0}", Math.Round(e.NewHeading.MagneticHeading, 1));
}
```

2. Compile and run the app on the device. Tap the start button and rotate the device to view the different heading values.

How it works...

To retrieve the heading information, we first need to subscribe to the location manager's `UpdatedHeading` event as follows:

```
this.locationManager.UpdatedHeading +=
  this.LocationManager_UpdatedHeading;
```

To initiate the delivery of heading information, we call the `StartUpdatingHeading` method as follows:

```
this.locationManager.StartUpdatingHeading();
```

Inside the `UpdatedHeading` event handler, we retrieve the heading information through the `MagneticHeading` property of the `CLHeading` object exposed through the event arguments' `NewHeading` property as follows:

```
this.lblOutput.Text = string.Format("Magnetic heading: {0}",
  Math.Round(e.NewHeading.MagneticHeading, 1));
```

To stop retrieving heading updates, we call the `StopUpdatingHeading` method with the help of the following code:

```
this.locationManager.StopUpdatingHeading();
```

There's more...

The heading is measured in degrees. The values for the four points of the horizon that can be viewed on a simple compass are the following:

- **0 or 360 degrees**: The magnetometer will return values of up to 359.99 degrees and then return 0 when the device is heading North.
- **90 degrees**: The device is heading East
- **180 degrees**: The device is heading South
- **270 degrees**: The device is heading West

Magnetic vs true heading

Magnetic heading is the heading that is based on what a normal compass will show as North. True heading is the true direction of North based on the actual position of the earth's North Pole. There is a slight difference between the two, which varies according to the earth's magnetic-field fluctuations, and it is usually about 2 degrees.

The `CLHeading` class provides both readings through the `MagneticHeading` and `TrueHeading` properties. This provides a significant help to developers, as calculating the difference between the two readings requires either expensive equipment or very difficult calculations based on the time of year and other factors.

Compass availability

The magnetometer, a module that can determine the heading in degrees and provides compass functionality to devices, is not available on all devices. To check if a device can provide heading information, retrieve the value from the `CLLocationManager.HeadingAvailable` static property as follows:

```
if (CLLocationManager.HeadingAvailable) {
  // Start updating heading
  //...
}
```

See also

▶ The *Determining location* and *Location services in the background* recipes

Using region monitoring

In this recipe, we will learn how to use GPS to respond to region-specific position changes.

Getting ready

Create a new **Single View Application** in Xamarin Studio and name it `RegionApp`. Add two buttons and a label on the view of the controller.

How to do it...

Perform the following steps:

1. Create two fields in the `RegionAppViewController` class as follows:

   ```
   private CLLocationManager locationManager;
   private CLCircularRegion region;
   ```

2. In the `ViewDidLoad` method, initialize the `RegionAppViewController` class, and subscribe to the `LocationsUpdated`, `RegionEntered`, and `RegionLeft` events as follows:

   ```
   this.locationManager.RegionEntered +=
     this.LocationManager_RegionEntered;
   this.locationManager.RegionLeft +=
     this.LocationManager_RegionLeft;
   this.locationManager.UpdatedLocation +=
     this.LocationManager_UpdatedLocation;
   ```

3. Enter the following event handlers in the class:

```
private void LocationManager_LocationsUpdated (object
   sender, CLLocationUpdatedEventArgs e)
{
   CLLocation location = e.Locations[0];
   if (location.HorizontalAccuracy < 100)
   {
      this.region = new CLCircularRegion(location.Coordinate,
         100, "Home");
      this.locationManager.StartMonitoring(this.region);
      this.locationManager.StopUpdatingLocation();
   }
}
private void LocationManager_RegionLeft (object sender,
   CLRegionEventArgs e)
{
   this.lblOutput.Text = string.Format("{0} region left.",
      e.Region.Identifier);
}
private void LocationManager_RegionEntered (object sender,
   CLRegionEventArgs e)
{
   this.lblOutput.Text = string.Format("{0} region
      entered.", e.Region.Identifier);
}
```

4. In the start button's `TouchUpInside` handler, call the `StartUpdatingLocation` method using the following code:

```
this.locationManager.StartUpdatingLocation();
```

5. In the stop button's `TouchUpInside` handler, call the `StopMonitoring` method using the following code:

```
this.locationManager.StopMonitoring(this.region);
```

6. Compile and run the app on the simulator. Navigate to **Debug | Location | Freeway drive** on the simulator's menu and tap the **Start region monitoring** button.

How it works...

Region monitoring is a feature that monitors boundary crossings. When a boundary of a specific region is crossed, the `CLLocationManager` object issues the appropriate events as follows:

```
this.locationManager.RegionEntered +=
   this.LocationManager_RegionEntered;
```

```
this.locationManager.RegionLeft +=
    this.LocationManager_RegionLeft;
```

In this example, we define the region based on the current location; hence, we also subscribe to the `LocationsUpdated` event.

When the app starts receiving location updates, it first checks for location accuracy using the following code:

```
if (location.HorizontalAccuracy < 100)
```

If the desired accuracy is achieved (<100 m, modify at your discretion), we initialize the `CLCircularRegion` object using the following line of code:

```
this.region = new CLRegion(e.NewLocation.Coordinate, 100, "Home");
```

The `CLCircularRegion` class is used to define circular regions and inherits the `CLRegion` class. Here, in the first parameter, we create the region to be monitored based on our current location. The second parameter declares the radius around the coordinate, in meters, defining the region's boundary. The third parameter is a string identifier we want to assign to the region.

To start monitoring the region, we call the `StartMonitoring` method using the following line of code:

```
this.locationManager.StartMonitoring(this.region);
```

When region monitoring has started, the appropriate events will be triggered when the device enters or leaves the region.

There's more...

Region monitoring is a very useful feature. For example, an app could provide specific information to users based on their proximity to various areas. Furthermore, it can notify of boundary crossings while the app is in the background.

Region monitoring availability

To check if a device supports region monitoring, call the `CLLocationManager.IsMonitoringAvailable` static method passing the type of the `CLRegion` object we want to use as follows:

```
if (CLLocationManager.IsMonitoringAvailable(typeof(CLCircularRegion))
{
  // Start monitoring a region
  //...
}
```

See also

▶ The *Using a significant-change location service* and *Location services in the background* recipes

Using a significant-change location service

In this chapter, we will learn how to use the significant location change monitoring feature.

Getting ready

Create a new **Single View Application** in Xamarin Studio and name it SLCApp. Add a label and two buttons on the view of the controller.

How to do it...

Perform the following steps:

1. Add the following ViewDidLoad method in the SLCAppViewController class:

```
private CLLocationManager locationManager;
public override void ViewDidLoad ()
{
  base.ViewDidLoad ();

  // Perform any additional setup after loading the view,
  typically from a nib.
  this.locationManager = new CLLocationManager();
  this.locationManager.LocationsUpdated +=
    LocationManager_LocationsUpdated;
  this.btnStart.TouchUpInside += (s, e) => {
    this.lblOutput.Text = "Starting monitoring significant
      location changes...";
    this.locationManager.
      StartMonitoringSignificantLocationChanges();
  } ;
  this.btnStop.TouchUpInside += (s, e) => {
    this.locationManager.
      StopMonitoringSignificantLocationChanges();
    this.lblOutput.Text = "Stopped monitoring significant
      location changes.";
  } ;
}
```

2. Add the following method:

```
private void LocationManager_LocationsUpdated (object sender,
CLLocationsUpdatedEventArgs e)
{
  CLLocation location = e.Locations[0];
  double latitude =
    Math.Round(location.Coordinate.Latitude, 4);
  double longitude =
    Math.Round(location.Coordinate.Longitude, 4);
  double accuracy = Math.Round(location.HorizontalAccuracy,
    0);
  this.lblOutput.Text = string.Format("Latitude:
    {0}\nLongitude: {1}\nAccuracy: {2}", latitude,
    longitude, accuracy);
}
```

3. In iOS Simulator, navigate to **Debug | Location | Freeway drive** on the menu.

4. Compile and run the app on the simulator. Tap the **Start monitoring** button to start monitoring for significant location changes.

How it works...

The significant-change location service monitors significant location changes and provides location information when these changes occur. In terms of power consumption, it is the less-demanding location service. It uses the device's cellular radio transceiver to determine the user's location. Only devices equipped with a cellular radio transceiver can use this service.

The code for using the significant-change location service is similar to the code of the standard location services. The only differences are the methods of starting and stopping the service. To start the service, we call the StartMonitoringSignificantLocationChanges method using the following line of code:

```
this.locationManager.StartMonitoringSignificantLocationChanges();
```

Location updates are issued through the LocationsUpdated event handler, which is the same event we use for the standard location service as follows:

```
this.locationManager.LocationsUpdated +=
  LocationManager_LocationsUpdated;
//...
private void LocationManager_LocationsUpdated (object sender,
  CLLocationUpdatedEventArgs e)
{
//...
}
```

There's more...

The significant-change location service can report location changes while in the background, waking up the app. It is very useful for apps that need to make use of location services, with a lower accuracy than that of the standard location services.

Significant-change location service availability

To determine if a device is capable of using the significant-change location service, retrieve the value of the `SignificantLocationChangeMonitoringAvailable` static property as follows:

```
if (CLLocationManager.SignificantLocationChangeMonitoringAvailable) {
  // Start monitoring for significant location changes.
  //...
}
```

See also

▸ The *Using region monitoring* and *Location services in the background* recipes

Location services in the background

In this recipe, we will discuss how to use location services while the app is in the background.

Getting ready

Create a new **Single View Application** in Xamarin Studio and name it `BackgroundLocationApp`. Just like we did in the previous recipes, add a label and two buttons on the view of the controller.

How to do it...

Perform the following steps to use the location services when the app is in the background:

1. In the **Solution** pane, double-click on the `Info.plist` file to open it. Under the **Source** tab, add a new key by clicking on the plus (**+**) sign or by right-clicking and selecting **New Key** from the context menu.

2. Select **Required background modes** from the drop-down list or just type `UIBackgroundModes` in the field.

3. Expand the key and right-click on the empty item below it. Click on **New Key** in the context menu. In its **Value** field, select **App registers for location updates**, or type the word `location`. Save the document. When done, you should have something similar to the following screenshot:

Property	Type	Value
BackgroundLocationAppViewCo ×	Info.plist	×
Bundle display name	String	BackgroundLocationApp
Bundle identifier	String	com.your-company.BackgroundLocationApp
Bundle versions string (short)	String	1.0
Bundle version	String	1.0
iPhone OS required	Boolean	Yes
Minimum system version	String	7.0
▸ Targeted device family	Array	(1 item)
▸ Required device capabilities	Array	(1 item)
▸ Supported interface orientations	Array	(3 items)
▾ Required background modes	Array	(1 item)
—	String	App registers for location updates

4. In the `BackgroundLocationAppViewController` class, enter the same code as the one used in the *Determining location* recipe of this chapter.

5. At the bottom of the `LocationManager_LocationsUpdated` method, add the following line:

```
Console.WriteLine("{0}:\n\t{1} ", DateTime.Now,
    this.lblOutput.Text);
```

6. Compile and run the app on the simulator. Tap the **Start** button to start receiving location updates.

7. With the simulator window active, press *Cmd + Shift + H*. This key combination simulates pressing the home button on a device and will move the app to the background. Watch Xamarin Studio's **Application Output** pad continuing the display of location updates.

How it works...

To receive location updates while the app is in the background, we need to set the `location` value to the `UIBackgroundModes` key in the `Info.plist` file. This basically makes sure that the app has the appropriate permission to receive location updates while it is in the background and that it will not get suspended.

If you open the `Info.plist` file in a text editor, this is what has been added:

```
<key>UIBackgroundModes</key>
  <array>
    <string>location</string>
  </array>
</key>
```

To make sure that the app is receiving location updates, check the status bar. The location services icon should be displayed even if the app is in the background.

There's more...

Setting the `UIBackgroundModes` key for location services is only needed for the standard location service. Both the region monitoring and significant-change location services support delivery of location updates while the app is in the background, by default. While one of these location services has started updating location data, the app can even be terminated. When a location update is received, the app is started or woken up from the suspended state and is given a limited amount of time to execute code.

To determine if an app has been started by one of these two location services, check the `options` parameter of the `FinishedLaunching` method in the `AppDelegate` class as follows:

```
if (null != options)
{
  if (options.ContainsKey
    (UIApplication.LaunchOptionsLocationKey))
  {
    Console.WriteLine ("Woken from location service!");
    CLLocationManager locationManager = new CLLocationManager();
    locationManager.UpdatedLocation +=
      this.LocationUpdatedHandler;
    locationManager.StartMonitoringSignificantLocationChanges();
  }
}
```

The `options` parameter is of the `NSDictionary` type. If this dictionary contains `UIApplication.LaunchOptionsLocationKey`, then the app has been started or woken up from the suspended state due to a location service. When this is the case, we need to call the `StartMonitoringSignificantLocationChanges` method on a `CLLocationManager` instance again, to retrieve location data.

The same applies to region-monitoring location service. Note that if we use either of these two location services, but our app does not support the background delivery of a location's events, we have to make sure that we stop monitoring location updates when they are no longer needed. If we do not, the location services will continue to run, causing significant battery drain.

Restricting to supported hardware

If our app's features are fully dependent on location services and cannot operate correctly on devices that do not support them, we have to add the `UIRequiredDeviceCapabilities` key in the `Info.plist` file with the `location-services` value.

Furthermore, when the app requires the use of the standard location service, which uses the GPS hardware, we need to add the `gps` value to the `UIRequiredDeviceCapabilities` key. This way, we make sure that the app will not be available through the App Store to the devices that are not equipped with the appropriate hardware.

UI updates while in the background

In this recipe, we deliberately set a value to the label's **Text** property while the app is in the background. However, updating the UI while the app is in the background should be avoided, because the iOS might terminate our app if there are too many updates. Furthermore, UI updates that occur in the background are basically being queued for when the app returns to the foreground and take place instantaneously when this happens. This may result in unexpected behavior in our app.

See also

▶ The *Determining location* recipe
▶ The *Creating an iOS project with Xamarin Studio* recipe in *Chapter 1, Development Tools*

Displaying maps

In this recipe, we will learn how to display maps in our app.

Getting ready

Create a new **Single View Application** in Xamarin Studio and name it `MapDisplayApp`.

How to do it...

Perform the following steps to display maps in the app:

1. Add `MKMapView` on the controller. The following screenshot shows the symbol for `MKMapView` in Xcode's object library:

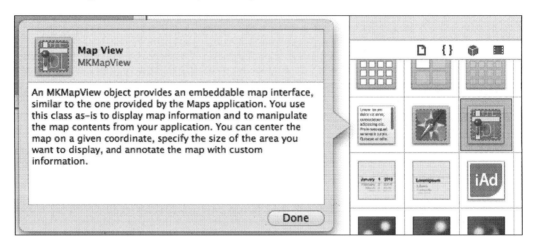

2. Add the following `using` directives in the `MapDisplayAppViewController.cs` file:

   ```
   using MonoTouch.MapKit;
   using MonoTouch.CoreLocation;
   ```

3. Enter the following code in the `MapDisplayAppViewController` class:

   ```
   public override void ViewDidLoad ()
   {
     base.ViewDidLoad ();
     this.mapView.ShowsUserLocation = true;
     this.mapView.RegionChanged += this.MapView_RegionChanged;
   }
   private void MapView_RegionChanged (object sender,
     MKMapViewChangeEventArgs e)
   {
     if (this.mapView.UserLocation.Location != null)
     {
       CLLocationCoordinate2D mapCoordinate =
         this.mapView.UserLocation.Location.Coordinate;
       Console.WriteLine("Current coordinates: LAT: {0}, LON:
         {1}", mapCoordinate.Latitude,
         mapCoordinate.Longitude);
     }
   }
   ```

4. Compile and run the app either on the simulator or on the device.

5. Zoom or pan the map by pinching on the screen (press *Option* and click-and-drag on the simulator) to output the current location in the **Application Output** pad.

How it works...

The `MonoTouch.MapKit` namespace wraps all the objects contained in the MapKit framework. The MapKit framework uses Apple maps to display maps.

`MKMapView` is the default iOS view that displays maps. It is especially designed for this purpose, and it should not be subclassed.

To display the user's location on the map, we set its `ShowsUserLocation` property to `true` using the following line of code:

```
this.mapView.ShowsUserLocation = true;
```

This activates the standard location service to start receiving location updates and handing them over to the `MKMapView` object internally.

 When `MKMapView` is first shown in an app, the system will prompt the user for the permission to use location services, just as if we were trying to use location services directly.

To determine when the user zooms or pans the map, we subscribe to the `RegionChanged` event using the following code:

```
this.mapView.RegionChanged += this.MapView_RegionChanged;
```

Inside the event handler, we retrieve the current location through the `UserLocation` property as follows:

```
if (this.mapView.UserLocation.Location != null)
{
  CLLocationCoordinate2D mapCoordinate =
    this.mapView.UserLocation.Location.Coordinate;
  Console.WriteLine("Current coordinates: LAT: {0}, LON: {1}",
    mapCoordinate.Latitude, mapCoordinate.Longitude);
}
```

If the `ShowsUserLocation` property is set to `false`, the location services will not be activated, and the `UserLocation.Location` property will return `null`. It will also return `null` when the app runs for the first time, as it will ask the user for permission to use location services. However, a map will be displayed as long as the device or simulator has an active Internet connection.

There's more...

We can set the center coordinate of the map to be displayed with the `SetCenterCoordinate` method as follows:

```
CLLocationCoordinate2D mapCoordinates =
    new CLLocationCoordinate2D(0, 0);
this.mapView.SetCenterCoordinate(mapCoordinates, true);
```

The first parameter is the map coordinates where we want the map to be centered at, represented by an object of the `CLLocationCoordinate2D` type. The second parameter declares if we want the centering of the map to be animated or not.

Apart from centering the map, we can also set its zoom level. We do this through the `SetRegion` method as follows:

```
this.mapView.SetRegion(MKCoordinateRegion.FromDistance(
    mapCoordinates, 1000, 1000), true);
```

The first parameter is of the `MKCoordinateRegion` type. Here, its `FromDistance` static method is used to create an instance. Its first parameter is the coordinate of the region's center, while the next two parameters represent the horizontal and vertical span of the map to display, in meters. It basically means that the region represented by this `MKCoordinateRegion` instance will have `mapCoordinates` at the center, and the horizontal and vertical part of the map will each represent 1000 meters on the map.

Note that `MKMapView` will set the actual region to an approximation of the values of `MKCoordinateRegion`. This is because the dimensions of `MKMapView` cannot always match the horizontal and vertical span values provided. For example, here, we set a square region of 1000 x 1000 meters, but our `MKMapView` layout is not an absolute square, as it basically takes over the entire screen. We can retrieve the actual region of the map that the `MKMapView` is displaying through its `Region` property.

See also

> ▸ The *Geocoding, Adding map annotations*, and *Adding map overlays* recipes

Geocoding

In this recipe, we will learn how to provide information about an address, city, or country based on location coordinates.

Getting ready

Create a new **Single View Application** in Xamarin Studio and name it `GeocodingApp`.

How to do it...

Perform the following steps:

1. Add an `MKMapView` on the top half of the view of `MainController`, a label, and a button on the bottom half.

2. Add the `MonoTouch.MapKit` and `MonoTouch.CoreLocation` namespaces in the `GeocodingAppViewController.cs` file.

3. Enter the following `ViewDidLoad` method in the class:

```
private CLGeocoder geocoder;
public override void ViewDidLoad () {
  base.ViewDidLoad ();
  this.mapView.ShowsUserLocation = true;
  this.btnGeocode.TouchUpInside += async (sender, e) => {
    this.lblOutput.Text = "Reverse geocoding location...";
    this.btnGeocode.Enabled = false;
    CLLocation currentLocation =
      this.mapView.UserLocation.Location;
    this.mapView.SetRegion(MKCoordinateRegion.FromDistance(
      currentLocation.Coordinate, 1000, 1000), true);
    this.geocoder = new CLGeocoder();
    try      {
      CLPlacemark[] placemarks =
        await this.geocoder.
          ReverseGeocodeLocationAsync(currentLocation);
      if (null != placemarks)   {
        CLPlacemark placemark = placemarks[0];
        this.lblOutput.Text =
          string.Format("Locality: {0},
            Administrative area: {1}",
            placemark.Locality,
            placemark.AdministrativeArea);
      }
    } catch (Exception ex) {
      Console.WriteLine("Error reverse geocoding location!
        {0}", ex.Message);
    } finally {
      this.btnGeocode.Enabled = true;
    }
  };
}
```

4. Make sure that the simulator's location is set to a stationary position. Navigate to **Debug | Location | Custom** (or **Apple**).

5. Compile and run the app either on the simulator or on the device. The result should be similar to the following screenshot:

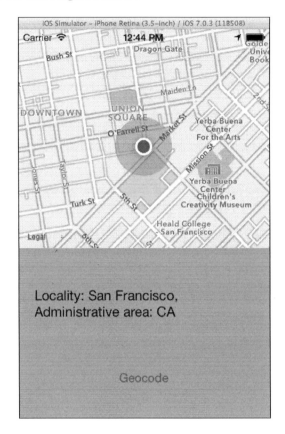

How it works...

Geocoding is the process of matching address information to geographic coordinates. Reverse geocoding is the opposite, matching geographic coordinates to address information. In this recipe, we are using reverse geocoding through the CLGeocoder class as follows:

```
private CLGeocoder geocoder;
```

After initializing the geocoder object, we call the ReverseGeocodeAsync method as follows:

```
CLPlacemark[] placemarks =
        await this.geocoder.
            ReverseGeocodeLocationAsync(currentLocation);
```

The method accepts a `CLLocation` parameter, which represents the location for which we want to retrieve geocoding data. The `return` value is an array of the CLPlacemark objects. The `CLPlacemark` class contains the reverse-geocoded information, such as the country, city, and address of the coordinates as shown in the following code:

```
CLPlacemark placemark = placemarks[0];
this.lblOutput.Text =
    string.Format("Locality: {0}, Administrative area: {1}",
            placemark.Locality,
            placemark.AdministrativeArea);
```

When reverse-geocoding a location, the array will always contain one item. If the return value is null, then an error has occurred.

There's more...

We can also use the `CLGeocoder` class for forward geocoding. For example, to get the coordinates of Apple's central offices, we use the `GeocodeAddressAsync` method as follows:

```
CLPlacemark[] forward =
    await this.geocoder.GeocodeAddressAsync("Infinite Loop, 1-5,
    Cupertino, CA, USA");
```

The method will give more accurate results when we pass as all the information that we have to it.

 Forward geocoding with the `GeocodeAddressAsync` method might return more than one item in the resulting `CLPlacemark[]` object. This is because the geocoder might not be able to determine the exact location through the passed information, so a set of possible results will be returned.

Things to have in mind for CLGeocoder

Apple provides the geocoding feature with a rate limit. Although the exact limit is not documented, it is recommended that you do not make more than one geocoding request per minute. If the rate limit is exceeded, the geocoder will fail with an error.

Obsolete API

The `CLGeocoder` class basically replaces `MKReverseGeocoder`, which only offered reverse geocoding until iOS 5.

See also

▶ The *Displaying maps*, *Adding map annotations*, and *Adding map overlays* recipes

Adding map annotations

In this recipe, we will discuss annotating a map to provide a variety of information to the user.

Getting ready

Create a new **Single View Application** in Xamarin Studio and name it `MapAnnotateApp`. Add `MKMapView` and a button on the view of the controller.

How to do it...

Perform the following steps to add annotations to a map:

1. Add the `MonoTouch.MapKit` and `MonoTouch.CoreLocation` namespaces in the `MapAnnotateAppViewController.cs` file.

2. Add the `IMKMapViewDelegate` interface to the `MapAnnotateAppViewController` class declaration using the following code:

   ```
   public partial class MapAnnotateAppViewController :
       UIViewController, IMKMapViewDelegate
   ```

3. Add the following code in the `ViewDidLoad` method:

   ```
   this.mapView.ShowsUserLocation = true;
   this.mapView.WeakDelegate = this;
   this.btnAddPin.TouchUpInside += (sender, e) => {
     CLLocationCoordinate2D mapCoordinate =
       this.mapView.UserLocation.Coordinate;
     this.mapView.SetRegion(MKCoordinateRegion.
       FromDistance(mapCoordinate, 1000, 1000), true);
     MKPointAnnotation myAnnotation = new MKPointAnnotation();
     myAnnotation.Coordinate = mapCoordinate;
     myAnnotation.Title = "My Annotation";
     myAnnotation.Subtitle = "Standard pin with Xamarin";
     this.mapView.AddAnnotation(myAnnotation);
   };
   ```

4. Add the following method in the `MapAnnotateAppViewController` class:

   ```
   [Export ("mapView:viewForAnnotation:")]
   public MKAnnotationView GetViewForAnnotation (MKMapView
     mapView, NSObject annotation)
   {
   ```

```
  if (annotation is MKUserLocation)
  {
    return null;
  } else
  {
    string reuseID = "myAnnotation";
    MKPinAnnotationView pinView =
      mapView.DequeueReusableAnnotation(reuseID) as
        MKPinAnnotationView;
    if (null == pinView)
    {
      pinView = new MKPinAnnotationView(annotation,
        reuseID);
      pinView.PinColor = MKPinAnnotationColor.Purple;
      pinView.AnimatesDrop = true;
      pinView.CanShowCallout = true;

    }
    return pinView;
  }
}
```

5. Compile and run the app either on the simulator or on the device. Tap the button to add a pin on the map. The result should be similar to the following screenshot:

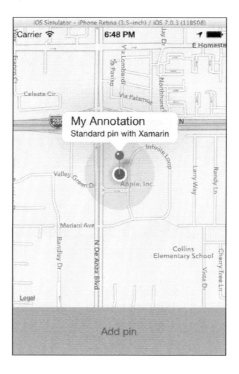

Tapping on the pin displays the callout bubble with the annotation title and subtitle.

How it works...

Annotating maps is very useful for providing a variety of information along with the map data. We can use the `MKPointAnnotation` class to create a simple annotation as follows:

```
MKPointAnnotation myAnnotation = new MKPointAnnotation();
myAnnotation.Coordinate = mapCoordinate;
myAnnotation.Title = "MyAnnotation";
myAnnotation.Subtitle = "Standard annotation";
this.mapView.AddAnnotation(myAnnotation);
```

We assign the annotation that will appear on the map coordinates, and optionally, a title and subtitle might also appear. We then add the annotation to the map view with the `AddAnnotation` method.

Just adding an annotation object to a map view is not enough. The annotation needs a view that will display its information. To provide a view for the annotation, we need to assign a delegate object to our map view. In this recipe, we are using our controller class as a delegate object for the map view as follows:

```
this.mapView.WeakDelegate = this;
```

We can assign any object that derives from `NSObject` to the `WeakDelegate` property. All we need to make it work properly is to make sure that we provide the necessary methods. Here is where the `GetViewForAnnotation` method comes in as follows:

```
[Export ("mapView:viewForAnnotation:")]
public MKAnnotationView GetViewForAnnotation (MKMapView mapView,
  NSObject annotation)
```

This method is found in the `MKMapViewDelegate` class and is called by the system when it needs to get a view for an annotation. The main difference in our implementation here is that instead of subclassing `MKMapViewDelegate`, we just use our controller as a delegate for our map view.

Inside the `GetViewForAnnotation` method, we need to make sure that we create and return a view for our annotation. As the map displays the user's location, there are two annotations on the map. We first need to check if the annotation object is `MKUserLocation` using the following code:

```
if (annotation is MKUserLocation)
```

In this case, we just return null. If the annotation parameter is of the `MKPointAnnotation` type, we first try to retrieve the view for it in a fashion similar to `UITableView` that creates the cells it contains, as follows:

```
MKPinAnnotationView pinView =
  mapView.DequeueReusableAnnotation(reuseIdentifier) as
  MKPinAnnotationView;
```

If the result of the `DequeueReusableAnnotation` method is `null`, we initialize a new instance for our annotation view using the following code:

```
pinView = new MKPinAnnotationView(annotation, reuseIdentifier);
pinView.PinColor = MKPinAnnotationColor.Purple;
pinView.AnimatesDrop = true;
pinView.CanShowCallout = true;
```

The view we create for the annotation here is of the `MKPinAnnotationView` type. This is the standard view that is represented by a pin on the map. The properties we set are pretty straightforward and define its appearance and behavior. The `PinColor` property defines the color of the pin, the `AnimatesDrop` property defines if the pin will be displayed on the map with an animation, and the `CanShowCallout` property defines if the annotation view will display the information of its underlying annotation in a callout bubble.

After we have created the view for the annotation, we just return it from the method using the following line of code:

```
return pinView;
```

There's more...

We can also create custom annotations and annotation views. For annotations, we have to override the `MKAnnotation` class, while for annotation views, we can override the `MKAnnotationView` class.

An annotation's performance

Theoretically, we can add as many annotations as we want to a map view. Although `MKMapView` can manage a large amount of annotations efficiently, it is strongly advised to take performance degradation into account. A way to overcome this is to display only the required annotations, instead of all of them. To do this, we can call the `ShowAnnotations` method, passing the specific annotation objects as an array using the following code:

```
this.mapView.ShowAnnotations(myAnnotationsArray, true);
```

See also

▸ The *Displaying maps* and *Adding map overlays* recipes

▸ The *Displaying data in a table* recipe in *Chapter 5, Displaying Data*

Adding map overlays

In this recipe, we will learn how to add a red circle overlay over a point on the map.

Getting ready

Create a new **Single View Application** in Xamarin Studio and name it `MapOverlayApp`. Add `MKMapView` and a button on the controller.

How to do it...

Perform the following steps to add overlays on the map:

1. Add the `MonoTouch.MapKit` and `MonoTouch.CoreLocation` namespaces in the `MapOverlayAppViewController.cs` file.

2. Add the `IMKMapViewDelegate` interface to the class declaration using the following code:

```
public partial class MapOverlayAppViewController :
  UIViewController, IMKMapViewDelegate
```

3. Add the following code in the `ViewDidLoad` method:

```
this.mapView.ShowsUserLocation = true;
this.mapView.WeakDelegate = this;
this.btnAddOverlay.TouchUpInside += (sender, e) => {
  CLLocationCoordinate2D mapCoordinate =
    this.mapView.UserLocation.Coordinate;
  this.mapView.SetRegion(MKCoordinateRegion.FromDistance(
    mapCoordinate, 1000, 1000), true);
  MKCircle circle =
    MKCircle.Circle(mapCoordinate, 250);
  this.mapView.AddOverlay(circle,
    MKOverlayLevel.AboveRoads);
};
```

4. Add the following method to the class:

```
[Export ("mapView:rendererForOverlay:")]
public MKOverlayRenderer OverlayRenderer (MKMapView
  mapView, IMKOverlay overlay)
{
  MKCircle circle = overlay as MKCircle;
  if (null != circle)
  {
    MKCircleRenderer renderer =
      new MKCircleRenderer(circle);
```

```
    renderer.FillColor = UIColor.FromRGBA(1.0f, 0.5f, 0.5f,
        0.5f);
    renderer.StrokeColor = UIColor.Red;
    renderer.LineWidth = 2f;
    return renderer;
  } else
  {
    return null;
  }
}
```

5. Compile and run the app either on the simulator or on the device. When you tap the
    button, the result should be similar to the following screenshot:

How it works...

While an MK MKAnnotation represents a point on a map, an MKOverlay object can
represent an area on a map. In this example, we use the MKCircle class, which inherits
from MKOverlay, to display a circle over an area on the map.

We initialize an `MKCircle` instance with its `Circle` static method using the following code:

```
MKCircle circle = MKCircle.Circle(mapCoordinate, 250);
```

The first parameter represents the coordinates of the center of the circle, while the second parameter represents the radius of the circle, in meters. After initialization, we add the overlay to the map view with the `AddOverlay` method as follows:

```
this.mapView.AddOverlay(circle, MKOverlayLevel.AboveRoads);
```

The second parameter of the `AddOverlay` method determines how the overlay should be rendered in relation to the map's information. There are two possible values, which are explained with the following accompanying screenshots:

- ▶ `MKOverlayLevel.AboveRoads`: This overlay will be displayed above the roads of the map, but below the map labels, as shown in the following screenshot:

- ▶ `MKOverlayLevel.AboveLabels`: This overlay will be displayed above both roads and labels on the map, but below annotations and 3D projections of the buildings, as shown in the following screenshot:

Unlike annotations, overlays require `MKOverlayRenderer` to display their information.

 Prior to iOS 7, overlays were shown with a view of the `MKOverlayView` type. This class is now deprecated.

To provide a renderer for our overlay, we use the `OverlayRenderer` method as follows:

```
public override MKOverlayRenderer OverlayRenderer (MKMapView
    mapView, IMKOverlay overlay)
```

Inside this method, we first check if the `overlay` parameter is of the type we want (in this case, an `MKCircle`) using the following code:

```
MKCircle circleOverlay = overlay as MKCircle;
if (null != circleOverlay)
```

Then, we create an instance of the `MKCircleView` class and return it as follows:

```
MKCircleRenderer renderer = new MKCircleRenderer(circle);
renderer.FillColor = UIColor.FromRGBA(1.0f, 0.5f, 0.5f, 0.5f);
renderer.StrokeColor = UIColor.Red;
renderer.LineWidth = 2f;
return renderer;
```

We set the appropriate properties that will define the appearance of our overlay. In this case, we set the `FillColor`, `StrokeColor`, and `LineWidth` properties.

There's more...

Overlays are handled efficiently by the map view. One important thing that the map view takes care of for us is that when we scale the map, the overlay is automatically scaled to match each zoom level. This way, we do not need to scale the overlay manually in code.

Creating custom overlays

We can create our own custom overlays. To do this, we need to override the `MKOverlay` class for the overlay and the `MKOverlayRenderer` class for the renderer.

Standard overlay objects

Apart from `MKCircle`, the other standard overlay objects are `MKPolygon` for creating polygon shapes and `MKPolyline` for creating polylines, like in a track-recording application.

See also

▸ The *Displaying maps* and *Adding map annotations* recipes

11

Graphics and Animation

In this chapter, we will cover the following topics:

- ▸ Animating views
- ▸ Transforming views
- ▸ Animating images
- ▸ Animating layers
- ▸ Drawing lines and curves
- ▸ Drawing shapes
- ▸ Drawing text
- ▸ A simple drawing app
- ▸ Creating an image context

Introduction

In this chapter, we are going to discuss custom drawing and animations. The iOS SDK contains two very useful frameworks for these tasks: Core Graphics and Core Animation.

These two frameworks simplify the process of animating UI elements and drawing 2D graphics on them. The effective usage of these two frameworks will make a difference between a dull and stunning app. After all, these two frameworks play a very important role in making the iOS platform unique in its kind.

We will learn how to provide simple or even more complicated animations for controls to provide a unique user experience. We will also see how to custom draw lines, curves, shapes, and text on the screen. Finally, with all the examples provided, we will create two drawing apps.

Animating views

In this recipe, we will learn how to take advantage of UIKit animations to move a `UILabel` on the screen.

Getting ready

Create a new **Single View Application** in Xamarin Studio and name it `ViewAnimationApp`. Add a label and button on the view of the controller.

How to do it...

Perform the following steps:

1. Enter the following code in the `ViewDidLoad` method:

```
this.lblOutput.BackgroundColor = UIColor.Green;
this.btnAnimate.TouchUpInside += (sender, e) => {
  RectangleF labelFrame = this.lblOutput.Frame;
  labelFrame.Y = 380f;
  UIView.Animate(1d, 0d,
    UIViewAnimationOptions.CurveEaseInOut,
    () => this.lblOutput.Frame = labelFrame,
    () => {
      this.lblOutput.Text = "Animation ended!";
      this.lblOutput.BackgroundColor = UIColor.Red;
    });
};
```

2. Compile and run the app on the simulator. Tap on the **Animate!** button and watch the label transitioning to the lower part of the view.

How it works...

The `UIView` class contains a number of various static methods that provide animation functionality. In this example, we simply change the position of a label with an animation.

To animate the change of the view, we call the static `UIView.Animate` method as follows:

```
UIView.Animate(1d, 0d, UIViewAnimationOptions.CurveEaseInOut,
    () => this.lblOutput.Frame = labelFrame,
    () => {
      this.lblOutput.Text = "Animation ended!";
      this.lblOutput.BackgroundColor = UIColor.Red;
    });
```

The following list explains the parameters of the `UIView.Animate` method, individually:

- **Duration**: This specifies the duration of the animation in seconds.

- **Delay**: This indicates the number of seconds before the animation starts. Set it to zero for the animation to start immediately.

- **Options**: This includes the various options for animation. In this example, we pass `UIViewAnimationOptions.CurveEaseInOut`, which applies an easing curve to the animation.

- **Animation**: This is an `NSAction` delegate with the changes that will be animated. In this example, we set the modified frame to the label as follows:

  ```
  () => this.lblOutput.Frame = labelFrame,
  ```

- **Completion**: This is an `NSAction` delegate, which will be called after the animation is complete.

We can combine multiple `UIViewAnimationOptions` values. For example, if we wanted the animation to repeat indefinitely, we would pass `UIViewAnimationOptions.CurveEaseInOut | UIViewAnimationOptions.Repeat`.

There's more...

Xamarin.iOS also offers an asynchronous method for `UIView` animations. This method is as follows:

```
await UIView.AnimateAsync(1, () => this.lblOutput.Frame =
    labelFrame);
```

However, there are no `delay` and `options` parameters with the asynchronous method.

Animatable properties

UIKit animations support a specific set of `UIView` properties. These properties are called **animatable** properties. Following is a list of `UIView` properties that can be animated:

- Frame
- Bounds
- Center
- Transform
- Alpha
- BackgroundColor
- ContentStretch

Transforming views

In this recipe, we will rotate a `UILabel` by applying a transformation. Furthermore, the rotation will be animated.

Getting ready

Create a new **Single View Application** in Xamarin Studio and name it `TransformViewApp`. Add a label and a button on the controller.

How to do it...

Perform the following steps:

1. Add the `MonoTouch.CoreGraphics` namespace in the `TransformViewAppViewController.cs` file as follows:

   ```
   using MonoTouch.CoreGraphics;
   ```

2. Enter the following `ViewDidLoad` method in the `TransformViewAppViewController` class:

   ```
   private double rotationAngle;
   public override void ViewDidLoad ()
   {
     base.ViewDidLoad ();
     this.btnRotate.TouchUpInside += async (sender, e) => {
       this.rotationAngle += 90;
       CGAffineTransform rotation =
       CGAffineTransform.MakeRotation((float)this.
         DegreesToRadians(this.rotationAngle));
       await UIView.AnimateAsync(0.5d, () =>
         this.lblOutput.Transform = rotation);
       this.lblOutput.Text = string.Format("Rotated to {0}
         degrees.", this.rotationAngle);
       if (this.rotationAngle >= 360) {
         this.rotationAngle = 0;
         this.lblOutput.Transform =
           CGAffineTransform.MakeIdentity();
       }
     };
   }
   ```

3. Add the following method:

   ```
   public double DegreesToRadians(double degrees)
   {
     return (degrees * Math.PI / 180);
   }
   ```

4. Compile and run the app on the simulator. Tap the button and watch the label rotate. The following screenshot displays that the label rotated 270 degrees:

How it works...

The `MonoTouch.CoreGraphics` namespace is a wrapper around the `CoreGraphics` framework. This framework is the basic graphics framework of iOS.

To rotate a view, we need a transformation object that will be applied to the view through its `Transform` property as follows:

```
CGAffineTransform rotation = CGAffineTransform.MakeRotation
    ((float)this.DegreesToRadians(this.rotationAngle));
```

The transformation object is an instance of the `CGAffineTransform` class and is initialized through the `MakeRotation` static method. This method accepts a float value of the angle of rotation we want to be applied, in radians. The `DegreesToRadians` method can be used to convert degrees to radians. After creating the transformation object, we assign it to the label's `Transform` property inside the animation handler as follows:

```
await UIView.AnimateAsync(0.5d, () => this.lblOutput.Transform =
    rotation);
```

Note that we need to increment the rotation angle each time the button is pressed, because the transformation we apply is not being autoincremented. If we apply another rotational transformation object with the same angle, there will be no effect since it is basically the same transformation.

When the label has been rotated to a full circle (360 degrees), we reset the `rotationAngle` value and the transformation object as follows:

```
this.rotationAngle = 0;
this.lblOutput.Transform = CGAffineTransform.MakeIdentity();
```

The `MakeIdentity` static method creates an identity transformation object, which is the default transformation of all views, before applying transformation objects to them.

There's more...

The `CGAffineTransform` class contains various static methods for creating transformation objects. These are as follows:

- `CGAffineTransformInvert`: This inverts a current transformation and returns the result
- `MakeIdentity`: This creates an identity transformation
- `MakeRotation`: This creates a rotation transformation
- `MakeScale`: This creates a scaling transformation
- `MakeTranslation`: This creates a translation transformation
- `Multiply`: This multiplies two transformations and returns the result

Transformation and Frame

After applying transformations on a view, its `Frame` property must not be taken into account, as its value will be undefined. If there is a need for altering the view's size or position after a transformation has been applied, use the `Bounds` and `Center` properties, respectively.

See also

- The *Animating views* and *Animating layers* recipes

Animating images

In this recipe, we will create a simple slideshow of images using the built-in animation feature of `UIImageView`.

Getting ready

Create a new **Single View Application** in Xamarin Studio and name it `ImageAnimationApp`. Add a `UIImageView` and two buttons on the controller. The sample project for this task contains three images. Add two or more images to the project and make sure that their **Build Action** is set to **Content**.

How to do it...

Perform the following steps:

1. Enter the following code in the `ViewDidLoad` method:

```
this.imgView.ContentMode = UIViewContentMode.ScaleAspectFit;
this.imgView.AnimationImages = new UIImage[] {
    UIImage.FromFile("Kastoria.jpg"),
    UIImage.FromFile("Parga02.jpg"),
    UIImage.FromFile("Toroni.jpg")
};
this.imgView.AnimationDuration = 3;
this.imgView.AnimationRepeatCount = 10;
this.btnStart.TouchUpInside += (sender, e) => {
    if (!this.imgView.IsAnimating) {
        this.imgView.StartAnimating();
    }
};
this.btnStop.TouchUpInside += (sender, e) => {
    if (this.imgView.IsAnimating) {
        this.imgView.StopAnimating();
    }
};
```

2. Compile and run the app on the simulator. Tap the **Start animating** button to start the animation.

How it works...

The `UIImageView` class can accept an array of `UIImage` objects and automatically display them in a sequence.

To load the images that the view will animate, assign an array of the images to its `AnimationImages` property as follows:

```
this.imageView.AnimationImages = new UIImage[] {
    UIImage.FromFile("Kastoria.jpg"),
    UIImage.FromFile("Parga02.jpg"),
    UIImage.FromFile("Toroni.jpg")
};
```

The sequence in which the images will be displayed is defined by their order in the array. After setting the images that will be animated, we set the duration of the animation in seconds and the number of times it will occur as follows:

```
this.imageView.AnimationDuration = 3;
this.imageView.AnimationRepeatCount = 10;
```

To start or stop the animation, call the `StartAnimating` or `StopAnimating` methods, respectively.

There's more...

There is no relation between the `AnimationImages` and `Image` properties of the `UIImageView` class. The image set to the `Image` property of the `UIImageView` class will not be displayed while the animation takes place.

Checking for animation

To determine if an animation is taking place, check the `IsAnimating` property of `UIImageView`.

See also

▶   The *Animating views* recipe

▶   The *Displaying images* recipe in *Chapter 2, User Interface – Views*

Animating layers

In this recipe, we will learn how to use the Core Animation framework to copy a `UILabel` on the screen by animating its layer.

Getting ready

Create a new **Single View Application** in Xamarin Studio and name it `LayerAnimation`. Add two labels and a button on the controller. Set the text and background color for the first label and a different background color for the second label.

How to do it...

Perform the following steps:

1. Add the `MonoTouch.CoreAnimation` namespace in the `LayerAnimationViewController.cs` file as follows:

   ```
   using MonoTouch.CoreAnimation;
   ```

2. Add a field of the `CALayer` type in the class as follows:

   ```
   private CALayer copyLayer;
   ```

3. Add the following code in the `ViewDidLoad` method:

   ```
   this.btnCopy.TouchUpInside += (s, e) => {
     this.lblTarget.Text = string.Empty;
     this.lblTarget.BackgroundColor = UIColor.Blue;
     this.copyLayer = new CALayer();
     this.copyLayer.Frame = this.lblSource.Frame;
     this.copyLayer.Contents = this.lblSource.Layer.Contents;
     this.View.Layer.AddSublayer(this.copyLayer);
     CABasicAnimation positionAnimation =
       CABasicAnimation.FromKeyPath("position");
     positionAnimation.To =
       NSValue.FromPointF(this.lblTarget.Center);
     positionAnimation.Duration = 1;
     positionAnimation.RemovedOnCompletion = true;
     positionAnimation.TimingFunction =
       CAMediaTimingFunction.FromName
       (CAMediaTimingFunction.EaseInEaseOut);
     positionAnimation.AnimationStopped += delegate {
       this.lblTarget.BackgroundColor =
         this.lblSource.BackgroundColor;
       this.lblTarget.Text = this.lblSource.Text;
       this.lblTarget.TextColor = this.lblSource.TextColor;
      this.copyLayer.RemoveFromSuperLayer();
     } ;
     CABasicAnimation sizeAnimation =
       CABasicAnimation.FromKeyPath("bounds");
     sizeAnimation.To = NSValue.FromRectangleF(new
       RectangleF(0f, 0f, this.lblSource.Bounds.Width * 2f,
       this.lblSource.Bounds.Height * 2));
     sizeAnimation.Duration = positionAnimation.Duration / 2;
     sizeAnimation.RemovedOnCompletion = true;
     sizeAnimation.AutoReverses = true;
     this.copyLayer.AddAnimation(positionAnimation,
       "PositionAnimation");
   this.copyLayer.AddAnimation(sizeAnimation, "SizeAnimation");
   } ;
   ```

4. Compile and run the app on the simulator. Tap the **Copy label** button to copy the contents of the first label to the second label, with animation. The following screenshot was captured while the process of copying was taking place:

How it works...

The `MonoTouch.CoreAnimation` namespace is a wrapper around the Core Animation framework.

Every view has a `Layer` property, which returns the view's `CALayer` object. In this task, we are creating an animation that graphically displays the contents of the label that are being copied from one label to another.

Instead of creating another label and moving it with a `UIView` animation, we will create a layer and move that instead. We create the layer by setting its `Frame` and `Contents` property; the latter is set from the source label's layer. We then add the layer to the main view's layer with the `AddSublayer` method. After this point, the main view contains a layer that displays the same contents and is on top of the source label. We will do all this with the help of the following code:

```
this.copyLayer = new CALayer();
this.copyLayer.Frame = this.lblSource.Frame;
this.copyLayer.Contents = this.lblSource.Layer.Contents;
this.View.Layer.AddSublayer(this.copyLayer);
```

To animate the transition from the source label to the target label, we will use the CABasicAnimation class. The highlighted part of the code in step 3 shows how to initialize and set up the instances of the class. The FromKeyPath static method creates a new instance, accepting the name of the layer's property as a parameter; this name will be animated. The To property represents the value to which the property will be animated. The Duration property represents the duration of the animation in seconds, while the RemovedOnCompletion property declares that the animation object should be removed from the layer when the animation finishes. The TimingFunction property sets the behavior of the animation. The AnimationStopped event is triggered when the animation finishes. Inside the handler we assign to it, we set the contents of the source label to the target label, thus completing the copy. The AutoReverses property states that when the value of the To property has been reached, the animation should be reversed. It is this property that gives the effect of the label getting bigger and subsequently smaller when it reaches its final position.

The animations start when they are added to the layer as follows:

```
this.copyLayer.AddAnimation(positionAnimation,
    "PositionAnimation");
this.copyLayer.AddAnimation(sizeAnimation, "SizeAnimation");
```

There's more...

A list of strings that the FromKeyPath method accepts can be found at https://developer. apple.com/library/ios/documentation/Cocoa/Conceptual/CoreAnimation_ guide/Key-ValueCodingExtensions/Key-ValueCodingExtensions.html#// apple_ref/doc/uid/TP40004514-CH12-SW2.

Apart from the To property, the CABasicAnimation class has two more properties for defining the animation: From and By. They are all of the NSObject type, but the actual values that should be assigned to them should be of the NSValue type. The NSValue class contains various static methods for creating instances of it.

Layers

Layers are very powerful and efficient objects that can be used for both drawing and animations. Using layers to perform animations on views, instead of the actual views themselves, is strongly suggested.

See also

▶ The *Animating views* recipe

Drawing lines and curves

In this recipe, we will implement custom drawing to draw two lines on a `UIView` class.

Getting ready

Create a new **Single View Application** in Xamarin Studio and name it `DrawLineApp`.

How to do it...

Perform the following steps:

1. Add a new class to the project and name it `DrawingView`. Derive it from `UIView` as follows:

    ```
    public class DrawingView : UIView
    ```

2. Add the following `using` directives in the `DrawingView.cs` file:

    ```
    using MonoTouch.CoreGraphics;
    using MonoTouch.UIKit;
    using System.Drawing;
    ```

3. Add the following constructor to the class:

    ```
    public DrawingView(RectangleF frame) : base(frame) {}
    ```

4. Override the `Draw` method of `UIView` and implement it with the following code:

    ```
    public override void Draw (RectangleF rect)
    {
      base.Draw (rect);
      Console.WriteLine("DrawingView draw!");
      CGContext context = UIGraphics.GetCurrentContext();
      context.SetLineWidth(5f);
      context.SetStrokeColorWithColor(UIColor.Green.CGColor);
      context.AddLines(new PointF[] {
        new PointF(0f, this.Bounds.Height),
        new PointF(this.Bounds.Width, 0f)
      } );
      context.StrokePath();
      context.SetStrokeColorWithColor(UIColor.Red.CGColor);
      context.MoveTo(0, this.Bounds.Height);
      context.AddCurveToPoint(0f, this.Bounds.Height, 50f,
        this.Bounds.Height / 2f, this.Bounds.Width, 0f);
      context.StrokePath();
    }
    ```

5. In the `ViewDidLoad` override of `DrawLineAppViewController`, initialize and add the view as follows:

```
DrawingView drawingView = new DrawingView(new
   RectangleF(0f, 20f, this.View.Bounds.Width,
   this.View.Bounds.Height));
drawingView.BackgroundColor = UIColor.Gray;
this.View.AddSubview(drawingView);
```

6. Compile and run the app on the simulator. The result should be similar to the one shown in the following screenshot:

How it works...

The `MonoTouch.CoreGraphics` namespace is a wrapper around the native Core Graphics framework. The Core Graphics framework contains the necessary objects for custom drawing on views.

To draw on a view, we have to override its `Draw(RectangleF)` method as follows:

```
public override void Draw (RectangleF rect)
```

Inside the `Draw` method, we need an instance of the current graphics context as follows:

```
CGContext context = UIGraphics.GetCurrentContext();
```

A graphics context is represented by the `CGContext` class. The `UIGraphics.GetCurrentContext` static method returns an instance of the current context.

The `CGContext` class contains various methods that allow us to draw on the view. We need to set the line width, the color, and then add the type of drawing as follows:

```
context.SetLineWidth(5f);
context.SetStrokeColorWithColor(UIColor.Green.CGColor);
context.AddLines(new PointF[] {
   new PointF(0f, this.Bounds.Height),
   new PointF(this.Bounds.Width, 0f)
} );
```

To add a line, we use the `AddLines` method that accepts an array of `PointF` structs, containing the start and end points of each line. Just adding the lines to the context is not enough. To present the drawing on the view, we call the `StrokePath` method as follows:

```
context.StrokePath();
```

To add another item to the drawing, we repeat the steps accordingly. The `MoveTo` method moves the current point so that the additional item will have a starting point for the curve.

There's more...

The `Draw` method is being called by the runtime when it needs to draw the contents of a view. We can only get the instance of the current graphics context inside the `Draw` method. We should not call it directly, since the `UIGraphics.GetCurrentContext` method will return `null` if we do. If we need to force the runtime to call the `Draw` method, we need to call `SetNeedsDisplay()`. Care should be taken when calling it, since drawing operations are expensive in terms of CPU usage.

When there is no need for causing the entire view area to be redrawn, we can call the `SetNeedsDisplayInRect` method, passing a `RectangleF` object in the coordinate system of the view area that we want to update.

Graphics context on a UIImageView class

The current graphics context of a `UIImageView` object is reserved for drawing the contents of the image. Calling `SetNeedsDisplay` on a custom view deriving from `UIImageView` has the same effect as calling the `Draw` method directly. If we need to draw on a custom image view, we have to either add another view on top of it and draw on that or draw on a custom layer and add it to the view's main layer.

See also

▸ The *Drawing text* recipe

▸ The *Creating a custom view* recipe in *Chapter 2, User Interfaces – Views*

Drawing shapes

Following the example from the previous recipe, we will draw a circle and square on the screen.

Getting ready

Create a new **Single View Application** in Xamarin Studio and name it `DrawShapeApp`. Add a custom view to the project, like we did in the previous task, and name it `DrawingView`.

How to do it...

Perform the following steps:

1. Override the `Draw` method of the `DrawingView` class and implement it with the following code:

    ```
    CGContext context = UIGraphics.GetCurrentContext();
    context.SetFillColorWithColor(UIColor.Blue.CGColor);
    context.SetShadow(new SizeF(10f, 10f), 5f);
    context.AddEllipseInRect(new RectangleF(100f, 100f, 100f,
        100f));
    context.FillPath();
    context.SetFillColorWithColor(UIColor.Red.CGColor);
    context.AddRect(new RectangleF(150f, 150f, 100f, 100f));
    context.FillPath();
    ```

2. In the `ViewDidLoad` method of the `DrawShapeAppViewController` class, initialize and display the view with the following code:

    ```
    DrawingView drawView = new DrawingView(new RectangleF(0f,
        20f, this.View.Bounds.Width, this.View.Bounds.Height));
    drawView.BackgroundColor = UIColor.DarkGray;
    this.View.AddSubview(drawView);
    ```

3. Compile and run the app on the simulator. The result on the screen should be similar to the one shown in the following screenshot:

How it works...

To draw shapes on a view, we need to call the appropriate method. We first set the fill color of the CGContext instance as follows:

```
context.SetFillColorWithColor(UIColor.Blue.CGColor);
```

To draw a circle, we call the AddEllipseInRect method, passing a RectangleF object that contains the bounding rectangle of the circle as follows:

```
context.AddEllipseInRect(new RectangleF(100f, 100f, 100f, 100f));
```

Whether the shape will be an ellipse or an absolute circle is defined through the bounding rectangle's size. We then call the FillPath method as follows:

```
context.FillPath();
```

The shadow effect is defined by the SetShadow method as follows:

```
context.SetShadow(new SizeF(10f, 10f), 5f);
```

The first parameter, which is of the SizeF type, defines the offset of the shadow, while the second parameter defines the amount of blur, in points.

There's more...

When the SetShadow method is called, all objects that are added to the context are displayed with a shadow. To remove the shadow, call the SetShadowWithColor method, passing either a fully transparent color or null for the color parameter.

Transparent colors

To fill a shape with a transparent color, create a `CGColor` instance with the appropriate values as follows:

```
context.SetFillColorWithColor(new CGColor(1f, 0f, 0f, 0.5f));
```

This will create a red color with its alpha value set to 50 percent.

See also

▶ The *Drawing lines and curves* recipe

Drawing text

In this recipe, we will learn how to draw styled text with an outline on a view.

Getting ready

Create a new **Single View Application** in Xamarin Studio and name it `DrawTextApp`. Add a custom view to the project, similar to the one we created in the previous recipe, and name it `DrawingView`.

How to do it...

Perform the following steps:

1. Implement the following `Draw` method override in the `DrawingView` class:

    ```
    CGContext context = UIGraphics.GetCurrentContext();
    PointF location = new PointF(10f, 100f);
    UIFont font = UIFont.FromName("Verdana-Bold", 28f);
    NSString drawText = new NSString("This text is drawn!");
    context.SetTextDrawingMode(CGTextDrawingMode.Stroke);
    context.SetStrokeColorWithColor(UIColor.Black.CGColor);
    context.SetLineWidth(4f);
    drawText.DrawString(location, font);
    context.SetTextDrawingMode(CGTextDrawingMode.Fill);
    context.SetFillColorWithColor(UIColor.Yellow.CGColor);
    drawText.DrawString(location, font);
    ```

2. In the `ViewDidLoad` method of the controller, initialize and display the `DrawingView` method as follows:

    ```
    DrawingView drawView = new DrawingView(new RectangleF(0f,
        20f, this.View.Bounds.Width, this.View.Bounds.Height));
    drawView.BackgroundColor = UIColor.DarkGray;
    this.View.AddSubview(drawView);
    ```

3. Compile and run the app on the simulator. The text will be displayed on the screen. The result should be similar to the following screenshot:

How it works...

The `NSString` class contains the very useful `DrawString` method, which draws the text it contains to the current context. To provide the outline effect, we call the `SetTextDrawingMode` method as follows:

```
context.SetTextDrawingMode(CGTextDrawingMode.Stroke);
```

We pass the `CGTextDrawingMode.Stroke` value. We then set the color and width of the outline to the graphics context and draw it text on the screen as follows:

```
context.SetStrokeColorWithColor(UIColor.Black.CGColor);
context.SetLineWidth(4f);
drawText.DrawString(location, font);
```

The `SetStrokeColorWithColor` method sets the color of the stroke, and the `SetLineWidth` method sets the width of the stroke. Calling the `DrawString` method of `NSString` draws the text in the graphics context in the specified location and with the specified font.

Similarly, to fill the text, we set the text drawing mode to `Fill` as follows:

```
context.SetTextDrawingMode(CGTextDrawingMode.Fill);
```

For the fill, we are not concerned about the line's width, so we just need to call the `DrawString` method once more as follows:

```
drawText.DrawString(location, font);
```

The `DrawString` method is overloaded. The overload we use here accepts a `PointF` struct, which represents the location of the string in the view's coordinate system and a `UIFont` instance that represents the font by which the text will be rendered on the screen.

There's more...

Drawing text on the screen with the `DrawString` method is very simple and the quickest way to do it. For more complex functionality, such as customizing the layout of the text, its appearance, and many more, we need to use the **CoreText framework**. This is accessible in Xamarin.iOS through the `MonoTouch.CoreText` namespace.

Size of the drawn text

The `DrawString` method of the `NSString` class returns the size of the bounding rectangle of the text. We can, however, get the size of the text before drawing it through the `StringSize` method as follows:

```
Console.WriteLine("Text size: {0}",
  drawText.StringSize(UIFont.FromName("Verdana-Bold", 28f)));
```

See also

▶ The *Drawing lines and curves* and *Drawing shapes* recipes

A simple drawing app

In this recipe, we will use the techniques we learned to create a drawing app.

Getting ready

Create a new **Single View Application** in Xamarin Studio and name it `FingerDrawingApp`. Once again, we will need a custom view. Add a class deriving from `UIView` and name it `CanvasView`.

How to do it...

Perform the following steps:

1. Implement the `CanvasView` class with the following code:

```
public class CanvasView : UIView
{
  public CanvasView (RectangleF frame) : base(frame)
  {
    this.drawPath = new CGPath();
  }
  private PointF touchLocation;
  private PointF previousTouchLocation;
  private CGPath drawPath;
```

```
private bool fingerDraw;
public override void TouchesBegan (NSSet touches, UIEvent
  evt)
{
  base.TouchesBegan (touches, evt);
  UITouch touch = touches.AnyObject as UITouch;
  this.fingerDraw = true;
  this.touchLocation = touch.LocationInView(this);
  this.previousTouchLocation =
    touch.PreviousLocationInView(this);
  this.SetNeedsDisplay();
}
public override void TouchesMoved (NSSet touches, UIEvent
  evt)
{
  base.TouchesMoved (touches, evt);
  UITouch touch = touches.AnyObject as UITouch;
  this.touchLocation = touch.LocationInView(this);
  this.previousTouchLocation =
    touch.PreviousLocationInView(this);
  this.SetNeedsDisplay();
}
public override void Draw (RectangleF rect)
{
  base.Draw (rect);
  if (this.fingerDraw)
  {
    using (CGContext context =
      UIGraphics.GetCurrentContext())
    {
      context.SetStrokeColorWithColor
        (UIColor.Blue.CGColor);
      context.SetLineWidth(5f);
      context.SetLineJoin(CGLineJoin.Round);
      context.SetLineCap(CGLineCap.Round);
      this.drawPath.MoveToPoint
        (this.previousTouchLocation);
      this.drawPath.AddLineToPoint(this.touchLocation);
      context.AddPath(this.drawPath);
      context.DrawPath(CGPathDrawingMode.Stroke);
    }
  }
}
}
```

2. In the `ViewDidLoad` method of the `FingerDrawingAppViewController` class, initialize and show the canvas as follows:

```
CanvasView canvasView = new CanvasView(new RectangleF(0f,
    20f, this.View.Bounds.Width, this.View.Bounds.Height));
canvasView.BackgroundColor = UIColor.Gray;
this.View.AddSubview(canvasView);
```

3. Compile and run the app on the simulator or on the device. Touch-and-drag your finger (or click-and-drag with the cursor) and start drawing. The following screenshot displays a sketch drawn in this app:

How it works...

In this task, we are combining touch events and custom drawing to create a simple drawing app. When the user touches and moves the finger on the screen, we keep the information of the touch location points and use them in the `Draw` method to draw lines.

After setting the touch locations to the class fields, we call `SetNeedsDisplay` to force the `Draw` method to be called. The `fingerDraw` variable is used to determine that the `Draw` method was called by a touch on the screen and not by the runtime when the view is first loaded.

Every time we call a method to draw something to a graphics context, the previous drawings in this context are cleared. To avoid this behavior, we use a CGPath object. We can add various drawing objects in CGPath and display these object on the screen by adding it to the graphics context. So, every time the user moves their finger on the screen, the new lines defined by the touch location points are added to the path, and the path is drawn on the current context.

Note that we need to hold information of both the current touch location and the previous one. This is because the AddLineToPoint method accepts one point, which defines the end point of the line, assuming that there already is a point in the path. The starting point of each line is defined by calling MoveToPoint, passing the previous touch location point.

The path that is drawn on the screen by sliding the finger on it is basically comprised of a series of consecutive straight lines. The result, however, is a smooth path that follows the finger movement, because the TouchesMoved method is triggered every time there is a single movement of the finger on the screen.

After adding the line to the path, we add it to the context and draw it in the graphics context, hence showing it on the screen as follows:

```
context.AddPath(this.drawPath);
context.DrawPath(CGPathDrawingMode.Stroke);
```

There's more...

Two new CGContext methods are introduced in this task: SetLineJoin and SetLineCap. The SetLineJoin method sets how each line will be joined to the previous one, while the SetLineCap method sets the appearance of the endpoint of a line.

The values that they accept are explained in the following two tables:

SetLineJoin	Description
CGLineJoin.Miter	Joins two lines with an angled corner
CGLineJoin.Round	Joins two lines with a rounded end
CGLineJoin.Bevel	Joins two lines with a squared end

SetLineCap	Description
CGLineCap.Butt	The line will end with a squared edge on the endpoint
CGLineCap.Round	The line will end with a rounded edge that expands beyond the endpoint
CGLineCap.Square	The line will end with a squared edge that expands beyond the endpoint

Clear the drawing

To clear the drawing, we simply have to set the `fingerDraw` variable to `false` and call `SetNeedsDisplay`. This way, the `Draw` method will be called without our custom drawing code, clearing the current context.

See also

▶ The *Drawing lines and curves*, *Drawing shapes*, and *Drawing text* recipes

Creating an image context

In this recipe, we will extend the finger-drawing app we created earlier by providing a save functionality for the drawings that the user will create.

Getting ready

Create a new **Single View Application** in Xamarin Studio and name it `ImageContextApp`. Add the `CanvasView` class we created in the earlier task to the project. Don't forget to change the namespace in the `CanvasView.cs` file to correspond to the namespace of the new project.

How to do it...

Perform the following steps:

1. Add the following methods in the `CanvasView` class:

```
public UIImage GetDrawingImage()
{
  UIImage toReturn = null;
  UIGraphics.BeginImageContext(this.Bounds.Size);
  using (CGContext context =
    UIGraphics.GetCurrentContext())
  {
    context.SetStrokeColorWithColor(UIColor.Blue.CGColor);
    context.SetLineWidth(10f);
    context.SetLineJoin(CGLineJoin.Round);
    context.SetLineCap(CGLineCap.Round);
    context.AddPath(this.drawPath);
    context.DrawPath(CGPathDrawingMode.Stroke);
    toReturn =
      UIGraphics.GetImageFromCurrentImageContext();
  }
  UIGraphics.EndImageContext();
```

```
        return toReturn;
    }
    public void ClearDrawing()
    {
        this.fingerDraw = false;
        this.drawPath.Dispose();
        this.drawPath = new CGPath();
        this.SetNeedsDisplay();
    }
```

2. Add two buttons on the view of the controller. One button will be used for saving the drawing and the other one for clearing the canvas.

3. Add the following code in the `ViewDidLoad` method of the `ImageContextAppViewController` class:

```
CanvasView canvasView = new CanvasView(new RectangleF(0f, 0f,
this.btnSave.Frame.Top - 10f, this.View.Bounds.Width));
canvasView.BackgroundColor = UIColor.Gray;
this.View.AddSubview(canvasView);
this.btnSave.TouchUpInside += (sender, e) => {
    UIImage drawingImage = canvasView.GetDrawingImage();
    drawingImage.SaveToPhotosAlbum((img, err) => {
        if (null != err)
        {
            Console.WriteLine("Error saving image! {0}",
                err.LocalizedDescription);
        }
    });
};
this.btnClear.TouchUpInside += (sender, e) => canvasView.
ClearDrawing ();
```

4. Compile and run the app on the simulator. Draw something on the canvas and tap the **Save drawing** button to save your drawing. Tap on the **Clear canvas** button to clear the canvas. You can then check the simulator's photo albums for your drawing.

How it works...

Using the `UIGraphics` class, we can create an image context through which we can retrieve our drawing in a `UIImage` object.

To create an image context, we call the `BeginImageContext` static method inside the `GetDrawingImage` method, passing the size that we want the image context to have, as follows:

```
UIGraphics.BeginImageContext(this.Bounds.Size);
```

The current context is now the image context we created with the `BeginImageContext` call. We then repeat the code we have in the `Draw` method; only this time, there is no need to add new lines to the path. We simply add the path that we already have to the context and draw it.

After adding the path, we get the context image by calling the `GetImageFromCurrentContext` method as follows:

```
toReturn = UIGraphics.GetImageFromCurrentImageContext();
```

Finally, we have to end the image context block and return the `UIImage` object as follows:

```
UIGraphics.EndImageContext();
return toReturn;
```

To clear the drawing from the screen, we simply have to set the `fingerDraw` variable to `false` and dispose and prepare our `CGPath` object for reuse inside the `ClearDrawing` method as follows:

```
this.fingerDraw = false;
this.drawPath.Dispose();
this.drawPath = new CGPath();
```

To reflect the clearing on the screen immediately, we call the `SetNeedsDisplay` method as follows:

```
this.SetNeedsDisplay();
```

There's more...

We cannot create an image context inside the `Draw` method. This is because when we call the `BeginImageContext` method, a context is actually created, but the view's default context remains as the current context. Hence, the `GetImageFromCurrentImageContext` method would return `null`.

Drawing on UIImageView

The technique discussed here can be used to draw on custom `UIImageView` objects. To display the drawing when the finger slides on the screen, we would simply have to set its `Image` property to the image we get from the image context.

Background on saved drawings

You will notice that although we are setting the `CanvasView` background to gray, the saved drawings are with a white background. This is because the view's background color is not included in the drawing. To include it, we would just have to draw a rectangle to the graphics context. This rectangle should be of the same color as the background color.

See also

▸ The *Drawing lines and curves, Drawing shapes, Drawing text,* and *A simple drawing app* recipes

12
Multitasking

In this chapter, we will cover the following topics:

- ▸ Detecting application states
- ▸ Receiving notifications for the application states
- ▸ Running code in the background
- ▸ Playing audio in the background
- ▸ Updating data in the background

Introduction

When the iOS platform was introduced in 2007, it brought lots of exciting new features for users and drastically changed the concept of mobile devices.

Despite its huge success, it lacked some features at the time, which were considered *basic*. One of these features was multitasking, that is, support for running multiple processes at the same time. The platform actually did support multitasking to system processes internally, but it was not available to developers. Starting with iOS 4, Apple provided support for multitasking, although it is still quite different from what most developers are accustomed to.

In this chapter, we will discuss how to make use of the platform's multitasking features. We will see under what circumstances we can use these features and what functionality we can provide to the users of our apps through multitasking. Specifically, we will learn about an application's states and its runtime lifecycle. Through a series of detailed example projects, we will be able to execute code while an app is in the background, support audio playback, and receive data updates.

Detecting application states

In this recipe, we will discuss how to detect the state of the application and respond accordingly when an application is transited from the active to the inactive state and vice versa.

Getting ready

Create a new **Single View Application** in Xamarin Studio and name it `AppStateApp`.

How to do it...

Perform the following steps:

1. Add the following method override to the `AppDelegate` class:

    ```
    public override void OnActivated (UIApplication
      application)
    {
      Console.WriteLine("Activated, application state: {0}",
        application.ApplicationState);
    }
    public override void OnResignActivation (UIApplication
      application)
    {
      Console.WriteLine("Resign activation, application state:
        {0}", application.ApplicationState);
    }
    public override void DidEnterBackground (UIApplication
      application)
    {
      Console.WriteLine("Entered background, application state:
        {0}", application.ApplicationState);
    }
    public override void WillEnterForeground (UIApplication
      application)
    {
      Console.WriteLine("Will enter foreground, application
        state: {0}", application.ApplicationState);
    }
    ```

2. Compile and run the app either on the simulator or on the device. Press the home button (or press *Shift* + *Command* + *H* on the keyboard for the simulator) to suspend the app and watch the **Application Output** pad in Xamarin Studio.

How it works...

The `UIApplicationDelegate` class contains methods that are triggered at specific notifications issued by the runtime. These methods are as follows:

- ▶ `OnActivated`: This method is called when the app is made active, for example, when unlocking the screen.

- ▶ `OnResignActivation`: This method is called when the app is about to become inactive, for example, when the screen is locked or when an incoming call takes place.

- ▶ `DidEnterBackground`: This method is called when the app has entered the background, for example, when pressing the home button. At this time, the app is suspended.

- ▶ `WillEnterForeground`: This method is called when the app is about to return to the foreground.

Note that when the app is moved to the background, both the `OnResignActivation` and `DidEnterBackground` methods are called. Similarly, when the app is moved to the foreground, both the `WillEnterForeground` and `OnActivated` methods are called.

All these methods contain one parameter, which contains the `UIApplication` instance of the app. The `UIApplication` class contains the `ApplicationState` property, which returns the state of the app as values of the `UIApplicationState` property. These values are as follows:

- ▶ **Active**: This indicates that the app is active

- ▶ **Inactive**: This indicates that the app is inactive, for example, when a notification alert is displayed

- ▶ **Background**: This indicates that the app is in the background

There's more...

There are cases where iOS will kill your app, for example, when a memory warning is issued and your app does not free up resources. The `WillTerminate` method will be called in these cases.

Proper usage

The preceding methods are very useful because they allow us to save the current data that is presented to the user when the app changes its state. When the app is transited to an inactive or background state, each method is given a limited amount of time to execute, so we should make sure that it does not perform long-running operations, or else, iOS will kill the app.

Receiving notifications for app states

In this recipe, we will discuss how to get notified when the application's state changes outside the scope of the `UIApplicationDelegate` implementation.

Getting ready

Create a new **Single View Application** in Xamarin Studio and name it `NotifyStatesApp`.

How to do it...

Perform the following steps:

1. Enter the following fields in the `NotifyStatesAppViewController` class:

    ```
    private NSObject appDidEnterBackgroundObserver,
      appWillEnterForegroundObserver;
    ```

2. Create the following methods:

    ```
    private void AddNotificationObservers()
    {
      this.appDidEnterBackgroundObserver =
        UIApplication.Notifications.
        ObserveDidEnterBackground((s, e) =>
        Console.WriteLine("App did enter background! App state:
        {0}", UIApplication.SharedApplication.
        ApplicationState));
      this.appWillEnterForegroundObserver =
        UIApplication.Notifications.
        ObserveWillEnterForeground((s, e) =>
        Console.WriteLine("App will enter foreground! App
        state: {0}", UIApplication.SharedApplication.
        ApplicationState));
    }
    private void RemoveNotificationObservers()
    {
      NSNotificationCenter.DefaultCenter.RemoveObservers(new []
        {
        this.appDidEnterBackgroundObserver,
        this.appWillEnterForegroundObserver
      });
    }
    ```

3. In the `ViewWillAppear` override, call the `AddNotificationObservers` method as follows:

    ```
    public override void ViewWillAppear(bool animated) {
      base.ViewWillAppear(animated);
    ```

```
    this.AddNotificationObservers();
}
```

4. In the `ViewWillDisappear` override, call the `RemoveNotificationObservers` method as follows:

```
public override void ViewWillDisappear(bool animated) {
    base.ViewWillDisappear(animated);
    this.RemoveNotificationObservers();
}
```

5. Compile and run the app on the simulator. Press the home button (or press *Shift + Command + H*), and watch the output in the **Application Output** pad.

How it works...

Apart from calling the methods of the `UIApplicationDelegate` object for app states, iOS issues notifications that we can receive. This is very useful, because in most cases, we need to be notified when the app's state changes outside the scope of the `AppDelegate` class.

To accomplish this, we use the `NSNotificationCenter` method through the `UIApplication.Notifications` class as follows:

```
this.appDidEnterBackgroundObserver =
    UIApplication.Notifications.ObserveDidEnterBackground((s, e) =>
    Console.WriteLine("App did enter background! App state: {0}",
    UIApplication.SharedApplication.ApplicationState));
```

This example only adds notification observers for the transition between the background and foreground. We can add more notification observers through the other available `Observe*` methods.

The result is similar to the example used in the previous recipe, but in this case, we get notified inside the scope of our view controller.

There's more...

To add notification observers when the app is activated or when it resigns activation, we use the `UIApplication.Notifications.ObserveDidBecomeActive` and `UIApplication.Notifications.ObserveWillResignActive` methods, respectively.

Removing notification observers

In this example, we call `RemoveNotificaitonObservers` inside the `ViewWillAppear` method. However, the method is not being called when the app is transited to the background but only when we display another view controller.

See also

▶ The *Detecting application states* recipe

Running code in the background

In this recipe, we will learn how to execute code in the background, taking full advantage of iOS's multitasking feature.

Getting ready

Create a new **Single View Application** in Xamarin Studio and name it `BackgroundCodeApp`.

How to do it...

Perform the following steps:

1. Enter the following code in the `AppDelegate` class:

```
private int taskID;
public override void DidEnterBackground (UIApplication
application)
{
  if (this.taskID == 0)
  {
    this.taskID = application.BeginBackgroundTask(() => {
      application.EndBackgroundTask(this.taskID);
      this.taskID = 0;
    });
    ThreadPool.QueueUserWorkItem(delegate {
      for (int i = 0; i < 60; i++)
      {
        Console.WriteLine("Task {0} - Current time {1}",
          this.taskID, DateTime.Now);
        Thread.Sleep(1000);
      }
      application.EndBackgroundTask(this.taskID);
      this.taskID = 0;
    });
  }
}
public override void WillEnterForeground (UIApplication
  application)
{
  if (this.taskID != 0)
```

```
    {
      Console.WriteLine("Background task is running!");
    } else
    {
      Console.WriteLine("Background task completed!");
    }
}
```

2. Compile and run the app on the simulator. Press the home button (*Command* + *Shift* + *H*) to make the app enter the background and watch the **Application Output** pad. Before the background task is completed (1 minute), bring the app to the foreground by either tapping on its icon in the multitasking bar or on its icon on the home screen.

How it works...

In the previous tasks, we learned how to get informed when an app gets transited from the foreground to the background and vice versa.

Multitasking on iOS is not quite what we are used to on other platforms. The iOS platform helps us makes sure that the foreground app will have all the available resources at its disposal (and the user's). To accomplish this, when the app enters the background, it is being suspended by the operating system. When it is suspended, it does not execute any code whatsoever.

If we want to prevent the app from being suspended when the user presses the home button, we can ask for background time. The time we ask for is limited to 600 seconds (10 minutes), which is more than enough for the majority of tasks we are likely to perform in the background (for example, saving the UI state, completing a file download/upload, closing any open connections, and so on).

To ask for the background time, we call the BeginBackgroundTask method of our UIApplication instance as follows:

```
this.taskID = application.BeginBackgroundTask(() => {
  application.EndBackgroundTask(taskID);
  this.taskID = 0;
} );
```

The method accepts one parameter of the NSAction type and returns an integer, which corresponds to the task ID. The NSAction parameter represents the block of code that will be executed just before the background time elapses. Inside that block of code, we have to call the EndBackgroundTask method, passing the ID of the task that was started, which will inform the runtime that we no longer need the background time. Each call of BeginBackgroundTask should be followed by a call to EndBackgroundTask. If we do not call this method and the background time elapses, the app will be terminated.

After calling the `BeginBackgroundTask` method, we can execute the code we want. To allow the `DidEnterBackground` method to complete and to avoid blocking the main thread, we just enclose our code to either an asynchronous call or in a separate thread. In this example, we use a thread from `ThreadPool`. As this specific task will be completed before the time in which we have the elapses, we call the `EndBackgroundTask` method to let the system know that the job is done. The block of code that we passed to the `BeginBackgroundTask` method will not be executed as we ended the task.

There are cases however, where the user might bring the app to the foreground while a background task is still running. To cover this scenario, we need to override the `WillEnterForeground` method and handle it in an appropriate manner. We can either stop the background task (by calling `EndBackgroundTask`), or provide some sort of feedback to the user that a task is still running. This scenario also makes the use of an asynchronous call to our code, which is the best practice. If the code of our background task is synchronous, then when the user brings the app to the foreground and the task is still running, the app will be frozen until the task is completed.

There's more...

To know how much time is left to perform the background tasks, we can check the value of the `BackgroundTimeRemaining` property as follows:

```
Console.WriteLine("Remaining time: {0}",
    application.BackgroundTimeRemaining);
```

Important considerations for the background code

The following are the important points to be considered when you are working with the background code:

- Do not update the UI while the app is in the background. Doing so may cause your app to terminate or crash. Any updates to UI elements that take place while the app is in the background are queued to be performed when it returns to the foreground. This will surely make the app unresponsive.

- Do not inform the user to bring your app to the foreground just to give more time to the task. Doing so will surely get your app rejected from the app store's approval process. If a background task is in progress and the user brings the app to the foreground, moving the app back to the background again basically continues the remaining background time.

- Perform lightweight operations in the background to avoid the runtime from killing your app.

- Avoid using external resources (for example, resources from the assets library).

See also

▸ The *Detecting application states* recipe

Playing audio in the background

In this recipe, we will learn how to prevent the app from being suspended in order to allow audio playback.

Getting ready

Create a new **Single View Application** in Xamarin Studio and name it `BackgroundAudioApp`. Add a button on the view of the controller. You will also need an audio file. In this example, an M4A file with a duration of 21 seconds is used.

How to do it...

Perform the following steps:

1. Double-click on the `Info.plist` file to open it. Select the **Source** tab at the bottom and add the `UIBackgroundModes` key (**Required background modes**) with the string value audio. The following screenshot shows you how the key and value are shown in the editor after they have been set:

▼ Required background modes	Array	(1 item)
	▬ String	App plays audio

2. Add the `MonoTouch.AVFoundation` namespace in the `BackgroundAudioAppViewController.cs` file.

3. Enter the following `ViewDidLoad` method in the class:

```
private AVAudioPlayer audioPlayer;
public override void ViewDidLoad ()
{
  base.ViewDidLoad ();
  NSError error = null;
  AVAudioSession.SharedInstance ().SetCategory
    (AVAudioSession.CategoryPlayback, out error);
  if (error != null)
  {
    Console.WriteLine ("Error setting audio session
      category: {0}", error.LocalizedDescription);
  }
```

```
      this.audioPlayer = AVAudioPlayer.FromUrl
        (NSUrl.FromFilename("sound.m4a"));
      this.btnPlay.TouchUpInside += (sender, e) =>
        this.audioPlayer.Play();
}
```

4. Add a sound file to the project and set its **Build Action** to **Content**.

5. Compile and run the app on the device. Tap the **Play sound** button and press the home button to make the app enter the background. Notice that the sound continues playing.

How it works...

To make sure that our app will be able to play the audio while it is in the background, we have to set the audio item in the UIBackgroundModes key in the Info.plist file.

In this example, we used the AVAudioPlayer class to play a sound file. Just creating an instance of the class and calling its Play method is not enough, though. We have to set a specific type for the audio session category. We will do this with the help of the following code:

```
NSError error = null;
AVAudioSession.SharedInstance ().SetCategory
  (AVAudioSession.CategoryPlayback, out error);
```

The static AVAudioSession.SharedInstance method returns the current audio session object. The audio session category is set to AVAudioSession.CategoryPlayback, which allows the AVAudioPlayer class to play sounds while the app is in the background. This requirement is specific to objects in the MonoTouch.AVFoundation namespace.

There's more...

The following are the available audio session categories:

▶ CategoryAmbient: In this category, sounds are silenced when the device screen is locked or when the device's silence switch is on. Sounds from external resources (such as the iPod app) are mixed with this category.

▶ CategorySoloAmbient: This is the default category. Sounds from external resources are silenced with this category. Sounds are silenced when the screen is locked or when the device's silent switch is on.

▶ CategoryPlayback: In this category, sounds are not silenced when the screen is locked or when the silent switch is on. Sounds from external resources are silenced but can be mixed if the MonoTouch.AudioToolbox.AudioSession. OverrideCategoryMixWithOthers property is set to true.

- ► `CategoryRecord`: This category is for recording audio. All the audio playback is silenced. The recording continues even when the screen is locked.

- ► `CategoryPlayAndRecord`: This category is for apps that need to record and play audio. Sounds from external resources are silenced but can be mixed if the `MonoTouch.AudioToolbox.AudioSession.OverrideCategoryMixWithOthers` property is set to `true`. Sounds continue to play when the screen is locked or when the silent switch is on.

- ► `CategoryAudioProcessing`: This category is specific to processing audio. Sound playback and recording is disabled in this category.

The background state for audio

Even when the app is configured through the `Info.plist` file to support the background audio playback, the app will be suspended when the playback is completed.

See also

- ► The *Location services in the background* recipe in *Chapter 10, Location Services and Maps*

Updating data in the background

In this recipe, we will learn how to make use of iOS 7's **background fetch** feature. This feature automatically wakes up the app at system-managed intervals, giving it a specific amount of time to retrieve data and update the UI.

Getting ready

Create a new **Single View Application** in Xamarin Studio and name it `BackgroundFetchApp`. Add a label to the controller.

How to do it...

Perform the following steps:

1. We need access to the label from outside of the scope of the `BackgroundFetchAppViewController` class, so create a public property for it as follows:

   ```
   public UILabel LabelStatus {
     get { return this.lblStatus; }
   }
   ```

2. Open the `Info.plist` file and under the **Source** tab, add the `UIBackgroundModes` key (**Required background modes**) with the string value, `fetch`. The following screenshot shows you the editor after it has been set:

3. In the `FinishedLaunching` method of the `AppDelegate` class, enter the following line:

```
UIApplication.SharedApplication.SetMinimumBackgroundFetchIn
    terval(UIApplication.BackgroundFetchIntervalMinimum);
```

4. Enter the following code, again, in the `AppDelegate` class:

```
private int updateCount;
public override void PerformFetch (UIApplication application,
Action<UIBackgroundFetchResult> completionHandler)
{
    try {
        HttpWebRequest request = WebRequest.Create
            ("http://software.tavlikos.com") as HttpWebRequest;
        using (StreamReader sr = new StreamReader
            (request.GetResponse().GetResponseStream())) {
            Console.WriteLine("Received response: {0}",
                sr.ReadToEnd());
        }
        this.viewController.LabelStatus.Text =
            string.Format("Update count: {0}/n{1}",
            ++updateCount, DateTime.Now);
        completionHandler(UIBackgroundFetchResult.NewData);

    } catch {
        this.viewController.LabelStatus.Text =
            string.Format("Update {0} failed at {1}!",
            ++updateCount, DateTime.Now);
        completionHandler(UIBackgroundFetchResult.Failed);
    }
}
```

5. Compile and run the app on the simulator or on the device. Press the home button (or *Command + Shift + H*) to move the app to the background and wait for an output. This might take a while, though.

How it works...

The `UIBackgroundModes` key with the `fetch` value enables the background fetch functionality for our app. Without setting it, the app will not wake up in the background.

After setting the key in `Info.plist`, we override the `PerformFetch` method in the `AppDelegate` class, as follows:

```
public override void PerformFetch (UIApplication application,
    Action<UIBackgroundFetchResult> completionHandler)
```

This method is called whenever the system wakes up the app. Inside this method, we can connect to a server and retrieve the data we need. An important thing to note here is that we do not have to use iOS-specific APIs to connect to a server. In this example, a simple `HttpWebRequest` method is used to fetch the contents of this blog: `http://software.tavlikos.com`.

After we have received the data we need, we must call the callback that is passed to the method, as follows:

```
completionHandler(UIBackgroundFetchResult.NewData);
```

We also need to pass the result of the fetch. In this example, we pass `UIBackgroundFetchResult.NewData` if the update is successful and `UIBackgroundFetchResult.Failed` if an exception occurs.

If we do not call the callback in the specified amount of time, the app will be terminated. Furthermore, it might get fewer opportunities to fetch the data in the future.

Lastly, to make sure that everything works correctly, we have to set the interval at which the app will be woken up, as follows:

```
UIApplication.SharedApplication.SetMinimumBackgroundFetchInterval(
    UIApplication.BackgroundFetchIntervalMinimum);
```

The default interval is `UIApplication.BackgroundFetchIntervalNever`, so if we do not set an interval, the background fetch will never be triggered.

There's more

Except for the functionality we added in this project, the background fetch is completely managed by the system. The interval we set is merely an indication and the only guarantee we have is that it will not be triggered sooner than the interval. In general, the system monitors the usage of all apps and will make sure to trigger the background fetch according to how often the apps are used.

Apart from the predefined values, we can pass whatever value we want in seconds.

UI updates

We can update the UI in the `PerformFetch` method. iOS allows this so that the app's screenshot is updated while the app is in the background. However, note that we need to keep UI updates to the absolute minimum.

See also

▸ The *Running code in the background* recipe

13
Localization

In this chapter, we will cover the following topics:

- ▸ Creating an app for different languages
- ▸ Localizable resources
- ▸ Regional formatting

Introduction

With the release of the iOS platform and the global software marketplace in the form of the App Store, Apple has made it easier for developers to distribute applications worldwide.

However, users worldwide will not even bother to download and use an app that is released in a language they do not understand. To broaden the user base for their apps, developers have to localize it. Localization is the process of translating text into multiple languages, providing resources specific to multiple regions, and thus creating an app that will target audiences of different cultures.

In this chapter, we will discuss the best practices to provide translated text that will be displayed according to each user's locale preferences. We will also see how to provide resources (images and videos) based on these preferences. Finally, we will use common .NET practices to format dates, currencies, and numbers.

Creating an app for different languages

In this recipe, we will create an app that will support two different languages.

Getting ready

Create a new **Single View Application** in Xamarin Studio and name it `MultipleLanguageApp`.

How to do it...

Perform the following steps:

1. Add two labels on the view of `MultipleLanguageAppViewController`.

2. Add two folders to the project. Name them `en.lproj` and `es.lproj`, respectively.

3. Add a plain text file in the `en.lproj` folder and name it `Localizable.strings`. Enter the following in the file and save it:

   ```
   // Localized output on MultipleLanguageAppViewController
   "Have a nice day!" = "Have a nice day!";
   ```

4. Add another plain text file in the `es.lproj` folder and name it the same as before: `Localizable.strings`. Enter the following in the file and save it:

   ```
   // Localized output on MultipleLanguageAppViewController
   "Have a nice day!" = "¡Qué tenga un buen día!";
   ```

5. Enter the following code in the `MultipleLanguageAppViewController` class:

   ```
   public override void ViewWillAppear (bool animated)
   {
     base.ViewWillAppear (animated);
     this.lblLocale.Text = string.Format("Locale: {0} -
       Language: {1}", NSLocale.CurrentLocale.
       LocaleIdentifier, NSLocale.PreferredLanguages[0]);
     string resourcePath = NSBundle.MainBundle.PathForResource
       (NSLocale.PreferredLanguages[0], "lproj");
     NSBundle localeBundle = NSBundle.FromPath(resourcePath);
     this.lblLocalizedOutput.Text = localeBundle.
       LocalizedString("Have a nice day!", "Localized output
       on MultipleLanguageAppViewController");
   }
   ```

6. Through the settings app on the simulator, set the language to English (if it is not set already) and run the app. The message will be displayed in English. Try setting the language of the simulator to Spanish (**Español**) and run the app again. The message will be displayed in Spanish.

How it works...

To make it easy for developers to provide support for multiple languages in apps, iOS reads text in different languages from the corresponding language folder. In this app, we support both English and Spanish. Their corresponding folders are `en.lproj` and `es.lproj`, respectively. When we call the `LocalizedString` method, it looks for and parses the `Localizable.strings` file to return the appropriate text.

The contents of the string files are defined by a set of quoted key-value pairs in a C style syntax, ending each set with a semicolon, as shown in the following code:

```
// Localized output on MultipleLanguageAppViewController
"Have a nice day!" = "¡Qué tenga un buen día!";
```

As you can see, we can also provide comments to assist the job of the person who will translate the text, even if we do it ourselves.

The `NSLocale.PreferredLanguages` static property returns a string array of the user's preferred language identifiers. The first item in this array is the currently selected language. If the selected language is English, it will return `en`; if it is Spanish, it will return `es`, and so on.

> Both these language codes are based on the ISO 639-1 standard. The three-letter ISO 639-2 standard is also supported. A list of all the available language codes can be found at `http://www.loc.gov/standards/iso639-2/php/code_list.php`.

The `NSBundle.PathForResource` method returns the path of the app bundle for the parameters we pass to it. We use this path to get the appropriate `NSBundle` instance, according to the selected language, as follows:

```
string resourcePath =
  NSBundle.MainBundle.PathForResource
  (NSLocale.PreferredLanguages[0], "lproj");
NSBundle localeBundle = NSBundle.FromPath(resourcePath);
```

We then call the `LocalizedString` method to display the appropriate text, as follows:

```
this.lblLocalizedOutput.Text = localeBundle.LocalizedString("Have
  a nice day!", "Localized output on
  MultipleLanguageAppViewController");
```

The first parameter's purpose is dual. It is both the key to look for in order to return the translated text and also the text that will be displayed in case the specified localization path is not found. The second parameter is the comment or any instruction we want to give to the translator. It is not displayed and basically not used. We can pass null to this parameter, and no error will occur. However, it is wise to always include a comment or instruction since it will help avoid confusion when translating multiple strings.

There's more...

It is advised to always provide keys that can act as the fallback text to be displayed in English, in case the language that the user has selected is not included in our app.

However, the `LocalizedString` method is overloaded. The second overload accepts three parameters. Consider the following example:

```
this.lblLocalizedOutput.Text = localeBundle.LocalizedString("Have
    a nice day!", "Have a nice day!", "Localizable");
```

The first parameter is the key to look for. The second parameter is the fallback value in case the specified localization path is not found. The third parameter is the name of the file containing the strings without the `.strings` extension. This overload is more helpful, and we can use different keys for our strings, which will help us identify where that particular string is used in the code. For example, in this case, we could set the key in the strings file to `MultipleLanguageAppViewController.lblLocalizedOutput`:

```
// Localized output on MainController
"MultipleLanguageAppViewController.lblLocalizedOutput" = "Have a
    nice day!";
```

Then, use it in our code as follows:

```
this.lblLocalizedOutput.Text = localeBundle.LocalizedString
    ("MultipleLanguageAppViewController.lblLocalizedOutput", "Have a
    nice day!", "Localizable");
```

This overload also helps us to separate our strings into multiple `.strings` files, passing the corresponding filename as the third parameter.

The last overload contains four parameters. The first three are the same as the second overload. The fourth parameter is simply the comment that we want the particular string to have.

Localization in real-world app scenarios

In this example, we use the `PathForResource` method to get an instance of the current locale bundle. This is because the values returned from the `LocalizedString` method are cached. In real-world app scenarios, where the app would be downloaded in a specific language and the user would most likely never change the language of the device to use it, just calling `NSBundle.MainBundle.LocalizedString` would be enough.

The localizable.strings encoding

The encoding of the `Localizable.strings` file should always be either UTF-8 or UTF-16.

Localizable resources

A localizable resource is content, such as images and sound files, which is specific to a locale. In this recipe, we will learn how to load and display resources based on the user's localization preferences.

Getting ready

Create a new **Single View Application** in Xamarin Studio and name it `LocalizableResourcesApp`. Add a label and a `UIImageView` on the view of `LocalizableResourcesAppViewController`. Two different images will also be needed, one for each locale. The images of USA and Spain are used in this example.

How to do it...

Perform the following steps:

1. Add two folders for the English and Spanish locales to the project (`en.lproj` and `es.lproj`).

2. Add one image in each folder. Make sure that the filename for the images is the same within both the folders.

3. Enter the following code in the `LocalizableResourcesAppViewController` class:

```
public override void ViewWillAppear (bool animated)
{
  base.ViewWillAppear (animated);
  this.lblLocale.Text = NSLocale.PreferredLanguages[0];
  this.imageView.Image = UIImage.FromFile
    (NSBundle.MainBundle.PathForResource("flag", "jpg"));
}
```

4. Compile and run the app on the simulator with English as the language selected in the *Settings* app. The result should be similar to the following screenshot:

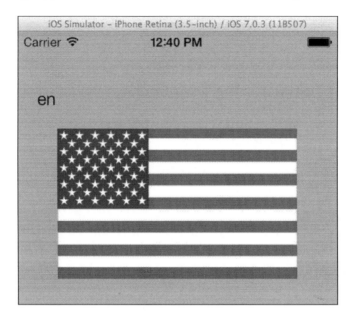

5. Now, set the simulator's language to Spanish and run the app again. The Spanish flag should be displayed instead, as shown in the following screenshot:

How it works...

The `PathForResource` method automatically searches for the appropriate language folder and loads the resource specified through its arguments. In this example, we pass the method's result to the `UIImage.FromFile` method in order to load the image and assign it to the image view's `Image` property.

There's more...

Apart from images, we can use the `PathForResource` method to load videos, PDF files, and any other localizable resource we need.

More information on localizable resources

We need to make sure the resource for the specific language folder exists. If it does not, an exception will occur. A way to avoid this is to add one universal image file in the project and use a `Localizable.strings` file inside each language folder, which contains the paths to the resources, as shown in the following code:

```
// US flag image
"flag_path"="en.lproj/flag.jpg";
```

To load the appropriate flag, we load the image with the `LocalizedString` method, as follows:

```
this.Image = UIImage.FromFile(NSBundle.MainBundle.
  LocalizedString("flag_path", "path/to/universal/image.jpg",
  "Localizable");
```

This way, the `image.jpg` image will be loaded if the corresponding language folder is not found.

See also

▸ The *Creating an app for different languages* recipe

Regional formatting

Regional formatting is the manner in which various information, such as currency, date, and time is displayed according to the different regions of the world. In this recipe, we will discuss how to display formatted numbers and dates according to the user's regional formatting settings.

Getting ready

Create a new **Single View Application** in Xamarin Studio and name it
`RegionalFormattingApp`.

How to do it...

Perform the following steps:

1. Add five labels on the view of `RegionalFormattingAppViewController`.

2. Enter the following code in the `RegionalFormattingAppViewController` class:

```
public override void ViewDidAppear (bool animated)
{
  base.ViewDidAppear (animated);
  this.lblLocale.Text = string.Format("Locale: {0}",
    NSLocale.CurrentLocale.LocaleIdentifier);
  this.lblDate.Text = string.Format("Date: {0}",
    DateTime.Now.ToLongDateString());
  this.lblTime.Text = string.Format("Time: {0}",
    DateTime.Now.ToLongTimeString());
  this.lblCurrency.Text = string.Format("Currency: {0:c}",
    250);
  this.lblNumber.Text = string.Format("Number: {0:n}",
    1350);
}
```

3. Compile and run the app on the simulator with regional formatting set to **United
   States** and **Spanish | Spain** under **Settings | General | International | Region
   Format**. The output for the United States regional format will be similar to what is
   shown in the following screenshot:

Locale: en_US
Date: Tuesday, March 18, 2014
Time: 1:09:47 PM
Currency: $250.00
Number: 1,350.00

The output for the Spanish regional format will be similar to what is shown in the
following screenshot:

Locale: es_ES
Date: martes, 18 de marzo de 2014
Time: 13:12:45
Currency: 250,00 €
Number: 1.350,00

How it works...

To format dates, currencies, and numbers, we use the standard .NET code. For date and time, the `DateTime.ToLongDateString` and `DateTime.ToLongTimeString` methods, respectively, return the values according to the locale.

For currency and numbers, we use C# numerical strings, as shown in the following code:

```
this.lblCurrency.Text = string.Format("Currency: {0:c}", 250);
this.lblNumber.Text = string.Format("Number: {0:n}", 1350);
```

There's more...

The `System.Globalization` namespace is supported in Xamarin.iOS. To display the current locale, consider the following line of code:

```
Console.WriteLine(CultureInfo.CurrentCulture.Name);
```

Note that there is one difference between the preceding code and `NSLocale.CurrentLocale.LocaleIdentifier`. The former uses a dash (-), while the latter uses an underscore (_) in the locale name.

14
Deploying

In this chapter, we will cover the following topics:

- ▶ Creating profiles
- ▶ Creating an ad hoc distribution bundle
- ▶ Preparing an app for the App Store
- ▶ Submitting an app to the App Store

Introduction

In this chapter, we will walk through all the required steps for preparing and installing the appropriate certificates on the development computer. We will also learn how to create the provisioning profiles that will allow us to deploy the app to a device, whether it is our own or someone else's, or send it to beta testers for installation on their devices.

Finally, we will see how to prepare the app for App Store submission and the process for its final release to the App Store.

Creating profiles

In this recipe, we will go through a step-by-step guide to creating and installing the appropriate certificates and provisioning profiles that are required for deploying an app to the device.

How to do it...

The following steps will guide you through the process of creating your developer certificate and appropriate provisioning profiles for an app.

We will start with the developer certificate, as follows:

1. Log in to the iOS Developer website at `http://developer.apple.com/ios`.

2. Go to the iOS **Provisioning Portal**.

3. Go to **Certificates, Identifiers & Profiles** from the menu on the right-hand side and click on **Certificates** on the next page.

4. Click on the plus (**+**) button on the right-hand side to add a new certificate. The following screenshot shows the settings page for the new certificate:

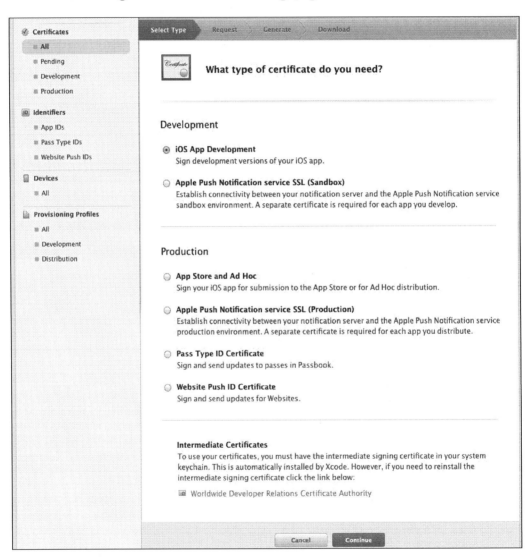

5. Select **iOS App Development** and click on **Continue**.

6. The next page provides information on creating a **Certificate Signing Request** (**CSR**) on your Mac. Follow the instructions to create a CSR and click on **Continue**.

7. On the next page, upload the CSR file and click on **Generate**.

8. After the certificate is generated, you will have the option of downloading it. Download it and double-click on the `.cer` file to install it. Keychain Access will open, showing the installed certificates on the machine.

Now that the certificate is installed, we need to set up Xamarin Studio to be able to use it. If you haven't already done so, close Keychain Access, as we don't need it. Perform the following steps:

1. Open Xamarin Studio.

2. Open **Preferences** (*Cmd + ,*).

3. Under the **Developer Accounts** option, click on the plus button to add your Apple Developer account.

4. Enter your Apple Developer account credentials and click on **OK**.

The following screenshot displays Xamarin Studio's **Preferences** window with a developer account already added:

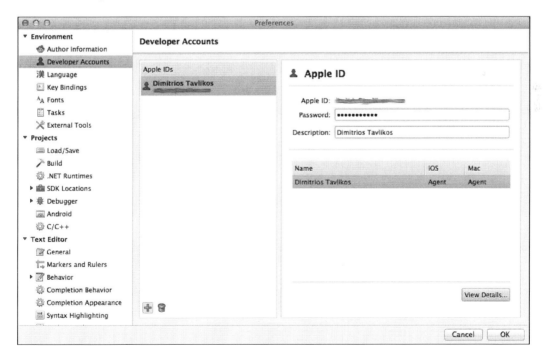

Now that we have issued and installed our developer certificate, we need to register the devices we will be using for debugging by performing the following steps:

1. Back in **Certificates, Identifiers & Profiles** of the Apple Developer portal, click on **Devices** on the left-hand side of the page.

2. Click on the plus button (**+**) to add a new device.

3. Enter a name for the device. If you are testing on multiple devices that do not belong to you, you will only be able to tell them apart by this name, so make sure it is something that will help you identify the device, for example, `Mike's iPhone 5s`.

4. Enter the device's **Unique Device Identifier** (**UDID**). You can find a device's UDID by connecting the device on your Mac and opening iTunes. Under the device's **Summary** tab, clicking on the serial number will display the UDID. Right-click on it and click on **Copy**. You can now paste it in the UDID field.

5. Click on **Continue**. The device is now added to your Apple Developer account and can be used for debugging and testing with your app.

We have created a development profile, set up Xamarin Studio, and added at least one device to our Apple Developer account. The next stage is to create an App ID and a provisioning profile, which will allow our app to be installed on a device.

Follow these steps to create an App ID:

1. In the **Certificates, Identifiers & Profiles** page, click on **App IDs** on the left-hand side of the page.

2. Click on the plus button (**+**) on the right-hand side to create a new App ID.

3. In the **App ID Description** section, enter a name for the App ID.

4. Select an **App ID Prefix**. If there is no available prefix, select **Generate New**.

5. In the **App ID Suffix** section, enter a bundle ID. As the instructions suggest, it is a good practice to use a reverse-domain name style string (for example, `com.mycompany.myapp`) for a bundle ID.

6. Click on **Continue**, and the App ID is created.

We are almost there. Now, it's time for the provisioning profile. Perform the following steps:

1. Click on **Provisioning Profiles** on the left-hand side of the page.

2. Click the plus (**+**) button on the right-hand side to create a new provisioning profile.

3. Check the **iOS App Development** option and click on **Continue**.

4. In the next page, select the App ID to which the provisioning profile will be bound and click on **Continue**.

5. After selecting an App ID, we need to select the developer certificate. After selecting the developer certificate we created earlier, click on **Continue**.

6. We now need to select the devices that the app can be installed on. Select one or more devices and click on **Continue**. It is important to note that the app will not be installed to devices that are not included here.

7. The final step is to give a name to the provisioning profile. Enter your preferred name and click on the **Generate** button.

8. After the provisioning profile is generated, we have the option of downloading it. Download and double-click on the `.mobileprovision` file to install it on your machine. Xcode will now open, with the **Organizer** window showing all the installed provisioning profiles on the machine.

We're done. We have successfully prepared our machine for iOS development and all the necessary provisioning profiles that will allow us to debug our app on a device!

How it works...

The process described in this recipe will allow you to deploy and debug your app on a device connected to your Mac. It will not allow you to distribute your app to beta testers or to the App Store.

The developer certificate is the certificate that allows the compilation of apps that will be deployed to devices. It is only meant for development, and one developer certificate corresponds to the enrollment of one iOS Developer Program.

Each provisioning profile holds information on what devices it can be installed on. An Apple Developer enrolled to the iOS Developer Program can add up to 100 devices and include them in a provisioning profile.

The App ID is the identifier of your app. Create one App ID for each of your apps.

The provisioning profile is the electronic signature that allows your app to be deployed to the device. Each provisioning profile corresponds to one app and holds all the appropriate permissions that will allow the app to execute on the device(s) included in it and the App ID information. It is also what distinguishes an app for development or distribution. Provisioning profiles are issued with an expiration time. At the time of writing this book, the duration of a provisioning profile is 1 year.

There's more...

To compile and debug an app on the device, select the developer certificate and provisioning profile in Xamarin Studio under the **iPhone Bundle Signing** node in project options, as shown in the following screenshot:

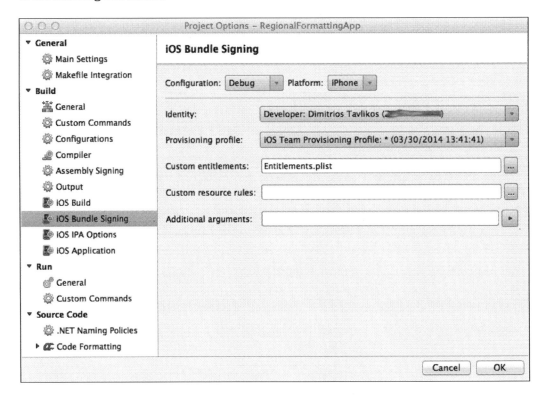

This has to be done for each build configuration (**Debug**, **Release**, and so on).

Under the **iPhone Application** node, set the **Display name**, **Bundle Identifier**, and **Bundle version** fields for your app. If you leave them blank, Xamarin Studio will set their values to default. Specifically, the **Bundle Identifier** field will be set to the one that is included in the App ID. However, if you set the **Bundle Identifier** field to something other than what is declared in the App ID, an error on compilation will occur.

Expiration of provisioning profiles

When a provisioning profile expires, the app does not work on the device any longer. You can either renew the existing profile or create a new one and install it on the device again.

See also

▸ The *Creating an ad hoc distribution bundle* recipe

▸ The *Compiling an iOS project* recipe in *Chapter 1, Development Tools*

Creating an ad hoc distribution bundle

In this recipe, we will learn how to create a bundle of our app. We will be able to send this bundle to beta testers so that they can test it on their devices.

Getting ready

To create an ad hoc distribution bundle, make sure you have created an App ID on the iOS Provisioning Portal for your app.

How to do it...

The process of creating ad hoc provisioning profiles is similar to the process of creating development distribution profiles. The following steps will guide you through the process:

1. Create a distribution certificate. For distributing apps to various devices that are not connected to your Mac, but also for submitting to the App Store, you need a distribution certificate to be installed. Follow the same steps described in the previous recipe for creating a developer certificate. This time though, select **App Store and Ad-Hoc** under the **Production** section when adding a new certificate. All the other required steps are the same.

2. Create a distribution provisioning profile. Follow the same steps described in the previous recipe to create a provisioning profile. This time though, select the **Ad Hoc** option in the **Distribution** section, instead of **iOS App Development**.

3. Download the provisioning profile and double-click on it to install it on your machine.

Now that we have all the distribution certificates and provisioning profiles ready, we need to create our ad hoc build by performing the following steps:

1. Open the project in Xamarin Studio. In this example, the `RegionalFormattingApp` project is used.

2. Select **Ad-Hoc** in the solution configuration combo box in the top-left corner, as shown in the following screenshot:

3. Open the project options, and under the **iPhone Bundle Signing** option, select the distribution certificate and provisioning profile in the list. Just make sure that you are selecting the certificate and provisioning profile for the **Ad-Hoc** configuration. In the following screenshot, the distribution certificate has been selected:

4. Under **iOS IPA Options**, make sure that **Build ad-hoc/enterprise package (IPA)** is checked.

5. Navigate to **Build | Rebuild All** on the menu bar to create the build.

The distribution build of our app is ready! It is time to share it with our testers. The following steps will guide you through the process:

1. On the Mac, open Finder and navigate to the `bin` folder of your project.

2. Open the `iPhone/Ad-Hoc` folder.

3. You can now send the `*.ipa` file, along with the provisioning profile file (`*.mobileprovision`) to the tester(s).

4. The tester(s) will be able to install the app by dragging-and-dropping both files in iTunes and syncing them with the device.

How it works...

For distributing apps, we need a distribution certificate. Just like the developer certificate, the distribution certificate is created once, but can be transferred to another Mac if needed.

The creation process of the ad hoc distribution provisioning profile is the same as the process of creating development provisioning profiles. The only difference is that we have the option of the type of distribution, which is either **App Store** or **Ad Hoc**. The `*.ipa` file is a file that is recognized by iTunes.

There's more...

There is also a third-party service that makes the distribution process very easy. You can create teams and upload different builds, notify your testers through e-mail whenever there is a new build, and most importantly, skip the iTunes syncing. You can find all the information at `http://www.testflightapp.com`. Note that TestFlight is for distribution only. The necessary certificates and provisioning profiles will still have to be created.

Syncing ad hoc app bundles with iTunes

Different users have different settings set up in their iTunes application. In case a user syncs the device and cannot find the app on the device, make sure the app is selected for syncing under the **Apps** tab of the selected device in iTunes.

See also

▸ The *Creating profiles* recipe

Preparing an app for the App Store

In this recipe, we will discuss the important steps we need to take for preparing an app for the App Store.

Getting ready

Follow the steps in the previous recipes to create an App Store distribution profile for your app.

How to do it...

One very important step in the preparation of the App Store regards the images that should be included in your app.

The most important image is the app icon. This is the icon that will represent your app on the users' devices. Depending on the target device, the dimensions of the icon should be different. Xamarin Studio makes this process easy by providing specific slots for assigning the icon for each target device/platform. For example, the icon size for an iPhone 3s is different from the size for an iPhone 4s, as is the icon for an iPhone 5 or a later device running on iOS 7.

The following steps will guide you through the process:

1. Double-click on the `Info.plist` file of your project to open the file in the embedded editor. The following screenshot shows all the available options for app icons in a universal (iPhone and iPad) app:

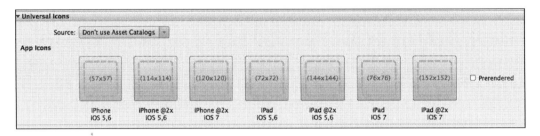

2. Click on each corresponding icon to assign the icon. The icons must be in the PNG format.

3. Now that we have set the app icon, we need to set a launch image.

4. The launch image is the first thing that is displayed when an app starts. Prepare a launch image in at least two dimensions for the iPhone and iPod Touch apps: 320 x 480 pixels for the lower resolution version, 640 x 960 pixels for the higher resolution version, and 640 x 1136 pixels for the 4-inch devices (iPhone 5, iPhone 5s, and so on).

5. Click on the corresponding box in the `Info.plist` editor to set the launch image.

We now have to set the iTunes Artwork image. This is a 512 x 512 and 1024 x 1024 image that will be displayed on our app's page on iTunes. It can be whatever you want; however, a good practice is to make it the same as the app icon. Just click on the corresponding button in the `Info.plist` file to assign the iTunes Artwork images.

How it works...

The application icons are very important. It is what the user will see on the device's screen and tap to start your app. Although all app icons appear as buttons with rounded corners and a lighting effect, you should not include these graphical features in your icons. These graphical features are automatically rendered upon app submission to the App Store. The icons should be perfect squares. Also, always provide a background for the icons. Do not use transparencies, because any transparencies on the icon will be displayed with black color, potentially destroying your intended icon appearance.

The launch image is displayed first when the app starts. When a screen goes blank at startup, it means there is no launch image. According to Apple's **iOS Human Interface Guidelines** (`https://developer.apple.com/library/ios/documentation/UserExperience/Conceptual/MobileHIG/index.html`), this image should be the first screen that is loaded when the app completes the launch process and is ready to accept input. It should only contain the static content of the first screen and not the content that is likely to change, like localized text.

There's more...

It is not mandatory to create your app icon for each available slot in the editor. In fact, even if you just create only one low-resolution icon, it will be acceptable, and you will be able to upload your app to the App Store. Its quality though, when installed on a high-resolution device such as the iPad Air, is not going to be top-notch. This is not good for the reputation of both the app and its developer, unfortunately.

The 4-inch screen launch image

As you may have already noticed, the `Info.plist` editor has a launch image already set for retina (4-inch) screens, which is a plain black background. This is because when the iPhone 5 was first launched, it was a device with a screen height that was different from that of the previous models.

The way Apple chose to help developers easily support the taller screen required developers to include a launch image in the dimensions of the new screen. This way, iOS automatically sizes the view controllers to the new screen size upon startup. By including this blank launch image by default, Xamarin Studio makes our life easier so that all our projects appear properly on the 4-inch devices.

See also

▸ The *Creating profiles* recipe

Submitting an app to the App Store

In this recipe, we will go through the required steps to submit an app to the App Store.

Getting ready

For this recipe, you will need to have your zipped distribution app bundle ready.

How to do it...

Perform the following steps for submitting your app to the App Store:

1. Prepare up to five screenshots that display various aspects of your app. For iPhone/iPod Touch apps, the dimensions should be 640 x 1136 px for portrait and 1136 x 640 px for landscape orientations.

2. Prepare the text that best describes your app. Try to include the most significant features. Remember, the description is what the users will read before downloading the app, so the more appealing it is, the better.

Prepare keywords that will help your app climb on top of the search results. Both app description and keywords are required.

3. iTunes Connect is the developer portal for managing and submitting apps (among other App Store-related stuff). Log in to iTunes Connect (`http://itunesconnect.apple.com`) with your Apple Developer ID. Click on the **Manage your Applications** link. Then, click on the **Add New App** button on the top-left corner. Follow the steps to complete the app's preparation on the portal. When you finish, make sure the app's status is **Waiting for Upload**.

4. After you have created a new app on the portal, you can upload the zipped app bundle with the Application Loader. It is installed by default with Xcode, and can be found under `/Developer/Application/Utilities`, or by searching through the Spotlight.

When you start Application Loader, it will ask you to log in with your Apple Developer ID. After logging in, you will be presented with the following window:

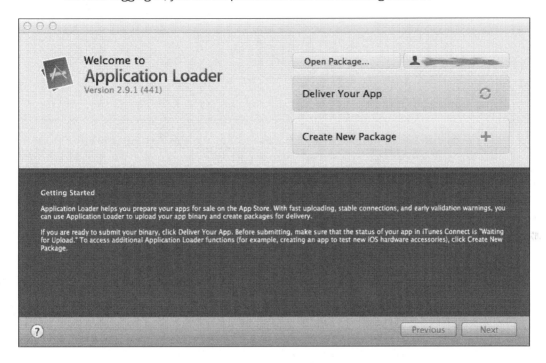

5. Click on the **Deliver Your App** button, and it will connect to iTunes Connect, find the apps you have in the **Waiting for Upload** status, and load them in the list box.

6. You will then be presented with a summary view of your app.

7. Click on the **Choose...** button, and a dialog box will appear that will allow you to select the zipped app bundle. After selecting it, proceed with the upload.

You are all set! If all steps have been completed correctly, the app will be uploaded, and it will be under review for release on the App Store.

How it works...

App screenshots can be in JPG, TIF, or PNG formats, in RGB color, and at a resolution of at least 72 DPI.

However, the images are important only when users are already viewing your app in the App Store. The keywords and description are the parameters that will allow your app to come up higher on search results and make the user decide whether the app is worth the download. Regarding the keywords, choose them wisely. Do not include as many as you can; fewer keywords that reflect the key aspects of the app are always better.

iTunes Connect is the developer portal for managing applications, reviewing financial data, app downloads, and it includes the contracts and agreements a developer needs to sign. Make sure you read and accept the contracts, or else you will not be able to proceed with the app's preparation process. During this process, you are required to provide the necessary information, for your app it includes, the price range if it is a paid app, the countries in which it will be available, as well as the release date for it if you do not want it to be released automatically as soon as it has passed through the App Store review process.

When everything is set up correctly and the app's status is **Waiting for Upload**, you can then run the Application Loader to upload it. Periodically and with each release of iOS and iOS SDK versions, various components or procedures change. Always make sure that your iOS SDK version is up-to-date.

There's more...

At some point in the app's preparation process, you will be required to enter a **Stock Keeping Unit (SKU)** number. This number is a unique identifier for each product or service. It can be any number you want, but keep a specific pattern to keep track of the identifiers, for example, when you develop additional apps.

See also

▶   The *Preparing an app for the App Store* recipe

15
Advanced Features

In this chapter, we will cover the following topics:

- ▶ Reproducing the page curl effect
- ▶ Integrating content sharing
- ▶ Implementing custom transitions
- ▶ Using physics in UI elements
- ▶ Implementing the text-to-speech feature

Introduction

In this chapter, we will explore only some of the huge variety of advanced features that the iOS platform has to offer.

Specifically, we will create a project that displays content separated into pages, which the user can navigate through like in a normal book, with the help of the newly introduced `UIPageViewController` class.

We will then discuss integrating content-sharing features and providing share/post functionality in our app with the help of `UIActivityViewController`. For the user interface, we will explore some basic aspects of **UIKit Dynamics** that allows rich animations for a better user experience. We will also learn how to provide custom transitions between view controllers.

In the last recipe of this chapter, we will work with the new text-to-speech feature and create an app that speaks, with the help of the `AVSpeechSynthesizer` class!

Reproducing the page curl effect

In this recipe, we will create an app that displays content like that of a book with the help of the `UIPageViewController` class.

Getting ready

Create a new **Single View Application** in Xamarin Studio and name it `BookApp`. Add another controller to the project and name it `Page`. Configure the appearance of the `Page` controller however you like. In the source code for this recipe, the contains a `UIImageView` and a `UILabel`.

How to do it...

Perform the following steps:

1. Enter the following code in the `BookAppViewController` class:

```
private UIPageViewController pageViewController;
private int pageCount = 3;
public override void ViewDidLoad ()
{
  base.ViewDidLoad ();
  Page firstPage = new Page(0);
  this.pageViewController = new
    UIPageViewController(
    UIPageViewControllerTransitionStyle.PageCurl,
    UIPageViewControllerNavigationOrientation.Horizontal,
    UIPageViewControllerSpineLocation.Min);
  this.pageViewController.SetViewControllers(new
    UIViewController[] { firstPage },
    UIPageViewControllerNavigationDirection.Forward,
    false, s => { });
  this.pageViewController.GetNextViewController =
    this.GetNextViewController;
  this.pageViewController.GetPreviousViewController =
    this.GetPreviousViewController;
  this.pageViewController.View.Frame = this.View.Bounds;
  this.View.AddSubview(this.pageViewController.View);
}

private UIViewController
  GetNextViewController(UIPageViewController
  pageController, UIViewController referenceViewController)
```

```
{

    Page currentPageController = referenceViewController as
      Page;

    if (currentPageController.PageIndex >= (this.pageCount -
      1))
    {

      return null;

    } else
    {
      int nextPageIndex = currentPageController.
        PageIndex + 1;
      return new Page(nextPageIndex);

    }
}

private UIViewController
  GetPreviousViewController(UIPageViewController
  pageController, UIViewController referenceViewController)
{

    Page currentPageController = referenceViewController as
      Page;
    if (currentPageController.PageIndex <= 0)
    {
      return null;
    } else
    {

      int previousPageIndex = currentPageController.
        PageIndex - 1;

      return new Page(previousPageIndex);

    }
}
```

2. Add a property to the `Page` class and change its constructor, as shown in the following code:

```
public Page (int pageIndex) : base ("Page", null)
{
```

```
        this.PageIndex = pageIndex;
    }

    public int PageIndex
    {
      get;
      private set;
    }
```

3. Finally, configure the content that will be displayed in `Page`, in the `ViewDidLoad` method:

```
this.imgView.Image =
  UIImage.FromFile(string.Format("images/{0}.jpg",
  this.PageIndex + 1));
  this.lblPageNumber.Text = string.Format("Page {0}",
    this.PageIndex + 1);
```

4. Compile and run the app on the simulator. Click-and-drag the cursor on the simulator's screen area to change the page. The result should look similar to the following screenshot:

How it works...

The `UIPageViewController` class introduced with iOS 5 was a desired component by many developers. It allows us to navigate through content with the effect of a real book, like in Apple's *iBooks* app.

We initialize it with the following line:

```
this.pageViewController = new
    UIPageViewController(UIPageViewControllerTransitionStyle.
    PageCurl, UIPageViewControllerNavigationOrientation.Horizontal,
    UIPageViewControllerSpineLocation.Min);
```

The first parameter of the constructor determines the type of the effect. The only available value right now is `PageCurl`. The second parameter determines the orientation of the effect. The `Horizontal` parameter is the value for the effect similar to a book, while `Vertical` is the value for the effect similar to a notebook, where the pages are bound at the top. The third parameter determines the position of the bind of the book. The `Min` parameter declares that the bind is on one edge of the screen (in this case, on the left-hand side).

After initializing the page controller, we need to set its first page by calling its `SetViewControllers` method, as shown in the following code:

```
this.pageViewController.SetViewControllers(new UIViewController[]
    { firstPage }, UIPageViewControllerNavigationDirection.Forward,
    false, s => { });
```

The method's first parameter is an array of `UIViewController` objects. We can set either one or two controllers for this parameter, depending on the device's orientation. For example, if the app supports landscape orientation, we might want to show two pages at the same time. The second parameter basically determines the navigation direction of the included pages. The `Forward` parameter means the next page will be loaded if we swipe from right to left on the screen, while `Reverse` means the previous page will be loaded for the same swipe. The last parameter is of delegate type `UICompletionHandler` and represents the handler to be executed after the controllers have been added. In this example, we do not need it, so we just pass an empty lambda.

Next, we need to provide the data source for the rest of the pages of our "book." Once again, Xamarin simplifies things for us by providing two very helpful properties for us to use: `GetNextViewController` and `GetPreviousViewController`. These properties merely represent the callback methods we would have to override if we were creating a delegate object for the page controller. Apart from their names, the signatures of these two methods are identical, as shown in the following code:

```
UIViewController GetNextViewController(UIPageViewController
    pageController, UIViewController referenceViewController);
UIViewController GetPreviousViewController(UIPageViewController
    pageController, UIViewController referenceViewController);
```

The first parameter gives us the page controller, while the second parameter gives us the controller that is currently displayed on screen when the method is called.

In the implementation of these methods, we simply have to return the controller that should be loaded after or before the current one. If we do not want the effect to be activated, we just return `null`.

Last but not least, we set the size of the page controller's view and add it to a superview so it will be displayed, using the following code:

```
this.pageViewController.View.Frame = this.View.Bounds;
    this.View.AddSubview(this.pageViewController.View);
```

There's more...

If we would like our app to support landscape orientation, we would first have to implement the `ShouldAutoRotate` and `GetSupportedInterfaceOrientations` methods in the `BookAppViewController` class. Secondly, we would have to provide two view controllers to the `SetViewControllers` method of the `UIPageViewController` class.

Double-sided pages

As you might have noticed in the previous screenshot of this recipe, when we turn a page, its content is displayed in reverse on the page's back, like when we see through a page in real books. We have the option of creating double-sided pages by setting the `UIPageViewController.DoubleSided` property to `true`.

Integrating content sharing

In this recipe, we will add the content-sharing functionality in an app. The app will be able to share content through social networks, e-mail, SMS, or **AirDrop**.

Getting ready

Create a new **Single View Application** in Xamarin Studio and name it `ContentShareApp`. The app will work on the simulator, but more sharing targets will be available on an actual device.

How to do it...

Perform the following steps:

1. Add a button to the controller.

2. Add the following code in the `ContentShareAppViewController` class:

```
private UIActivityViewController shareController;
public override void ViewDidLoad ()
{
  base.ViewDidLoad ();
  this.btnShare.TouchUpInside += async (sender, e) => {
    NSString link = new
      NSString ("http://software.tavlikos.com");
    this.shareController = new UIActivityViewController (new
      NSObject [] {
      link
    }, null);
    this.shareController.CompletionHandler =
      this.ActivityCompleted;

    await this.PresentViewControllerAsync (
      this.shareController, true);
  };
}
private void ActivityCompleted (NSString activityType, bool
  completed)
{
  Console.WriteLine ("Activity type: {0}", activityType);
  Console.WriteLine ("Completion: {0}", completed);
}
```

3.   Compile and run the app on a device. Tap the **Share link** button, and a screen similar to the following screenshot will appear:

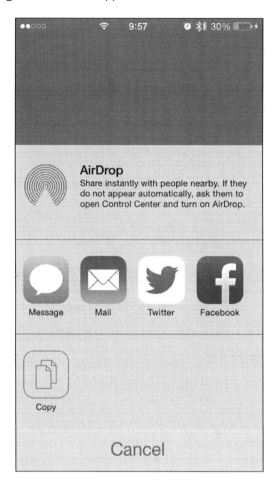

How it works...

The `UIActivityViewController` class is responsible for displaying the available sharing options, depending on the availability of these options on each device.

To initialize an instance of `UIActivityViewController`, we pass the following two arguments:

```
this.shareController = new UIActivityViewController(new NSObject[] {
  link
}, null);
```

The first parameter is an array of `NSObject` objects. In this example, we just pass one object of the `NSString` type. This object is a URL. The second parameter is an array of `UIActivity` objects. In this example, we pass `null`. The `UIActivity` class is meant to be subclassed so we can add our own custom activity "providers" to `UIActivityViewController`, with our own icon and functionality.

We then set the callback that will be called when the user completes the action, using the following code:

```
this.shareController.CompletionHandler = this.ActivityCompleted;
//..
private void ActivityCompleted(NSString activityType, bool
  completed)
{
  Console.WriteLine("Activity type: {0}", activityType);
  Console.WriteLine("Completion: {0}", completed);
}
```

Through the callback, we get an `NSString` representation of the type of activity and a bool indicating whether the user actually completed (`true`) or cancelled (`false`) the activity. Note that this parameter will be `false`, whether the user tapped the cancelled button on `UIActivityViewController` or actually cancelled the action later through the corresponding screen (for example, tapping the **Cancel** button in the mail-composition screen).

After we have set up `UIActivityViewController`, we present it modally using the following code:

```
await this.PresentViewControllerAsync(this.shareController, true);
```

The controller will be automatically dismissed whether the user has completed the action or cancelled it.

When we tap one of the available options, the corresponding screen will appear. The following screenshot shows the Facebook-share screen:

There's more...

We can exclude activities we do not want to display through the `ExcludeActivityTypes` property. For example, to remove the mail activity from the options, we set the following array of `NSString` objects to the property:

```
this.shareController.ExcludeActivityTypes = new NSString[] {
    "com.apple.UIKit.activity.Mail" };
```

Implementing custom transitions

In this recipe, we will create an app that displays a view controller modally but with our own custom-animated transition.

Getting ready

Create a new **Single View Application** in Xamarin Studio and name it `CustomTransitionApp`. Add another view controller to the project and name it `ModalController`. Finally, we will need a button on each of these controllers.

How to do it...

Perform the following steps:

1. Add the following classes to the project:

```
public class MyTransitionAnimator :
  UIViewControllerAnimatedTransitioning
{
  public bool IsPresenting { get; set; }
  public override double TransitionDuration
    (IUIViewControllerContextTransitioning
    transitionContext) {
    return 1;
  }
  public override void AnimateTransition
    (IUIViewControllerContextTransitioning
    transitionContext) {
    if (this.IsPresenting) {
      UIView containerView =
      transitionContext.ContainerView;
      UIViewController toViewController =
        transitionContext.GetViewControllerForKey(
          UITransitionContext.ToViewControllerKey);
      containerView.AddSubview(toViewController.View);
      RectangleF frame = toViewController.View.Frame;
      toViewController.View.Frame = RectangleF.Empty;
      UIView.Animate(this.TransitionDuration(
        transitionContext),
        () => toViewController.View.Frame = new RectangleF
        (20f, 20f, frame.Width - 40f, frame.Height - 40f),
        () => transitionContext.CompleteTransition (true));
    } else {
```

```
            UIViewController fromViewController =
              transitionContext.GetViewControllerForKey(
              UITransitionContext.FromViewControllerKey);
            RectangleF frame = fromViewController.View.Frame;
            frame = RectangleF.Empty;
            UIView.Animate(this.TransitionDuration(
              transitionContext),
              () => fromViewController.View.Frame = frame,
              () => transitionContext.CompleteTransition (true));
        }
    }
}
public class MyTransitionDelegate :
  UIViewControllerTransitioningDelegate
{
    private MyTransitionAnimator animator;
    public override IUIViewControllerAnimatedTransitioning
      PresentingController (UIViewController presented,
      UIViewController presenting, UIViewController source)
    {

        this.animator = new MyTransitionAnimator();
        this.animator.IsPresenting = true;
        return this.animator;
    }
    public override IUIViewControllerAnimatedTransitioning
      GetAnimationControllerForDismissedController
      (UIViewController dismissed) {
        this.animator.IsPresenting = false;
        return this.animator;
    }
}
```

2. Add the following code in the `ViewDidLoad` method of
    `CustomTransitionAppViewController`:

```
this.btnPresent.TouchUpInside += async (sender, e) => {
  ModalController modalController = new ModalController();
  modalController.ModalPresentationStyle =
    UIModalPresentationStyle.Custom;
  modalController.TransitioningDelegate = new
    MyTransitionDelegate();
  await this.PresentViewControllerAsync(modalController,
    true);
};
```

3. Compile and run the app on the simulator. Tap the button and watch the modal controller being presented smoothly from the top-left corner. The result should be similar to the following screenshot:

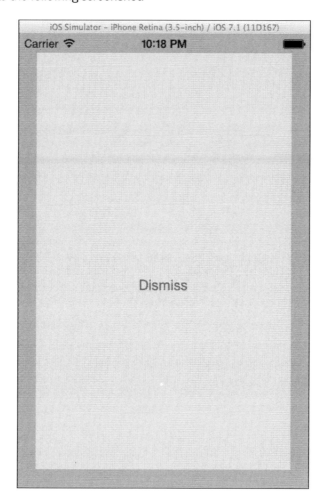

How it works...

To create our custom transition, we need to create two objects.

The first object is a subclass of `UIViewControllerAnimatedTransitioning` as shown in the following line of code:

```
public class MyTransitionAnimator :
UIViewControllerAnimatedTransitioning
```

This class contains two methods that we need: `TransitionDuration`, which specifies the duration of the animated transition, and `AnimateTransition`, where the actual animation takes place.

Inside the `AnimateTransition` method, we get a `IUIViewControllerContextTransitioning` object, which is responsible for the whole process. The animation will take place on a `UIView` that the object creates for this purpose. This `UIView` object is accessed through the transition context object's `ContainerView` property, as shown in the following line of code:

```
UIView containerView = transitionContext.ContainerView;
```

Through the transition context object, we can also get the controllers that take part in the transitioning. To get the target controller, we call the `GetViewControllerForKey` method, passing to it `UITransitionContext.ToViewControllerKey`, using the following code:

```
UIViewController toViewController =
    transitionContext.GetViewControllerForKey(
    UITransitionContext.ToViewControllerKey);
```

After we get the objects we need, we add the target controller's view to the transition context's view and change its frame with the `UIView.Animate` method. When all animations are executed, we need to call the `CompleteTransition` method on the transition context, as shown in the following code:

```
containerView.AddSubview(toViewController.View);
//..
UIView.Animate(this.TransitionDuration(transitionContext), () =>
    toViewController.View.Frame = new RectangleF(20f, 20f,
    frame.Width, frame.Height), () =>
    transitionContext.CompleteTransition(true));
```

The second object is a subclass of `UIViewControllerTransitioningDelegate`. The declaration of the class is shown in the following line of code:

```
public class MyTransitionDelegate :
    UIViewControllerTransitioningDelegate
```

Inside the `MyTransitionDelegate` subclass, we override the `PresentingController` method and return an instance of `MyTransitionAnimator` that we created earlier, as shown in the following code:

```
this.animator = new MyTransitionAnimator();
this.animator.IsPresenting = true;
return this.animator;
```

The `IsPresenting` property of `MyTransitionAnimator` is used as a flag so the animator will know if the transition is for presenting a controller or dismissing it. We set it to `false` inside the `GetAnimationControllerForDismissedController` method from which we return the same `MyTransitionAnimator` instance, using the following code:

```
this.animator.IsPresenting = false;
return this.animator;
```

It is clear that one method will be called when the controller is to be presented and the other is to be dismissed.

Finally, to enable everything, we set the `ModalPresentationStyle` property to `UIModalPresentationStyle.Custom`, and a new instance of `MyTransitioningDelegate` to the `TransitioningDelegate` property of the controller that will be presented, using the following code:

```
modalController.ModalPresentationStyle =
   UIModalPresentationStyle.Custom;
modalController.TransitioningDelegate = new
   MyTransitionDelegate();
```

There's more...

Custom transitions are not limited to modal controllers. We can use custom transitions for pushing controllers into the navigation stack of a navigation controller or completely create our own navigation stack.

Transitioning between child controllers

The `UIViewController` class contains the `Transition` method that allows us to transition from one child controller to another, inside the parent controller.

 Child controllers are controllers whose views are part of the hierarchy of a third controller's view. This controller is the parent controller.

See also

▸ The *Animating views* recipe in *Chapter 11, Graphics and Animation*

Using physics in UI elements

In this recipe, we will use UIKit Dynamics to add the properties of physics to an image view. The image view will drop from its initial position to the bottom of the screen, simulating the effect of an object dropping on the floor.

Getting ready

Create a new **Single View Application** in Xamarin Studio and name it `ViewPhysicsApp`. Add `UIImageView` and two buttons to the controller. We will also need an image to show in the image view.

How to do it...

Perform the following steps:

1. Add the following fields in the `ViewPhysicsAppViewController` class:

    ```
    private RectangleF imageRect;
    private UIDynamicAnimator animator;
    ```

2. Add the following code in the `ViewDidLoad` method:

    ```
    this.View.InsertSubviewBelow(this.imgView, this.btnReset);
    this.imageRect = this.imgView.Frame;
    this.imgView.Image = UIImage.FromFile("1.jpg");
    this.animator = new UIDynamicAnimator(this.View);
    ```

3. Next, in the `ViewDidLoad` method again, add the following button handlers:

    ```
    this.btnDrop.TouchUpInside += (sender, e) => {
      UIGravityBehavior gravity = new
        UIGravityBehavior(this.imgView);
      UICollisionBehavior collision = new
        UICollisionBehavior(this.imgView);
      collision.TranslatesReferenceBoundsIntoBoundary = true;
      this.animator.AddBehaviors(gravity, collision);
    };
    this.btnReset.TouchUpInside += (sender, e) => {
      this.animator.RemoveAllBehaviors();
      this.imgView.Frame = this.imageRect;
    };
    ```

4. Compile and run the app on the simulator. Tap the **Drop!** button and watch the image view drop to the bottom of the screen. Tap the **Reset** button to reset it back to its original position. The following screenshot shows the app in its initial state and after the **Drop!** button is tapped:

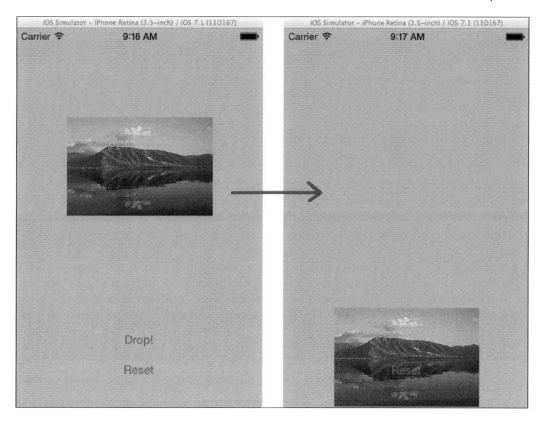

How it works...

UIKit Dynamics offers a variety of objects that allow us to add the properties of physics to UIKit objects.

The first thing we need to do is to initialize a `UIDynamicAnimator` object. This class provides the context in which all the physics animations will take place. We pass the controller's view, which automatically makes it our 2D "physics world," using the following line of code:

```
this.animator = new UIDynamicAnimator(this.View);
```

After we have created the dynamic animator, we need to add some behavior to it. Inside the `btnDrop` handler, we first make sure the image view will be affected by gravity by creating a `UIGravityBehavior` instance, as shown in the following code:

```
UIGravityBehavior gravity = new UIGravityBehavior(this.imgView);
```

If we leave it as it is, the image view will just drop below the bottom boundary of the screen. So, we also need a collision behavior, which we can add using the following code:

```
UICollisionBehavior collision = new
  UICollisionBehavior(this.imgView);
collision.TranslatesReferenceBoundsIntoBoundary = true;
```

Note that the collision also needs a boundary to collide with, or it will have the same effect if it was not there. In this case, we use the boundary of our animator object, as indicated in the preceding highlighted code.

Now that we have our behavior set up, we add them to our animator to put everything into motion, using the following code:

```
this.animator.AddBehaviors(gravity, collision);
```

There's more...

We can also modify how the image view will bounce when it hits the ground. Try adding the following code below the `UICollisionBehavior` initialization line:

```
UIDynamicItemBehavior dynBehavior = new
  UIDynamicItemBehavior(this.imgView);
dynBehavior.Density = 1f;
dynBehavior.Elasticity = 0.7f;
dynBehavior.Friction = 1f;
```

Of course, don't forget to add the new behavior to the animator, as shown in the following line of code:

```
this.animator.AddBehaviors(gravity, collision, dynBehavior);
```

If you run the app and tap the **Drop!** button, the image will bounce more when it hits the ground!

UIKit Dynamics usage

UIKit Dynamics was designed to provide simple 2D physics to `UIView` objects or to every object that implements the Objective-C `UIDynamicItem` protocol (`IUIDynamicItem` interface in C#). It was not designed to develop games with `UIView` objects. For this purpose, we have the **SpriteKit framework**, which is available through the `MonoTouch.SpriteKit` namespace. This is outside the scope of this book.

Implementing the text-to-speech feature

In this recipe, we will learn to work with `AVSpeechSynthesizer`, the class that provides the **Text-To-Speech** (**TTS**) functionality for many different languages.

Getting ready

Create a new **Single View Application** in Xamarin Studio and name it `SpeechApp`. Add a `UITextField` and a button to the controller.

How to do it...

Perform the following steps:

1. Add the `MonoTouch.AVFoundation` namespace in the `SpeechAppViewController.cs` file, using the following code:

   ```
   using MonoTouch.AVFoundation;
   ```

2. Add the following code in the `ViewDidLoad` method:

   ```
   this.txtEntry.ShouldReturn = (textField) =>
     textField.ResignFirstResponder();
   this.btnSpeak.TouchUpInside += (sender, e) => {
     AVSpeechSynthesizer synth = new AVSpeechSynthesizer();
     AVSpeechUtterance utterance = new
       AVSpeechUtterance(this.txtEntry.Text);
     utterance.Rate = 0.3f;
     utterance.Voice = AVSpeechSynthesisVoice.
       FromLanguage("en-US");
     synth.SpeakUtterance(utterance);
   };
   ```

3. Compile and run the app on the simulator. Type some text in English in the text field and tap the **Speak** button. Listen while your app speaks!

How it works...

The `AVSpeechSynthesizer` class was introduced with iOS 7. It provides very simple and practical TTS functionality.

After initializing an instance of the class, we create an `AVSpeechUtterance` object, passing it to the text we want it to process, as shown in the following code:

```
AVSpeechSynthesizer synth = new AVSpeechSynthesizer();
AVSpeechUtterance utterance = new
  AVSpeechUtterance(this.txtEntry.Text);
```

We then set the rate of the speech and assign a voice to the utterance, using the following code:

```
utterance.Rate = 0.3f;
utterance.Voice = AVSpeechSynthesisVoice.FromLanguage("en-US");
```

The rate adjusts the speed at which the text will be spoken. You can test various speeds to suit your needs.

The voice is an instance of `AVSpeechSynthesisVoice`. To initialize it, we call the `FromLanguage` static method, passing the BCP-47 language code. Unfortunately, there is only one type of voice for each available language, and we have no control over it.

Finally, to start the speech, we call the `SpeakUtterance` method to the synthesizer, passing the utterance object to it using the following code:

```
synth.SpeakUtterance(utterance);
```

 We can call the `SpeakUtterance` method multiple subsequent times, passing a different utterance object each time. The speech synthesizer will queue each utterance and play it in sequence.

There's more...

We can enumerate the available language codes that the speech synthesizer supports by enumerating the return value of the `AVSpeechSynthesisVoice.GetSpeechVoices()` method, as shown in the following code:

```
foreach (AVSpeechSynthesisVoice eachVoice in
    AVSpeechSynthesisVoice.GetSpeechVoices()) {
    Console.WriteLine(eachVoice.Description);
}
```

Adjusting the utterance

We can make more adjustments to how the speech will be performed through the following properties of the `AVSpeechUtterance` class:

- `PitchMultiplier`: This is the pitch of the utterance. It is a float whose values are in the range of `0.5` and `2`.
- `PostUtteranceDelay`, `PreUtteranceDelay`: This is the amount of time to wait after (post) and/or before (pre) each utterance is spoken, in seconds.
- `Volume`: This is the audio volume of the speech. It is in the range of `0.0` (silent) to `1.0` (loudest).

Index

P

page curl effect
reproducing 344-348
page navigation
content, viewing with 70-73
phone calls
starting 194, 195
photo album
EXIF data, reading 192
individual assets, retrieving 192
managing 189-191
permission, checking 192
physics
adding, UIKit Dynamics used 358-360
prerequisites, Xamarin.iOS app
installing 8
iOS SDK 9
Xamarin Starter Edition 10
Xcode 9
progress
displaying, of known length 64-67
height, setting 67
project template
Empty project 22
Master-detail application 22
OpenGL application 23
Single view application 22
Tabbed application 23
Utility application 22
provisioning profile
creating 329-334
expiration 334
proximity sensor
using 224, 225

R

radian 245
regional formatting 325-327
region monitoring service
about 248
availability 257
using 255, 256
REST services
consuming 163-165
rows
customizing 136-139

S

SDK 7
segue 107
ServiceStack.Text
URL 165
shapes
drawing 293, 294
drawing, with transparent colors 295
significant-change location service
about 248
availability 260
using 258-260
simple web browser
content, scaling 150
creating 149, 150
supported files 150
soft debugger 40
Software Development Kit. *See* **SDK**
sounds
playing 185
recording, for specific time 189
recording, with microphone 185-188
SpriteKit framework 360
SQLite
about 113
URL 113
SQLite database
about 113
creating 116-120
table, creating 121
standard location service 248
Stock Keeping Unit (SKU) 342
storyboards
about 105
creating 105-107
data, passing 108
unwinding 109, 110
unwind segue, creating 111

T

table
content, adding 140
data, displaying in 132-135
data, searching 145-149
editing 140-142
editing mode, enabling of rows 142

About Packt Publishing

Packt, pronounced 'packed', published its first book "*Mastering phpMyAdmin for Effective MySQL Management*" in April 2004 and subsequently continued to specialize in publishing highly focused books on specific technologies and solutions.

Our books and publications share the experiences of your fellow IT professionals in adapting and customizing today's systems, applications, and frameworks. Our solution based books give you the knowledge and power to customize the software and technologies you're using to get the job done. Packt books are more specific and less general than the IT books you have seen in the past. Our unique business model allows us to bring you more focused information, giving you more of what you need to know, and less of what you don't.

Packt is a modern, yet unique publishing company, which focuses on producing quality, cutting-edge books for communities of developers, administrators, and newbies alike. For more information, please visit our website: www.packtpub.com.

Writing for Packt

We welcome all inquiries from people who are interested in authoring. Book proposals should be sent to author@packtpub.com. If your book idea is still at an early stage and you would like to discuss it first before writing a formal book proposal, contact us; one of our commissioning editors will get in touch with you.

We're not just looking for published authors; if you have strong technical skills but no writing experience, our experienced editors can help you develop a writing career, or simply get some additional reward for your expertise.

Xamarin Mobile Application Development for iOS

ISBN: 978-1-78355-918-3   Paperback: 222 pages

If you know C# and have an iOS device, learn to use one language for multiple devices with Xamarin

1. A clear and concise look at how to create your own apps building on what you already know of C#.

2. Create advanced and elegant apps by yourself.

3. Ensure that the majority of your code can also be used with Android and Windows Mobile 8 devices.

Xamarin Mobile Application Development for Android

ISBN: 978-1-78355-916-9   Paperback: 168 pages

Learn to develop full featured Android apps using your existing C# skills with Xamarin.Android

1. Gain an understanding of both the Android and Xamarin platforms.

2. Build a working multi-view Android app incrementally throughout the book.

3. Work with device capabilities such as location sensors and the camera.

Please check **www.PacktPub.com** for information on our titles

iOS Development using MonoTouch Cookbook

ISBN: 978-1-84969-146-8   Paperback: 384 pages

109 simple but incredibly effective recipes for developing and deploying applications for iOS using C# and .NET

1. Detailed examples covering every aspect of iOS development using MonoTouch and C#/.NET.

2. Create fully working MonoTouch projects using step-by-step instructions.

3. Recipes for creating iOS applications meeting Apple's guidelines.

iOS 7 Game Development

ISBN: 978-1-78355-157-6   Paperback: 120 pages

Develop powerful, engaging games with ready-to-use utilities from Sprite Kit

1. Pen your own endless runner game using Apple's new Sprite Kit framework.

2. Enhance your user experience with easy-to-use animations and particle effects using Xcode 5.

3. Utilize particle systems and create custom particle effects.

Please check **www.PacktPub.com** for information on our titles

Made in the USA
Lexington, KY
10 September 2014